LIBERAL ARTS AT THE BRINK

LIBERAL ARTS
AT THE BRINK

✦

VICTOR E. FERRALL, JR.

Harvard University Press
Cambridge, Massachusetts
London, England
2011

Library of Congress Cataloging-in-Publication Data

Ferrall, Victor E., Jr., 1936–
Liberal arts at the brink / Victor E. Ferrall, Jr.
p.   cm.
Includes bibliographical references and index.
ISBN 978-0-674-04972-7 (cloth : alk. paper)
1. Education, Humanistic—United States.   2. Small colleges—
United States.   3. United States—Intellectual life.   I. Title.
LC1011.F47 2011
370.11'2—dc22   2010041633

To Linda

Contents

Preface   *ix*

Introduction   *1*

1. Liberal Arts Colleges and Why We Should Care about Them   *7*

2. The Economic Health of Liberal Arts Colleges   *23*

3. The Declining Demand for Liberal Arts Education   *40*

4. Competing   *60*

5. Cooperating   *81*

6. Recruiting Students   *105*

7. Liberal Arts Teachers: A Profile   *113*

8. Employing and Deploying Faculty for Teaching Excellence   *126*

9. Tenure   *138*

10. Curriculums   *147*

11. At the Brink   *154*

Epilogue: A Fable   *163*

Appendix: Data on the 225 Colleges   *169*

Notes   *257*

Acknowledgments   *277*

Index   *279*

Preface

In my junior year in high school, I won a Ford Scholarship to attend college the following fall. To be a winner, one had to meet two requirements: do acceptably well on a written test and be of an age to be less than sixteen and a half years old on the day one would enter college. The Ford Foundation's idea was to accelerate the training of needed leaders in post–World War II America by getting them off to an early college start. The idea was probably misguided, but there it was. I became a Ford Scholar.

The year I received the Ford Scholarship, four institutions of higher education were participating in the program: the University of Chicago, Yale University, the University of Wisconsin, and Oberlin College. My parents had a friend who had been involved in experimental education at the University of Chicago. He told them Chicago could derail a sixteen-year-old faster than any college or university in the country. My parents accepted his advice and told me of course I could go to Chicago, but not until I was at least seventeen. They found a way to tell me no by saying yes—a parenting masterpiece.

Yale had a special program for its young Ford freshmen. It kept them separate from the other students and sought to integrate them gradually into the life of the university. I wanted to drink beer and chase girls, not be kept separate, so Yale was out. Living in New Jersey, I could not imagine why anyone would want to go to the University of Wisconsin, so it was out too. (Later, I learned that UW was an outstanding venue for drinking beer and chasing girls, but by then it was too late.) That left Oberlin College.

In the 1950s and early 1960s, if one wanted to attend a small, liberal arts college that was coed, the top choices were Swarthmore and Oberlin, with Carleton a distant third (because of the snowed-in winters in Northfield, Minnesota). I have never regretted choosing a liberal arts college in general, nor Oberlin in particular. My children also attended liberal arts colleges (Dickinson, Kenyon, and Oberlin). When I had the opportunity to become the president of Beloit College, I jumped at it. I have never regretted going to Beloit, either.

Looking back, I don't believe that, at barely sixteen, I could have handled the social pressures at Yale; I'm afraid I might have handled the social life at Wisconsin all too well, and heaven knows what would have become of me at Chicago. So a small, residential liberal arts college was the right choice for me. It was and still is the right choice for many young men and women, for many reasons. Let me mention a few personal ones.

At Oberlin, I learned who Mahler was before Leonard Bernstein introduced him to America. Even though I was only sixteen, an inch too short, and a half step too slow, I made all but the final cut for the freshman basketball team. I made close friends who were women (which was hard to do if the only time you saw them was at weekend mixers at the Seven Sisters colleges) and African Americans (which was hard to do anywhere in those days). I discovered I could be—and wanted to be—interested in almost anything. I learned how to deal with failing, an extraordinarily valuable skill that fewer and fewer individuals seem to possess these days. I got to know professors well, in and out of the classroom, who were life models for me—of both what I wanted and did not want to be. One became my mentor. And I developed the skills necessary to foil an attempt by Oberlin trustee (then dean of Harvard Law School and later U.S. solicitor general) Erwin Griswold to have me kicked out of college for a student prank (mine, not his) that particularly angered him. This last point was especially consequential because, years later, I became Erwin's law partner and took great delight in reminding him of the misguided harm he almost caused.

This book is about liberal arts education as it is offered at liberal arts colleges. Relatively little is written about liberal arts colleges, perhaps because of their small size and enrollments, or their singular commitment to undergraduate liberal arts education. Then again, it may be because great research laboratories, prestigious graduate and professional schools, and big-name scholars are at universities, not liberal arts colleges. Or it may be because most liberal arts college professors spend most of their time teaching, not trying to get published. Whatever the reason, most writers on higher education write about universities.

Universities, of course, offer liberal arts instruction, but they also provide an array of services, including vocational, technical, and professional programs at the graduate as well as the undergraduate level. Much of this book deals with the demand for liberal arts education. Changes in that demand are most starkly exposed at liberal arts colleges because of the singularity of their educational offering. While the analysis that follows focuses on liberal arts colleges, universities doubtless confront the same winds of change.

I was a practicing attorney for thirty years before spending nine years as the president of Beloit College, so this book about liberal arts colleges is written from the perspective of an outsider with some inside knowledge. It is, of course, also written from the point of view of a college president, which may not be a good thing. More than seventy-five years ago, in *The Goose-Step: A Study of American Education* (1923), muckraker Upton Sinclair explained that a college president fulfills his duties "by being the most universal faker and the most variegated prevaricator that has yet appeared in the civilized world . . . , by making his entire being a conglomeration of hypocrisies and stultifications, so that by the time he has been in office a year or two he has told so many different kinds of falsehoods and made so many different kinds of pretenses to so many different people, that he has lost all understanding of what truth is, or how a man could speak it."

It has been my experience that some academics are more comfortable reporting and analyzing others' observations than their own. They view accurately assessing the observations of others as scholarship, accurately assessing one's own as somehow indulgent. This confuses me. In any case, while I have read widely about liberal education, done research, and interviewed students, teachers, and administrators, this is not a scholarly book. It grows out of and is based on my own observations and experience as a liberal arts college president.

A brilliant thirty-five-year-old philosophy professor I know is writing his first (tenure) book about the philosophy of a nineteenth-century thinker. I asked why he did not instead write about his own

philosophy. "It would not be published," he explained. "You must dem-
onstrate your ability to analyze and criticize the philosophies of others
before anyone will listen to yours." If my young philosophy-professor
friend is correct, it may partially explain the reluctance to rely on one's
own observations.

Discussions of liberal arts education tend to center on pedagogical
issues. Economic factors—aside from observing that tuitions are too
high—are typically not the focus. They *are* a focus in this book. Further, most persons interested in liberal arts education have in mind an
image of what a liberal arts college is. For many, the image looks like
Williams or Swarthmore. This book looks at those schools and 223
other liberal arts colleges, most of which are strikingly different from
and face challenges dramatically unlike those confronting Williams
and Swarthmore.

A thesis of this book is that liberal arts colleges are at risk—the poor
colleges, of slipping away into vocational instruction or disappearing
altogether; the rich colleges, of becoming irrelevant. In Chapter 1, I attempt to spell out why I believe this matters and should not be permitted to happen. While I have tried to subject my reasons to postmod-
ernist skepticism, it is true that liberal arts colleges have been a part of
my life since I was a teenager: as a student, an alumnus, a parent, a
spouse, a trustee, and a president. The educational experience they
provide is what I know best. I reject, however, the assertion that the
validity of a thesis can only be gauged on the basis of who is propound-
ing it. I prefer the view reflected in the assertion that "just because you
are paranoid doesn't mean no one is following you."

It has been suggested that a better title for this book would be "Liberal Arts Colleges: Why I Love Them and Why They Can't Be Saved,"
and it is true that the situation liberal arts colleges confront is dire.
They are, sadly, *not* the canaries in the higher-education mine. If they
are snuffed out, the likelihood is that most of the miners will not notice or, if they do, will not care. But liberal arts colleges are far too valuable to give up on. A more optimistic alternative title might be, "Liberal
Arts Colleges: Before It Is Too Late, Get Your Act Together and Make
Common Cause to Save Yourselves, Because No One Else Is Going to
Do It."

LIBERAL ARTS AT THE BRINK

Introduction

✦

Postsecondary education is big business. In 2007, 4,352 accredited public and private degree-granting institutions enrolled 18.2 million students (15.6 million of whom were undergraduates and 11.3 million of whom were full-time students) and the year before, those institutions had enjoyed total revenues of more than $410 billion. The enrolled students represented 39 percent of all eighteen- to twenty-four-year-olds (and 46 percent of those who had graduated from high school). Approximately 3.6 million people were employed at colleges and universities in 2007, 1.4 million as faculty members.[1] Undergraduate education is also a growth industry. In 1960, 392,000 students earned bachelor degrees. By 2007, that number had nearly quadrupled, to 1.52 million.[2]

When I think about the evolution of U.S. higher education, an image recurs in my mind: an armada of education institutions slowly being assembled over more than two hundred years, then, beginning in the late nineteenth century, surging forward, propelled by the winds of societal change, large squadrons peeling off in different directions with different academic armaments and objectives, leaving behind a tiny portion of the original force—the liberal arts colleges. Liberal arts colleges form by far the smallest piece of the vast higher-education armada, and the one with the least growth. Depending on how one classifies them, there are roughly 125 to 250 private liberal arts colleges serving between 100,000 and 350,000 undergraduates, less than 2 percent of all postsecondary students. Table I.1, which includes enrollment data for several different groups of institutions at points between 2007

Table I.1   Various total enrollments (2007–2009)

All accredited degree-granting postsecondary institutions[a]	18,200,000
U.S. for-profit colleges[b]	1,200,000
Florida community colleges[c]	831,000
University System of Ohio[d]	473,000
University of Phoenix[e]	384,900
10 single-campus universities (undergraduate only)[f]	379,000
3 community colleges[g]	350,000
225 private liberal arts colleges[h]	349,000
51 highest-rated private liberal arts colleges[i]	103,000

a. National Center for Education Statistics, *Digest of Education Statistics 2008*, www.nces.ed.gov.

b. Ibid.

c. Florida Department of Education, www.fldoe.org/cc/facts_glance.asp (accessed 2/13/10).

d. www.uso.edu/strategicplan (accessed 2/13/10).

e. University of Phoenix reported total enrollment of 455,600 in the first quarter of 2010, up from 384,900 in the first quarter of 2009. "Apollo Group, Inc. Reports Fiscal 2010 First Quarter Results," January 7, 2010, www.apollogrp.edu (accessed 2/10/10).

f. University of Central Florida (Orlando), www.iroffice.ucf.edu/enrollment/2008–09/index.html; University of Texas (Austin), www.utexas.edu/opa/pubs/facts/enrollment.php; Arizona State University (Tempe), www.educationportal.com/directory/school/Arizona_State_University; Ohio State University (Columbus), www.osu.edu/enroll; Texas A&M University (College Station), www.tamu.edu/oisp/student-reports/enrollment-profile-fall-2008-certified.pdf; Penn State University (University Park), www.budget.psu.edu/; University of Florida (Gainesville), www.ir.ufl.edu/fall/sus3.xls; Michigan State University (East Lansing), www.opbweb.opb.msu.edu/docs/CommonDataSet/2008/Default.htm; Purdue University (West Lafayette), www.admissions.purdue.edu/Academic_Profile/Student_Enrollment.html; Florida State University (Tallahassee), http://dof.fsu.edu/forms/BarnhillFall08.pdf (all accessed 2/13/10).

g. Miami-Dade College, www.mdc.edu/ir/datapages/headcounts.pdf; Northern Virginia Community College, www.nvcc.edu/about-nova/directories—offices/administrative offices/oir/vccs/files/VCCSfall08profile.pdf; Houston Community College System, www.hccs.edu/hcc/System%20Home/Departments/OIR/Publications/Publication_PDFS/Factsheet_PDFs/QuickFacts.pdf (all accessed 2/13/10).

h. The 225 private liberal arts colleges analyzed in this book. *America's Best Colleges*, 2009 ed. (New York: U.S. News and World Report); see Appendix, Table A.1, and Chap. 1, n. 28.

i. The 50 private liberal arts colleges ranked highest by *U.S. News* plus Sarah Lawrence College; Appendix, Table A.1.

and 2009, gives an impression of the relative scale of private liberal arts college enrollment.

Today, liberal arts colleges are in trouble. In the face of steadily declining demand for liberal arts education (the only service they provide) and surging demand for career-oriented, vocational instruction, they are struggling with inadequate financing to provide their extremely costly services, grappling with the growth of tax-supported public institutions intent on capturing a larger share of the already small and shrinking market for liberal arts education, and forced to wrestle with the crippling burden of recession. Most liberal arts colleges must also contend with relentless price cutting by the richest colleges and universities, obliging them either to offer tuition discounts they simply cannot afford or fall further behind. This book seeks to explain how all this has come to pass, by examining the economic circumstances of liberal arts colleges, explaining how they have come to confront such seemingly intractable obstacles to their future viability, and exploring whether there is a way for them to overcome those obstacles.

Chapter 1 defines *liberal arts*, gives a brief history of liberal arts colleges, and identifies the 225 colleges that are analyzed in this book. It then discusses the great and continuing value—to students and to society as a whole—of the unique educational experience liberal arts colleges provide.

Chapter 2 spells out the resources available to the colleges—wealth (endowment) and revenues—and the costs of operation (including financial aid). Chapter 3 distinguishes the demand for the degrees these colleges confer from the demand for the liberal arts education they offer, and examines in detail the declining demand for liberal arts education and the rising demand for vocational instruction. It then outlines key tactics the colleges have employed to meet changing demand, especially admitting more (and often less-qualified) students and offering more vocational and fewer liberal arts courses and majors, and explores the implications of these moves. Data provided for the 225 colleges show that, over the twenty-one years between 1986–1987 and 2007–2008, the number of colleges graduating at least 90 percent liberal arts majors fell by more than half, and the number graduating 30 percent or more vocational majors nearly quadrupled. Financially struggling colleges may be able to survive by shifting to more vocational curriculums, but when they do, the liberal arts education they provided is lost.

Generally, free-market competition between sellers of goods and services yields lower prices, higher output, and better quality, but for this to happen, certain marketplace requirements must be met. Chapter 4 explains the many ways they are *not* met in the liberal arts education market and how, as a result, competition among liberal arts institutions has been a destructive force, increasing the cost of providing educational services and raising the price that poorer students must pay for them.

Liberal arts colleges and universities could reduce expenses by collaborating rather than competing, and, as discussed in Chapter 5, to some extent they have. For the most part, however, the colleges have been extremely wary about giving up any measure of curriculum autonomy and have followed an ill-advised, go-it-alone strategy. Mergers, in effect the ultimate collaboration, have been largely limited to the acquisition of failing colleges by for-profit, primarily online, universities. More of these acquisitions can be expected in the future. The one major, successful cooperative undertaking by liberal arts institutions—an agreement among colleges belonging to the so-called Overlap Group to limit financial aid to wealthy students—was blocked by the U.S. Department of Justice. To date, the only national consortium of liberal arts colleges, the Annapolis Group, has not played an effective leadership role for cooperation.

Resuscitating demand for liberal arts education is the single greatest challenge liberal arts colleges face. Chapter 6 examines how they have gone about it—on their own, not collaboratively, and not effectively.

It is abundantly clear that some liberal arts colleges are not going to survive, at least not without abandoning their liberal arts mission. Those that do survive will do so only if they are at the top of their game. Above all, this means providing excellent teaching, the one area of natural advantage they enjoy. Two chapters are devoted to teaching. Chapter 7 describes the unique qualities of and circumstances faced by liberal arts college teachers. Chapter 8 outlines actions colleges should take to maintain and improve the quality of teaching.

A view held by many higher education critics is that tenure undercuts teaching quality by limiting the incentives to pursue excellence and providing a safe haven for inferior teachers. Chapter 9 does not contend that abolishing tenure is necessary but does insist that the tenure process must be better managed if it is not to impede teaching quality.

Liberal arts colleges are actively concerned with their own excellence, but their concern is too often expressed by revising—or arguing about revising—their curriculum. Chapter 10 contends that, to a substantial extent, curriculum reviews are a misplaced expenditure of faculty time and effort.

The concluding chapter, Chapter 11, explores what, if anything, liberal arts colleges can do to save themselves—that is, to stay, if not reverse, falling demand for their liberal arts education services.

A Note on Data

The U.S. Department of Education collects an astonishing array of data on all levels and aspects of U.S. education. Each year its National Center for Education Statistics (NCES) collects a large amount of statistical information about higher education institutions as a part of its Integrated Postsecondary Education Data System (IPEDS). All of the data set out in the eight tables that make up the Appendix, and much of the data contained in the tables included in the text, are taken from that collection.

All higher education institutions that accept federal funding—so-called Title 4 funding—such as Pell Grants, Perkins and Stafford Loans, PLUS Loans (for parents), and the Science and Mathematics Access to Retain Talent (SMART), Academic Competitiveness (ACG), and Federal Supplemental Educational Opportunity (FSEOG) Grants, are required annually to provide information about virtually every aspect of their operations, including enrollment, tuition and fees, graduation rate, student financial aid, completions (degrees conferred, by major), expenses, revenues, and endowment. Since almost every college accepts federal funding, such data are reported to NCES by almost every college.

The reporting period is the academic year. Because college academic years vary slightly—for example, some end on May 31, others on June 30—there are slight variations in the periods covered by their reports. In addition, colleges maintain their records in slightly different ways. For example, while most colleges record tuition and required fees separately, a few record only comprehensive fees, which include room and board as well as tuition and fees. The result is that, in an IPEDS table showing tuition and fees, data for colleges reporting only comprehensive fees will be shown as "not available." Overall, however, the data collected by NCES are extraordinarily complete, comparable, and reliable. As a practical matter, without them the analysis provided in this book would not have been possible.

It typically takes each college three to four months to gather and record its data and submit it to NCES. There are different due dates for submitting different types of information. For example, completions data are collected and submitted in the fall following the end of the academic year in which they occurred, while fall enrollment data are collected and reported the following spring. After data are collected, it can take NCES as long as a year to correlate, process, assemble, prepare summaries, and finally release the full data collection to the public.

IPEDS data analyzed in this book are from the academic year 2007–2008, the most recent data available at the time the analysis was completed. They are compared with data from the 1986–1987 academic year, twenty-one years earlier, the earliest year for which comparable IPEDS data are available.

Readers can review the entire IPEDS data collection by going to http://nces.ed.gov/ipeds/datacenter.

CHAPTER 1

Liberal Arts Colleges and
Why We Should Care about Them

⁛

Which colleges are liberal arts colleges seems a simple question to answer: "They're, you know, like Oberlin or Wellesley." Actually, it isn't simple. The word *liberal* used in the context of education has not been well understood and is a source of confusion, especially outside the academy. Former Lawrence University president Rik Warch recalls a graduating senior who told him, "When I came to college, I really had no idea what the liberal arts were. I just thought there would be a lot of Democrats here."

Defining the Term

Webster's Third New International Dictionary has a long entry for the word *liberal* and, happily, the first definition is right on the money: "of, belonging to, being, or consisting of liberal arts or one of the liberal arts." *Webster's* adds another definition: "of, belonging to, or befitting a man of free birth, also, of, belonging to, or befitting one that is a gentleman in social rank."[1] This latter definition, however, is said to be archaic, something those who have read Cardinal Newman on the subject already suspected ("Liberal education makes not the Christian, nor the Catholic, but the gentleman").[2]

What does "belonging to the liberal arts" mean? *Webster's* is ready with an answer—the liberal arts are "studies . . . not in one of the technical fields."[3] Definitions such as this are known to rhetoricians as definitions by negation, like defining tiddledywinks as a game not played with a ball and bat.[4] *Webster's* explains that "technical" fields are "practical knowledge" fields, leaving us with the following: liberal arts are fields of knowledge that are not practical.

The dictionary includes a separate entry for *liberal arts,* but it is not entirely helpful either. We can safely pass over the first definition, "the studies comprising the trivium and quadrivium in the middle ages" (although it is the most explicit and straightforward definition we have encountered thus far) and go straight to the second, "the studies (as language, philosophy, history, literature, abstract science) especially in a college or university, that are presumed to provide chiefly general knowledge and to develop the general intellectual capacities (as reason or judgment)."[5] Unhappily, however, *Webster's* feels constrained to clarify the second definition by adding "as opposed to professional, vocational or technical studies," and we are back to defining liberal by what it is not. Like it or not, "not practical knowledge" has long been the basic descriptor of liberal education, at least for persons of common sense and sensibility.[6]

The day the word *liberal* stopped being used to describe education "befitting a gentleman in social rank," it should have been scrapped by the academic community. If academics want nonacademics to understand what they are talking about when they refer to liberal education, they would do well to find a different adjective. Almost anything— *broad, open, inclusive, general*—would be more descriptive.[7] (One person has suggested calling it "awesome education.")

The best plan, in my view, would be for liberal arts institutions to take exclusive possession of the word *education* by dropping the word *liberal* altogether and assigning the word *training* or *instruction* to professional, technical, and vocational fields. Even without the adjective *liberal,* embedded in the noun *education* is the implication of liberal education. When we refer to an "educated person," we do not think of someone who possesses a vocational skill or trade. Rather, again following *Webster's,* we have in mind a person of expanded "knowledge, wisdom, desirable qualities of mind or character, . . . or general competence."

In 1970 Clark Kerr developed a classification of higher education groups to improve the precision of research at the Carnegie Foundation for the Advancement of Teaching.[8] Since then, Carnegie has taken responsibility for classifying higher education institutions, including defining liberal arts colleges. Obviously, liberal arts colleges are ones that offer courses in liberal arts fields of study. What constitutes a liberal arts field has stayed strikingly constant over the years, although a few new disciplines have been added. Carnegie has identified the following broad fields of study as liberal arts disciplines:[9]

English language and literature	Psychology
Foreign languages	Social sciences
Letters	Visual and performing arts
Liberal and general studies	Area and ethnic studies
Life sciences	Multi- and interdisciplinary
Mathematics	studies
Physical sciences	Philosophy and religion

There is also broad consensus about the disciplines Carnegie has identified as vocational:[10]

Agriculture	Home economics
Allied health	Law and legal studies
Business and management	Library and archival sciences
Communications	Marketing and distribution
Conservation and natural	Military sciences
resources	Protective services
Education	Public administration and
Engineering	services
Health sciences	Theology

The difficulty, of course, is that there is a spectrum of colleges, ranging from those that offer only liberal arts courses to those whose offerings are 100 percent vocational. For example, even though few would dispute that Swarthmore and Smith are liberal arts colleges, both have engineering departments and engineering majors. Where should we place the cutoff between liberal arts and vocational colleges?

Readers not interested in the complexities of definition and classification may want to skip over the next few paragraphs devoted to the Carnegie Foundation's forty-year struggle to define a liberal arts college.

These paragraphs do, however, confirm how very difficult it is to say what a liberal arts college is.

Carnegie now classifies about 4,300 higher education institutions— public and private, nonprofit and for-profit, two-year and four-year schools, and undergraduate, master's, and doctoral programs. From 1970 until 1976, it identified 721 liberal arts colleges, 689 of which were private, 32 public. Carnegie divided them into two groups, Liberal Arts Colleges I and Liberal Arts Colleges II, both of which included institutions that were "primarily" undergraduate and awarded more than half of their degrees in liberal arts fields.[11] The 146 Liberal Arts Colleges I (2 of which were public) were said by Carnegie to be "highly selective"; the 575 Liberal Arts Colleges II, "less specialized." These quoted terms were not defined, perhaps because to do so would have been too obviously subjective.

By 1976, while Carnegie's classifications had not changed, the number of colleges included in the groups had. The total number of liberal arts colleges had fallen from 721 to 583, only 11 of which were public, and the number of group I colleges was down from 146 to 123, none of which was public. In 1987, the total number of colleges classified as liberal arts fell further, from 583 to 572, although the number of public colleges that were included rose from 11 back up to 32, and the number of group I colleges (highly selective) climbed from 123 to 142 (including 2 public schools).

In 1994, Carnegie completely revised its definitions, classifying all institutions on the basis of the highest degree they conferred. Liberal Arts Colleges I and II were replaced by Baccalaureate (Liberal Arts) Colleges I and Baccalaureate Colleges II. Both groups were described as "primarily" undergraduate colleges with a "major emphasis" on baccalaureate-degree programs. The group I colleges awarded 40 percent or more of their baccalaureate degrees in liberal arts fields and were "restrictive" in admissions. The group II colleges either awarded fewer than 40 percent of their degrees in those fields or were "less restrictive."[12] Again, the terms set off here in quotation marks were not defined.

The new classifications were, to say the least, as imprecise as the ones they replaced. What was clear was that the percentage of liberal arts degrees required for inclusion was reduced from 50 to 40 percent. What was less clear was why the Baccalaureate Colleges I category included the parenthetical notation "(Liberal Arts)" whereas the Baccalaureate Colleges II category did not. It seemed to indicate that, so far as Carnegie was concerned, only the 166 group I colleges (7 of which were public) were unequivocally liberal arts colleges. The 471 colleges in group II might or might not be, depending on how "restrictive" they were in their admissions. The definitions left open the possibility that group II colleges could grant higher percentages of baccalaureate degrees in liberal arts fields than group I colleges but still be excluded from the liberal arts identification because they were not sufficiently restrictive in their admissions. This was not helpful.

In 2001 the Carnegie Foundation tried again. The first thing it did was eliminate the word *liberal* from both its classification descriptions and its definitions. Given the confusion that word had caused, at first blush this seemed a sound move. Carnegie's new classification scheme, however, maintained the distinction between "arts and sciences" disciplines (leaving out "liberal") and "occupational and technical" disciplines (which it renamed "professional" disciplines), and added to it the extent to which institutions offer graduate degrees in the same fields in which they confer undergraduate degrees.[13]

The new classification structure radically increased the number of college categories. What were formerly either group I or II colleges can now fall into any of fifteen categories, including "arts and sciences focus" (A&S-F), that is, at least 80 percent of bachelor degrees go to majors in the arts and sciences); "arts and sciences plus professional" (A&S + Prof), meaning 60 to 79 percent of bachelor degrees are awarded in arts and sciences fields; or "balanced arts and sciences/professions" (Bal), indicating that 41 to 59 percent of degrees are awarded in either arts and sciences or professional fields. Each of these classifications is subdivided into NGC (no graduate degrees are awarded in fields corresponding to undergraduate majors), SGC (some such graduate degrees are awarded, but in less than half the fields), and HGC (some such graduate degrees are awarded in at least half the fields). (Bizarrely, in my view, NGC, SGC, and HGC stand for "no graduate coexistence," "some graduate coexistence," and "high graduate coexistence," respectively.)

With all respect to Carnegie, and recognizing that category design is extraordinarily complex, this restructuring seems at best less than a bold step forward, and at worst obscurantic. There are 89 private, not-for-profit colleges in the A&S-F/NGC category, all of which were included in the former Baccalaureate (Liberal Arts) Colleges I category.[14] The A&S-F/SGC subgroup includes more of the colleges from that prior category (e.g., Bard, Bryn Mawr, Middlebury, the two St. John's Colleges, Williams, and Wesleyan University), but also Dartmouth College, John F. Kennedy University, Maharishi University of Management, Naropa University, University of Judaism, and Xavier University of Louisiana, to mention a few. It is fair to say that the current Carnegie classification scheme is of little help in deciding which colleges are liberal arts colleges.

Until the second half of the nineteenth century, virtually every four-year, postsecondary institution that was not a trade or professional school offered a broad, nonvocational undergraduate curriculum and could reasonably be viewed as a liberal arts college. It was not until after Yale College became the first U.S. institution to grant a Ph.D. degree, in 1861, and passage of the first land-grant bill, the Morrill Act of 1862, launched the state universities, that undergraduate education outside the liberal arts began its ascent toward the preeminence it now enjoys.

Especially in the mid-nineteenth century, the founding of colleges spread rapidly across the United States. The Midwest proved particularly fertile ground for liberal arts colleges. Some were established, with missionary-like zeal, to bring East Coast–college liberal education to the frontier. Yale graduates were especially active, establishing a number of Midwest colleges designed to cleave faithfully to Yale's classical curriculum. Beloit College in Wisconsin, for example, was founded by Yale men in 1847 with the express mission of replicating the Yale curriculum for those who, for whatever reason, could not get to New Haven. Beloit was called "the Yale of the West," which was not a marketing slogan but a literal description of its educational offerings.

Colleges sprang up seemingly at every crossroad. Often, after the citizens of a new village built a lumber mill and a grain depot, the next

order of business was to found a local college. In 1851 Reverend Absalom Peters told the Society for the Promotion of Collegiate and Theological Education at the West, "Our Country, in the whole extent of
it, is to be a land of Colleges."[15] Frederick Rudolph has aptly observed
that "college-founding in the nineteenth century was undertaken in
the same spirit as canal-building, cotton-ginning, farming and gold-
mining": not "completely rational," but "touched by the American faith
in tomorrow, in the unquestionable capacity of Americans to achieve a
better world, . . . the romantic belief in endless progress."[16]

Today, most liberal arts colleges are small, residential, often located
in a rural setting, and devoted primarily to educating undergraduates.
Student enrollment is typically between 1,000 and 2,500. Students can,
and usually do, know a substantial percentage of their classmates. Students and faculty often interact outside the classroom. Most instruction is provided by full-time tenured or tenure-track professors, not
graduate students or teaching assistants. Classes tend to be small; large
lecture courses are the exception. Course enrollments of fifty students
are uncommon, and those with twenty or fewer are the norm. In contrast, in 2007 at the University of Colorado, there were 33 undergraduate courses that had 400 or more enrollees.[17] The numbers of majors
and courses offered at liberal arts colleges also tend to be small. In 2007,
for example, Beloit College's course catalog reported 56 majors and
543 courses. That same year, the University of Wisconsin–Madison offered 214 majors and 11,200 courses.[18]

Amherst College history professor emeritus Hugh Hawkins has offered the following succinct definition of a liberal arts college: "A four-
year institution of higher education, focusing its attention on candidates for the B.A. degree who are generally between the ages of eighteen
and twenty-one, an institution resistant to highly specific vocational
preparation and insisting on a considerable breadth of studies . . . [that
hopes to develop] interests and capabilities that will enrich both the
individual learner and future communities."[19]

Intimacy distinguishes the liberal arts college experience—intimacy
with the entire academic entity, because of the colleges' small size, and
especially with faculty members, most of whom are primarily engaged
in teaching rather than research and scholarship. In 1995, a Pew Chari-

table Trusts–sponsored Higher Education Roundtable of liberal arts college presidents put it this way:

> For many of those outside the academy and even more of us within, it is the liberal arts college—residential, devoted to instruction in a broad curriculum of the arts and sciences, designed as a place of growth and experimentation for the young—that remains the mind's shorthand for an undergraduate education at its best. Architecturally and philosophically, the liberal arts college embodies the ideal of learning as an act of community, in which students and faculty come together to explore and extend the foundations of knowledge. The intimacy of the residential setting, the emphasis placed on teaching, the celebration of the liberal arts as the foundation for a lifetime of learning—all define the ideal form of scholarly purpose and endeavor in undergraduate institutions. . . .
>
> When larger institutions wish to design special undergraduate environments that would provide a quality experience in residential learning and mentorship, they build small sub-communities that replicate the model of the liberal arts college.[20]

The other key distinguishing quality of liberal arts colleges is their singular commitment to teaching undergraduates. According to University of California, Berkeley, professor David Kirp, "Professors at liberal arts colleges, even[!] elite colleges like Swarthmore and Amherst, are expected to take their classroom obligations seriously."[21] In discussing the financial challenges facing Arizona State University and other public research universities, Jane Wellman observed, "Universities aspire to prestige that is achieved by increasing selectivity, getting a research mission and having faculty do as little teaching as possible, not by teaching and learning and taking students from Point A to Point B."[22]

There are now hundreds of small, private, residential colleges scattered around the country. Not all of them, of course, are liberal arts colleges, and there is no "official" list of the ones that are. Which colleges should be included in the analysis for this book?

In a thoughtful book on liberal arts colleges, David Breneman looked at 212 colleges with a combined enrollment of 260,000 students, among whom 40 percent or more majored in a liberal discipline as defined by the Carnegie Foundation in 1988.[23] In 2000, economists Michael McPherson and Morton Schapiro estimated that fewer than 100,000 students, less than 0.6 percent of all U.S. higher education enrollees, attended liberal arts colleges—colleges, as they put it, "where the majority of students major in the liberal arts and live on campus, and where admission is moderately selective (turning down, say, more than a third of those who apply)."[24] In 2004 the 89 private, not-for-profit colleges included in the Carnegie Foundation's A&S-F/NGC category had an undergraduate enrollment of 124,670.[25] All of them are unquestionably liberal arts colleges.

Another group of institutions that could be defined as liberal arts colleges are the members of the Annapolis Group. In 1993 a group of private-college presidents formed an organization they called the Annapolis Group, taking the name from the Maryland site of their first meeting. The group's express purpose is to strengthen and promote private, not-for-profit, residential liberal arts colleges. In 2007–2008, the combined full-time undergraduate enrollment of the 126 Annapolis Group–member colleges included in this book was about 218,000.[26]

In 1983, while the Carnegie Foundation was struggling with its definitions, *U.S. News and World Report* blithely began publishing its annual list of the "Best Liberal Arts Colleges." *U.S. News* claims the colleges on its list "award at least half of their degrees in the arts and sciences," although a close review reveals that more than a quarter of them do not. Nonetheless it is somehow comforting that, unlike the Carnegie Foundation, *U.S. News* has saved the word *liberal*, even if it does not define it. While college administrators love to complain about the inaccuracy of *U.S. News*'s rankings—and there are significant flaws in its methodology—it is hard to quarrel with the broad picture the rankings paint. Further, the magazine's "Best Liberal Arts Colleges" list is the most familiar, most often referred to, and most influential list of liberal arts colleges in the United States and, despite its flaws, it is no more arbitrary than any other list would be.[27]

In this book, the 225 private, not-for-profit colleges ranked in the 2009 *U.S. News* list of "Best Liberal Arts Colleges" are analyzed.[28] The Carnegie Foundation's A&S-F/NGC colleges and the Annapolis Group

Table 1.1   2007–2008 undergraduate enrollment at colleges included in
this study

Tier	Number of colleges	Total enrollment	Average enrollment
I	51	103,497	2,029
II	68	111,666	1,642
III	63	86,230	1,414
IV	43	47,258	1,099
Total	225	348,651	1,567

Note: See Appendix, Table A.1.

members list are too limited, as each omits colleges that are reasonably classified as liberal arts. Breneman's list is similar to the one used here but somewhat out of date.

Colleges included in the *U.S. News* ranking are usefully divided into four tiers. In this book, Tier I includes the 51 highest ranked, best known, and (for the most part) richest private liberal arts colleges. Sixty-eight colleges (ranked between 52 and 122 by *U.S. News*) make up Tier II. *U.S. News* does not publish numeric rankings for the colleges included in its Tiers III and IV but rather lists them alphabetically. Sixty-three of the colleges included in *U.S. News*'s Tier III and 43 of the colleges included in its Tier IV are included in the analysis here. Much of the discussion that follows distinguishes among the four tiers.

Table 1.1 summarizes the enrollment data for the 225 colleges included in this study.

Why Should We Care?

The thesis here is simple. Society needs well and broadly educated citizens. The more liberally educated citizens it has, the stronger it will be. Individuals benefit from being well and broadly educated. The more they are liberally educated, the stronger they will be in both their personal and their professional lives, and as citizens. Liberal arts colleges, while not the only vehicles for producing liberally educated citizens, are among the best.

Thoughtfulness as a "habit of mind" is what liberal education offers.[29] And as Lord Brougham neatly observed nearly two centuries ago, "Education makes a people easy to lead, but difficult to drive; easy to govern, but impossible to enslave."[30] In the ever more complex and contentious society in which we live, thoughtful citizens are a precious resource.

Certain qualities characterize the thoughtfulness of liberally educated persons. First and foremost is curiosity, a desire to know and, especially, to understand. From this flows a questioning attitude, a lack of self-certainty, and a propensity for unfettered inquiry. Full acceptance of the proposition "I may be wrong" is a baseline quality. Liberally educated persons are moved to ask such questions as, "What is good?" In addition to being drawn to explore what is, they ask, "What could be?"

A liberal education defines the relationship of its holders to the world around them. They are seldom satisfied with their level of knowing. They wonder, and bring their analytical resources and knowledge to bear on their wondering. The life of their minds is not limited by or to their daily experience. For them, the fact of not knowing can be a source of pleasurable challenge. Creativity is central to what they value.

These qualities, I have observed again and again, lead liberally educated persons to develop a set of skills that are broadly useful, fully transferable, and applicable to any challenge, vocational or other—skills that serve society as well as the individual. Liberally educated persons are capable and desirous of:

- Critical self-examination;
- Persuasive and graceful disputation;
- Effective written communication, that is, the ability to say in writing what is intended to be said;
- In Martha Nussbaum's phrase, "narrative imagination," that is, compassion and the inclination and ability to put oneself in another's shoes;[31]
- Sophisticated technology-based exploration;
- A continuing drive to generalize, to search for the common denominator;
- A well-developed understanding of the human condition, re-

flected in the ability to predict the conduct of others with substan-
tially better than average accuracy;
• An appreciation of creativity and beauty;
• An understanding of history and its consequences;
• An intellectually entrepreneurial spirit;
• A commitment to service to others and the community, that is, a
sense of social responsibility; and
• An examined life.

More than eighty years ago, while a Williams College freshman, film-
maker Elia Kazan told his immigrant father that he was studying math,
astronomy, English, Latin, and French. His father responded, "Why you
no study something use-eh-full?"[32] I believe the very fact that everything a liberal arts student studies is not "use-eh-full" is the genius of
the uniquely American liberal arts education. It is the nonvocational,
non-career-based "uselessness" of the subject matter that opens the
door to appreciating knowing for the sake of knowing and that drives
home the fact that learning is of value in and of itself, without regard
to whether it is directly linked to a marketable skill. It is possible to realize these things while studying vocational subjects but it is much
more difficult, because the student is constantly distracted from the
utility of acquiring knowledge by the utility of the knowledge being
acquired. Liberal arts education eliminates this distraction. Its lack of
career-directed purposefulness separates knowing from need to know,
learning from need to learn, and desire to understand from need to
understand.

It is often said that a liberal arts education well suits a few persons,
but for most, vocational courses of study are the right path. In my view,
this is elitist and wrong. Liberal arts education is not an alternative to
vocational training. Rather, it facilitates and enhances the vocational
experience by honing the way the mind works and stimulating enthusiasm for using it, and by enriching the entire life experience.

Today, for many persons, a high-paying job is a grail, not merely a
goal; self-certainty is admired and self-questioning derided; and much
contemporary "culture" is commercial, not creative. In a lecture she
delivered at Amherst College in 2007, novelist Marilynne Robinson
gloomily reported that "every aspect of contemporary life assumes a

lowest common denominator that is very low indeed."[33] (One of the currently popular cultural forms is "reality TV," the common denominator of which is that it is not real.) In this regard, I was heartened by a statement made by a Beloit College trustee, a highly successful corporate CEO whose formal education ended with high school. When I asked him whether he regretted not having gone to college, he answered in the affirmative. "Because you feel you lack critical thinking or communications skills?" I asked. "Not at all," he replied. "Then why?" I asked. "Because," he said, "I feel left out of art, music, literature, and culture."

Perhaps paradoxically, it may be business leaders who most persuasively articulate the value of a liberal arts education. A few years ago, history professor Warren Goldstein interviewed a number of executives who had attended Yale as undergraduates:

> "A liberal arts education teaches you how to think: how to analyze, how to read, how to write, how to develop a persuasive argument. These skills are used every day in business. A liberal arts education also offers the ability to focus on large ideas. We live in a world where everyone is multitasking, often skimming the surface and reacting to sound bites. But as undergraduates, we had the opportunity to read great literature and history, to focus and to consider. This developed a standard of depth and care that calibrates our work for the rest of our lives." (Susan Crown, principal, Henry Crown and Company investment firm.)

> "Because I was a well-educated person, I was able to use that education in the forging of relationships. I did a lot of business abroad, in cultures where being liberally educated matters more than it does here." (Robert M. Rubin, commodities and currency trader, Drexel Burnham.)

> "For leaders and managers, an undergraduate degree in business is a genuine, serious mistake. What you're going to learn is an advanced version of bookkeeping; you never learn the most rigorous thinking taught in professional business schools. I don't know anybody who recommends undergraduate study in business, certainly not over liberal arts, and I include science." (Donna Dubinsky, CEO, Numenta.)[34]

One can, of course, succeed in life without obtaining a liberal arts undergraduate degree. Bill Gates and Steve Jobs are famously successful college dropouts. Abraham Lincoln left school when he was fifteen years old. Even though Ben Franklin received his last schooling when he was eleven years old, he was a champion of formal liberal arts education as, among other things, the founder and first provost of the University of Pennsylvania:[35]

> Like many self-educated people, he was aware of the gaps in his education. He had filled most of them better than they would have been filled in school. But it had required a great deal of work, more than ought to have been necessary. And it required a sense of discipline, a devotion to learning, and a knack for absorbing information that were not given equally to all. Though he deliberately downplayed it, Franklin understood his own exceptionality; unlike many self-made men, he did not set his own experience as a standard for others.[36]

Former University of Chicago president Edward Levi correctly pointed out that universities and colleges are entitled to great credit for keeping liberal education alive:

> They have continued the traditions of culture and rediscovered cultures which had died. They have inculcated an appreciation for the works of the mind, developed the skills of the intellect, emphasized the continuing need for free inquiry and discussion, the importance of scientific discovery, the need to understand the nonrational. Thus they have stood for the concept of the wholeness of knowledge, the morality of that intellectual criticism which is so difficult because it is self-criticism, requiring the admission of error. They have helped to create thoughtfulness about values. They have held to the conception that these skills, this appreciation, this examination of values, this way of inquiry are the possession of the free man to be acquired through education. This is what a liberal education is about.[37]

A superb undergraduate liberal arts education is certainly available at the great private universities and at the honors colleges that an increasing number of distinguished public universities are creating. But the university undergraduate experience and the liberal arts college experience are different. Universities are diverse and complex. Their missions emphasize research and scholarship. Yale University history professor Jaroslav Pelikan pointed out that even when university professors divide their time equally between scholarship and teaching, and divide their teaching time equally between graduate and undergraduate students, the undergraduates get only one-quarter of their time.[38] In contrast, liberal arts colleges focus entirely on teaching undergraduates. Their goal is singular: to instill in their young students the capability and the desire to become liberally educated.

Society's need for thoughtful leaders has never been greater. Do liberal arts colleges have any special value in satisfying this need? The answer is a resounding *yes*. Even though their students represent no more than 1 or 2 percent of the total U.S. higher education enrollment, for two centuries tiny liberal arts colleges have produced a hugely disproportionately large percentage of leaders. Their graduates have been and continue to be at the forefront in every field: educators, scholars, jurists, statesmen, diplomats, politicians, scientists, business executives, artists, musicians, literary writers, journalists, and on and on. Many have received Nobel, MacArthur, Fulbright, Pulitzer, and other awards recognizing their high achievements. For example:

- Twelve U.S. presidents (27 percent) and six U.S. Supreme Court chief justices (35 percent) attended liberal arts colleges.[39] One president, James Garfield, attended two: Hiram College and Williams College.
- Three of the four first members of President Obama's transition team were liberal arts college graduates (from Sarah Lawrence, Knox, and Colby), as were three of the fifteen original executive department heads in his cabinet and two of the six holders of other cabinet-level positions.
- In the One Hundred Eleventh Congress (2009–2011), fifty-nine representatives (14 percent) and nine senators (9 percent) graduated from one of the liberal arts colleges analyzed in this book.[40]
- Over the ten years from 1999 to 2008, twelve of the fifty-three Nobel laureates (23 percent) who received their undergraduate education at a U.S. college or university received it at a liberal arts college.[41]
- Twelve of the ninety-nine recipients of MacArthur Fellowships

(so-called Genius Awards) over the four years from 2005 to 2008 attended a liberal arts college (Bates, Bennington, Calvin, Carleton, Hampshire, Haverford, Illinois Wesleyan, Kalamazoo, Oberlin, Smith, Trinity, and Wesleyan University).[42]

- In 2010 at least thirteen of the ninety-one tenured and tenure-track professors at Harvard Law School had graduated from a liberal arts college.[43]

- Harvard University president Drew Gilpin Faust is a liberal arts college graduate (Bryn Mawr College), as are two other presidents among the fifty highest-ranked national universities: Mary Sue Coleman, president of the University of Michigan (Grinnell College), and Nathan O. Hatch, president of Wake Forest University (Wheaton College).[44]

- Twenty-eight of the fifty baccalaureate-granting institutions that, proportionate to their size, graduated the most science and engineering doctorate recipients from 1997 to 2006 were liberal arts colleges. Five of them, Harvey Mudd, Reed, Swarthmore, Carleton, and Grinnell, ranked ahead of Harvard; nine of them ahead of Yale.[45]

It would be foolish to abandon such successful enterprises.[46]

The Pew-sponsored Higher Education Roundtable of college presidents neatly summarized the unique value of liberal arts colleges: "It is the liberal arts college that best retains the language and imagery of education as a social compact between a community and its individual members—even as 'community' has come to encompass a broad range of people and responsibilities. In this setting, acquiring knowledge is defined not just as a means to individual advancement but as a basis for assuming the mantle of social responsibility, of making constructive contributions to the community and larger society of which one is part."[47]

It would be a tragedy if, as the Roundtable participants said, the exceptional educational experience liberal arts colleges provide were to become "a quaint relic, more precious than important, pursued by a handful of students who seek mainly the status and credentialing that a degree from a private institution confers."[48]

CHAPTER 2

The Economic Health of Liberal Arts Colleges

✦

Liberal arts colleges' revenues have never covered their expenses. The colleges have always had to search for outside financial support. Church affiliations, which most colleges had at least at the outset, did not provide adequate revenue supplements (although they sometimes stimulated the eleemosynary instincts of church members) and colleges have eagerly sought wealthy donors, regardless of faith or denomination. From the beginning, the colleges showed entrepreneurial initiative in the pursuit of funding, for example renaming themselves after wealthy donors like William Denison (Granville College) and William Carleton (Northfield College).[1] In the eighteenth and early nineteenth centuries, states also provided needed funds to private colleges. Harvard, Yale, and Columbia would not have survived the colonial period without state support, and many other colleges also benefited from state largesse.[2] With the rise of the public universities after the Civil War, however, direct state subsidies for private institutions dried up.

Wealth (Endowment)

As everyone knows, it is the income from accumulated wealth—the endowment—that makes it possible for private institutions to sell their educational services at below-cost prices. Endowment size, perhaps more than any other single factor, determines the success and the perceived quality of private colleges and universities. By and large, the oldest institutions—the ones that have had the longest time to build an endowment—are the richest. There are, of course, exceptions, usually related to exceptionally large gifts from individual donors. Perhaps the most imposing gift a liberal arts college ever received, however, was not wealth but knowledge.

In 1968, when its endowment was about $10 million, Grinnell College alumnus and long-time trustee James Rosenfield, a brilliant investor in his own right, persuaded his even more financially astute friend Warren Buffett to join the Grinnell board of trustees. Together, Rosenfield and Buffett invested Grinnell's modest resources in daring ways. In 1968, for example, Grinnell put up 10 percent ($300,000) of the start-up money for a new company being formed by Grinnell alumnus Robert Noyce. Between 1974 and 1980 Grinnell sold its interest in that company, Intel, for $14 million, realizing a 4,600 percent profit. In 1977 Grinnell spent $12.9 million, a third of its endowment at the time, to purchase a television station in Dayton, Ohio, an unheard-of investment for a small liberal arts college. Four years later it sold the station for $49 million. In 1984, the college bought 30,000 shares of *Des Moines Register* stock for $16 per share. (Buffett owned a significant interest in the *Washington Post* and liked newspapers.) After two years, the college sold the *Register* stock for $140 per share. Grinnell also bought stock in Buffett's investment company, Berkshire Hathaway, for $5,252, which it later sold for $3.7 million; $200,000 worth of stock in another start-up company, Apple, which it sold after two years for $1.25 million; and made a $10 million investment in the Sequoia Fund that, twenty years later, was worth more than $600 million. Through extraordinarily canny investments such as these, Grinnell's endowment grew from $10 million in 1968 to $1.47 billion in 2008.[3]

A fundamental reality of endowments is, the rich almost always get richer. If College A's endowment is $100 million and College B's is $200 million, and both manage to increase their endowments at the rate of 7 percent per year, after ten years College A will have $200 million and College B, $400 million. Before, College B had $100 million more than College A; now it has $200 million more. The difference in their wealth has doubled.

A likely reason College B had more money than College A to begin with is that it is older and got started building its endowment earlier. Of course, there are other factors that affect wealth: adept fund-raising, investment-management skill, capturing megadonations, attracting students who go on after graduation to become rich, and luck, to mention only a few. But once a college has a head start, it is hard for others to catch up.

Colleges with small endowments try to catch up. They grind away, searching for six-figure donations and hoping for a seven-figure gift. They organize fund drives with optimistic gift pyramids showing how many five-, six-, and seven-figure gifts they need to make their goal. They hire experts to manage their endowments. But the richer institutions are doing the same thing, often using their superior wealth to employ superior fund-raisers and money managers. Yale University's in-house investment management department, for example, was long considered one of the best in the nation, nonprofit or commercial, and its investment strategies were followed by many universities and colleges. Historically, institutions with larger endowments have, on average, enjoyed higher rates of return.[4]

The National Association of College and University Business Officers' (NACUBO) *2008 NACUBO Endowment Study* covers the academic year immediately before the recession began in the second half of 2008. It reported the endowments of 791 participating colleges and universities, public and private, representing most U.S. institutions of higher learning with endowments of at least $100 million. It showed that institutions with more than $1 billion in endowment assets had, on average, a staff of seven managing their investments, and at least one institution, doubtless a university, employed thirty-one investment managers. In contrast, while some institutions with endowment assets of less than $100 million may have had investment-savvy trustees, most had no staff investment managers and relied instead on outside consultants for investment guidance, or had no professional support at all. Only half of the wealthiest institutions ($1 billion plus) felt a need to retain any outside consultants.[5]

Less wealthy schools have another serious disadvantage in managing their endowments. They need the money now. To paraphrase an old joke, while their wealthy competitors may occasionally dip into income, they may be forced to invade capital. A college that needs whatever money it manages to raise each year to cover operating expenses is ill equipped to build wealth.

Economic inequality among colleges and universities is dramatic, and increasing. Wealth is concentrated in a very few institutions. The *2008 NACUBO Endowment Study* showed that:

- The 5 wealthiest institutions—Harvard, Yale, Stanford, Princeton, and the University of Texas—each of which enjoyed an endowment of more than $10 billion, accounted for more than one-quarter of the combined endowments of all 791 institutions.
- The 21 richest institutions, all of which were universities and 15 of which were private, accounted for more than half.
- Seventy-seven institutions, including 50 private institutions (41 universities and 9 liberal arts colleges), had endowments of more than $1 billion, representing nearly three-quarters of the total endowment assets in the study ($412.8 billion).[6]
- Harvard University's wealth alone, $36.6 billion, was greater than the combined endowments of the 551 poorest colleges and universities, that is, the bottom two-thirds.
- Institutions with endowments of $100 million or less held only 4.4 percent of the study group's combined endowment assets.[7]

The tables that follow are drawn from the huge data bank collected by the National Center for Education Statistics, described in Chapter 1. Data for each of the 225 liberal arts colleges analyzed in this book are provided in the Appendix.

The huge disparity in wealth among liberal arts colleges is reflected here in Table 2.1, which shows the range, average, and median size of the endowment assets in each tier. Table 2.2 shows 2007–2008 endowment assets per full-time equivalent (FTE) undergraduate—that is, the size of the endowment relative to the college's enrollment.

To permit this wealth to grow, colleges and universities seek to spend only a portion of their endowments' annual appreciation. Typically the spending determination is made on the basis of a fixed percentage (often 4.5 to 5.0 percent), frequently of a rolling, three-year average of the total endowment. When spending is based on a multiyear average, a

Table 2.1   Market value of 2007–2008 endowment assets ($000)

Tier	Range	Average	Median
I	$78,000–$1,800,000	$662,000	$550,000
II	$14,000–$1,000,000	$184,000	$140,000
III	$13,000–$367,000	$70,000	$61,000
IV	$1,800–$75,000	$21,000	$15,000

Note: See Appendix, Table A.3.

Table 2.2   Market value of 2007–2008 endowment assets per full-time equivalent undergraduate (FTE)

Tier	Range	Average	Median
I	$58,000–$1,168,000	$338,000	$273,000
II	$20,000–$642,000	$119,000	$93,000
III	$12,000–$161,000	$57,000	$43,000
IV	$900–$110,000	$24,000	$19,000

Note: See Appendix, Table A.3.

college spends less than the fixed percentage in years when its endowment is growing; more when it is contracting.

For example, if a college's endowment is $100 million in Year 1 and it increases by $10 million in each of the next two years, the endowment at the end of Year 3 will be $120 million. At a 5-percent spending rate based on a three-year rolling average, the college will spend $5.5 million in Year 3, even though 5 percent of the Year 3 endowment ($120 million) is $6 million. If, during each of the next two years, the endowment declines $10 million, the college will still spend $5.5 million in Year 5, even though 5 percent of its endowment that year ($100 million) is only $5 million.

During fiscal 2007–2008, the average spending rate among all institutions that participated in the *2008 NACUBO Endowment Study* was 4.6 percent. The average spending rate for the richest institutions (those with more than $1 billion in endowment assets) was 4.3 percent, significantly lower than that of the poorest (those with less than $25 million), 4.8 percent.[8] Based on the 2008 NACUBO data, at a 4.6 percent spending rate, Tier I Pomona College would have had more than $54,000 available to spend for each of its 1,522 full-time students; Tier IV Marymount Manhattan College, only $383 for each of its 1,724 full-time students. (Princeton University, by way of comparison, would have had $104,000 for each of its 7,249 full-time undergraduate and graduate students.)

As readers have doubtless surmised, Pomona College could have provided tuition-free admission to all of its students. In contrast, many Tier III and IV colleges did not have enough spendable endowment revenue to cover annual increases in operating expenses—salaries, benefits, maintenance, utilities, and so forth—let alone to increase financial aid or grow their endowments.

Table 2.3 applies the 4.6 percent spending rate to the 2007–2008 endowment assets per FTE shown in Table 2.2, providing a rough estimate of the average spendable endowment monies available in that year to the colleges in each tier.

It might be expected that the investment policies of educational institutions would be quite conservative, and until the end of the twentieth century, they generally were. In 1998, colleges and universities as a group held 90 percent of their endowments in traditional assets—equities, fixed income, and cash. Between 1999 and 2008, however, equity and fixed-income holdings declined steadily, from 88 percent to 71 percent. For the most part following the so-called Yale Plan, many colleges replaced their more conservative investments with riskier alternative asset classes, primarily less liquid hedge funds, real estate, private equity, venture capital, and natural resources. In 2008, while the poor-

Table 2.3   4.6 percent of the market value of 2007–2008 endowment assets per undergraduate FTE

Tier	Range	Average
I	$2,700–$53,700	$15,500
II	$900–$29,500	$5,500
III	$600–$7,400	$2,600
IV	$40–$5,100	$1,100

Note: See Appendix, Table A.3.

est institutions in the NACUBO study still held 83 percent of their money in equities and fixed-income instruments, the richest institutions had barely 50 percent of their money invested in traditional assets.[9] Nearly one-quarter of the richest institutions' investments were in hedge funds alone. Institutions with endowments between $100 and $500 million, which included most of the Tier II colleges, had moved in the same direction, with nearly 30 percent of their endowments invested in nontraditional assets.[10]

One can reasonably speculate why the dramatic change in investment policies occurred. Rich colleges and universities doubtless observed the success that commercial investors were enjoying, had the resources to get into the game, and did so. The investment managers they hired were eager to play, to do their stuff. Tier II colleges saw what was happening and concluded that, if they failed to join in, they would fall even farther behind. And until the financial-market meltdown and recession in the second half of 2008, the investment strategy worked: endowments soared.

Between 2008 and 2009, however, the recession substantially cut into the endowments of almost every higher education institution, public and private, university and college. The average endowment of the 842 U.S. institutions that participated in the NACUBO's 2009 endowment study dropped 23 percent in value. The endowments of one-third of the participating liberal arts colleges dropped more than that amount. The average rate of return on endowments of all institutions also fell precipitously, an average of 18.7 percent, slightly more for the wealthiest colleges and universities (20.5 percent for institutions whose endowments exceeded $1 billion) than for the less well endowed (18.6 percent for those with endowments of $51 million to $100 million). Further, 43 percent of the 2009 NACUBO study participants reported increasing their endowment spending rate.[11]

Because many of the alternative assets that colleges and universities had acquired were not liquid, cash they had relied on to meet their ongoing expenses, including interest charges and principle repayments on their debt, became unavailable. Some institutions were forced to borrow; others found themselves obliged to sell assets at distress prices to meet their financial obligations.

The overwhelming economic inequality among higher education institutions has not been significantly changed by the recession, although it may have been lessened somewhat. If, for example, two colleges, one with an endowment of $200 million and the other $100 million, both lost 20 percent, the dollar gap between them dropped from $100 million to $80 million. What difference this will make, if any, remains to be seen. From the standpoint of the future of liberal arts education, the impact of recession on Tier II colleges is likely to be particularly adverse. As a group, they have struggled the hardest to remain true to the liberal arts mission, to resist the pressure to become more vocational. Losing a quarter of their endowment wealth—and in some cases more—makes their challenge more difficult, as will recession-generated increases in demand by students for more career-oriented courses, lower tuition, more financial aid, and cheaper educational alternatives, including community and technical colleges and online instruction.

Operating Expenses and Tuition Revenues

Liberal arts colleges, with their residential campuses, small classes, full-time tenured teaching faculties, lack of graduate student teaching assistants, expansive facilities (libraries, laboratories, athletics), and so on, provide the most expensive undergraduate education. Their total list prices (tuition, room, and board) reflect this fact. In 2009–2010, half of the 100 most expensive colleges and universities were liberal arts colleges—ranging from Sarah Lawrence College ($54,410 per year) to Colorado College ($46,902)—all of which are included in this study.[12]

It is difficult to compare the operating expenses of liberal arts colleges because their individual circumstances differ so greatly. Depreciation, interest, maintenance, and other expenditures vary widely among colleges and, from year to year, at any given college. The expense items most consistently comparable for all colleges are payments to faculty members and staff (that is, salaries, wages, and benefits), and there is strikingly little variation among colleges in the percentage of total expenses per FTE accounted for by these payments.

Rich or poor, in 2007–2008 most colleges devoted about 40 percent of their spending to payments to employees (see Table 2.4).[13] There were, however, major differences in the total amounts colleges spent on salaries, wages, and benefits per FTE. The ten highest-ranked colleges spent, on average, more than three times as much as did Tier IV colleges. One cannot conclude that the poorer colleges provided an inferior education to their students compared with the wealthy colleges, but from the data shown in Table 2.5 we can see that they did provide a much less costly one.

While there is substantial variation in the percentage of the colleges' total expenses covered by tuition and fee revenues, ranging from 3 percent to 83 percent in 2007–2008, the average in each of the four tiers is

Table 2.4   Average percentage of 2007–2008 total expenses per undergraduate FTE accounted for by faculty/staff salaries, wages, and benefits

Tier I	42.6%
Tier II	41.5%
Tier III	40.1%
Tier IV	40.6%

Note: See Appendix, Table A.7.

Table 2.5   Total 2007–2008 expenses for salaries, wages, and benefits per undergraduate FTE

Tier/rank[a]	Range	Average
I/1–10	$23,000–$36,300	$30,600
11–20	$21,900–$32,100	$26,200
21–30	$19,200–$30,200	$22,300
31–40	$17,800–$25,700	$19,600
41–50	$14,100–$21,900	$17,400
II	$10,100–$24,300	$14,900
III[b]	$6,500–$24,400	$12,700
IV	$5,000–$27,900	$9,700

Note: See Appendix, Table A.7.
   a. Tier I college rankings according to *America's Best Colleges,* 2009 ed. (New York: U.S. News and World Report).
   b. Excluding American Jewish University ($95,800).

surprisingly consistent (see Table 2.6), although the average for the eight Tier I colleges with endowments of more than $1 billion was significantly lower, 30.6 percent. The percentage is, of course, affected by both the amount of tuition discounting and the costliness of the educational services provided.

There also was little variation between tiers in the average amount of the colleges' 2007–2008 total revenues (including return on investments) required to cover their total expenses, although there was substantial variation between colleges in each tier. On average, the colleges in all four tiers came close to breaking even (Table 2.7). Fifty to 60 percent of the colleges in each tier, however, operated at a loss.[14] It is striking that, in the year before (2006–2007), only ten of the colleges—three in Tier III and seven in Tier IV—had operated at a loss.[15]

A study by economists Gordon Winston and Stephen Lewis ranked all U.S. colleges and universities, public and private, by the total subsidy students received—the costs of providing educational services minus net tuition revenues—in 1991. On average, each student at institutions in the top 10 percent (ranked by the total subsidy the institutions

Table 2.6   Average percentage of 2007–2008 total expenses covered by tuition and fees revenues

Tier I	44.5%
Tier II	50.1%
Tier III	50.6%
Tier IV	47.6%

Note: See Appendix, Table A.5.

Table 2.7   Average percentage of 2007–2008 total revenues expended to cover total expenses

Tier I	102.9%
Tier II	110.2%
Tier III	103.0%
Tier IV	100.4%

Note: See Appendix, Table A.8.

gave) received an education that cost their college or university more than $25,000 to provide, for which they paid $4,700. Students at institutions in the bottom 10 percent received an education that cost only $6,500, for which they paid an average of more than $5,000. Moreover, the institutions in the top 10 percent had nearly four times more resources supporting the education they gave their students than did the institutions in the bottom 10 percent.[16]

Financial Aid

In 2003–2004, according to the National Postsecondary Student Aid Study (NPSAS), 83 percent of all undergraduates attending a private, not-for-profit, four-year institution received some type of financial aid. Seventy-three percent of them received grants and 56 percent took out student loans. The average grant was $7,700, the average loan $6,900. Fifty percent of the grants students received came from their college; 28 percent included federal funds, 22 percent state funds, and 23 percent funds from other sources such as private organizations or employers. The average institutional grant was $7,100.[17]

On average, the financial aid grants from liberal arts colleges, especially those in Tiers I and II, were much higher than the national average. At Williams College, for example, where in 2008, 47 percent of the students received scholarship aid provided by the college, the average scholarship awarded to entering first-year students (the members of the class of 2012) was $37,003.[18] At Dickinson College, 57 percent of first-year students in 2008 received grants and scholarship aid from the college, averaging $22,700 per student.[19]

Tuition Discounting

As is well known, liberal arts colleges engage in extensive tuition discounting. Table 2.8 shows that, in 2007–2008, the average discount (the percentage of the list-price tuition and required fees not covered by the tuition and fees receipts) was more than one-third in all four tiers.

Table 2.8 also shows a significant increase in discounting between 2006–2007 and 2007–2008, especially among Tier II colleges. There are

Table 2.8   Average tuition (and required fees) discounts

Tier	2006–2007	2007–2008
I	19.7%	33.5%
II	30.2%	37.6%
III	30.6%	40.2%
IV	28.7%	37.6%

Note: See Appendix, Table A.6, and http://nces.ed.gov/ipeds/datacenter.

a number of possible explanations for this change, including normal year-to-year variation and an increase in direct lending to students by colleges, in lieu of bank and other third-party loans. Almost certainly, however, the dramatic move, especially among Tier I colleges, away from loans to outright grants—beginning in 2007 and accelerating in 2008—played a role.

After a few rumblings early in 2003, in 2007 the tuition-discounting world exploded. In increasing numbers, wealthy universities and colleges began announcing they would admit students from less and less poor families tuition-free. It is unclear why this happened. Was it simply a reflection of unbridled competition for top students? Did public anger about the high cost of college boil over? Did tight economic times and declining federal and state government support for higher education put new economic pressure on lower- and lower-middle-class families? Did the huge wealth of a growing number of universities and colleges create a revolt among parents? Did administrators start to feel guilty about charging $50,000 a year when their endowments were earning more than that per student every year? Was the pressure put on the richest institutions by Senator Grassley of Iowa to spend at least 5 percent of their huge endowments if they wanted to keep their tax-exempt status taken by them as a warning shot?[20] It is hard to know. (One cannot help wondering if Senator Grassley would be pleased if negative tuitions, paying students to attend, were to take root at the richest colleges and universities. It seems a safe bet that, with the possible exception of Grinnell, the private colleges in his home state would be devastated.)

In any case, in July 2007 Amherst College announced it was eliminating student loans. From now on, it said, all financial aid for Amherst students would be in the form of outright grants.[21] The events that captured the most media attention, however, were Harvard's announcement later that year that it would begin offering significant financial aid to families with annual incomes of up to $180,000, followed in short order by Yale's declaration that it would do the same for families with incomes as high as $200,000—that is, four times higher than the average income of an American family of four.

In no time at all, it seemed, the rich institutions were competing to see who could offer the sweetest deal. Dozens of wealthy universities and liberal arts colleges followed Amherst's lead and replaced student loans with outright grants. It was described as a "stampede" by the *New York Times*.[22] Stanford, MIT, Penn, and Dartmouth eliminated tuition altogether for families with incomes of $75,000 to $100,000. At Columbia, Harvard, Brown, Stanford, Yale, and Duke, families with incomes of less than $60,000 would pay nothing for their children's education. Even a few public universities, like the Universities of Indiana, Florida, North Carolina, and Virginia, got into the act, replacing loans with grants for poor students.

Other deal sweeteners were devised by affluent institutions. MIT upped its financial aid budget by $7 million and Bates College boosted its financial aid budget "a few points to keep ahead of the trend." Princeton announced it would pay for at least 10 percent of its incoming students to go abroad for a year to do social-service work before they entered the university, and Dartmouth reported offering scholarships worth nearly $3,000 to allow students who receive financial aid to take advantage of research and internship opportunities in their junior year. A number of colleges in the Northeast began providing free airline tickets to potential students and their parents for campus visits. Bucknell, Cornell University, Amherst, the University of Michigan, and four other institutions created partnerships with community colleges.

Cities joined in. Kalamazoo, Michigan; Davenport, Iowa; Dayton, Ohio; La Crosse, Wisconsin; Denver; Philadelphia; Pittsburgh; and San Francisco all established or were considering (before the 2008 recession) programs to pay some or all of the college expenses of graduates of local high schools. To do this, the cities solicited funding from private donors, in direct competition with private colleges and universities.

To top it all off, the 136 richest institutions were required to provide detailed information about their wealth to the Senate Finance Committee in Washington, on which Senator Grassley is the ranking minority member.[23] While nothing seems to have come of it yet, the recession has not softened the view of Senator Grassley, who has said, "I hope colleges won't rely on double-digit losses as a reason to raise tuition or freeze student aid. . . . A lot of colleges still have plenty of money in the bank," sending shivers up the spines of university presidents and trustees.[24]

The effects of tuition giveaways by the richest schools can trickle down and have an adverse impact on even the least prestigious, poorest liberal arts colleges. Reacting to the suggestion that the majority of liberal arts colleges do not compete with the wealthy highfliers for students, Dickinson College's former vice president for enrollment, Robert J. Massa, wrote:

> Within two months of Harvard's announcement, almost 20 affluent colleges followed suit. Among the first to say, "Me too," was Swarthmore College. Although Swarthmore is in our state and athletic conference, Dickinson does not significantly overlap with it for students. Swarthmore does compete with Harvard and other affluent schools and apparently assumed, with its financial largesse, that it needed to replace loans with grants to keep up. Bowdoin College overlaps with Swarthmore, and eventually it joined others in the move to eliminate loans. Bowdoin is not in Dickinson's top-10 overlap schools.
>
> But Colby College *is* one of our top-10 overlap schools and also overlaps with Bowdoin. While Colby's endowment is significantly lower than Swarthmore's and Bowdoin's, it felt compelled to eliminate loans as well. Now, within several months, Harvard's move to spend its money will certainly affect Dickinson's ability to attract students.[25]

Dickinson College, ranked 119th among private institutions by NACUBO on the basis of its 2008 endowment ($308 million), is by no means one of the poorest colleges.[26] At an annual spending rate of 4.6

percent, this represented $5,600 per student. After covering increases in operating costs, such as maintenance and salaries, little money was left for increasing scholarship aid to Dickinson students. When William Durden, Dickinson's president, was asked by a Dickinson student's father whether the college intended to follow Harvard's lead and provide aid to families with up to $180,000 in annual income, he responded that Dickinson could not afford to do so. The father replied, "I know this costs a lot of money, but you should do it anyway." Dickinson and other liberal arts colleges, Durden later told the *New York Times*, "are going to be under huge pressure to do these things that we just can't do."[27]

It remains to be seen how many of the financial aid initiatives described above, all of which occurred before June 2008, will survive the recession. Many have already been cut back or terminated. College and university officials are talking openly about returning to student-aid loans and showing renewed interest in students who can pay in full.[28] Scholarship initiatives undertaken or planned by cash-strapped cities are particularly vulnerable. Obviously, the new discounts most likely to be preserved are the ones put in place by the richest institutions.

Surviving

With the exception of the few very wealthy colleges, all liberal arts colleges have struggled financially for a long time. In 1971, Clark Kerr, then chairman of the Carnegie Commission on Higher Education, opined that, while 29 percent of 730 liberal arts colleges were not in financial trouble, 43 percent were headed for trouble and 28 percent were already in financial difficulty.[29] In 1975, Howard Bowen and W. John Minter concluded that 27 percent of all private colleges were in serious financial trouble.[30] In a 1980 report, Virginia Fadil and Nancy Carter said that 57 four-year private colleges had closed, 24 had merged, and 6 had become public between 1970 and 1979.[31] In 1994, Ernest Boyer reported that 200 institutions had merged, closed, or were otherwise no longer eligible for inclusion in the Carnegie Foundation's listing.[32] Amherst College historian Hugh Hawkins stated that "167 private four-year colleges . . . disappeared between 1967 and 1990."[33]

Given their constant state of financial distress, it was reasonable to expect that some colleges would be forced out of business.

The dire warnings, however, did not take into account liberal arts colleges' survival instinct. Between 1987 and 2008, only twenty-one four-year colleges, including nine religious schools and two women's colleges, disappeared from the Carnegie Foundation's list of higher education institutions. They included Mount Vernon College, a women's college in the District of Columbia that was purchased by George Washington University in 1999; Bradford College in Massachusetts, which, before it closed in 2000, had attempted to become a four-year coeducational, rather than a two-year women's, college; and religious colleges Barat College in Illinois, which was purchased by DePaul University in 2001 and had its operations discontinued and its assets sold in 2004; Marymount College in New York, which merged with Fordham University in 2002 and closed in 2007; and Trinity College in Vermont, which closed in 2001.

Not all of the colleges that disappeared from the Carnegie list, however, went out of business, at least not in the usual sense of the word. Radcliffe College, for example, was finally integrated into Harvard University in 1999. The tiny Shimer College, known for its fidelity to Robert Hutchins's Great Books curriculum, survived by abandoning its small residential campus in Waukegan, Illinois, in 2006, and moving to the Southside Chicago campus of the Illinois Institute of Technology.[34]

Perhaps the most publicized recent "closing" was of experimental Antioch College in Yellow Springs, Ohio, which suspended operation in 2008 (as a result, most believe, of egregious bad management), although some of its alumni are struggling to resurrect their alma mater.[35] At the time its trustees determined to close down Antioch College, Antioch University had five "units" scattered across the country. These university units, unlike the college, were "without significant physical plants to maintain, without residential students, without tenured faculty, and without strong systems of faculty governance."[36] Faced with financial crisis, Antioch's trustees apparently concluded they could save either the 20-year-old university units or the 155-year-old liberal arts college, but not both. They opted to sacrifice the college, the historic heart and soul of Antioch.

The case of Milton College in Milton, Wisconsin, is an interesting one. Founded in 1844, it received national press coverage when it closed its doors in 1982, 138 years later. Milton's demise was broadly attributed to unmanageable debt and loss of accreditation, but there were more factors behind its "slow agonizing decline" in the 1970s, including poor planning, excessive dependence on tuition revenues, inadequate fund-raising, unchecked growth, excessive reliance on debt, and ambiguity about its mission. At the end, its catalogue continued to describe Milton as a liberal arts college, but its major programs for the most part had come to be vocational—teacher training, nursing, criminal justice, social welfare, recreation, and communications.[37]

At roughly the same time Milton College was going under, Olivet College in Olivet, Michigan, was also struggling. Olivet was founded in the same year as Milton, 1844, by one of the founders of Oberlin College. In the early part of the twentieth century it had enjoyed a particularly rich literary history. For several years, Ford Madox Ford was on its faculty as, from time to time, were Gertrude Stein, Alice B. Toklas, Sherwood Anderson, and Katherine Anne Porter.

By the late 1970s, Olivet faced financial collapse. Staff reductions and across-the-board salary cuts were implemented to keep the college afloat. I served on the Olivet College board of trustees from 1978 to 1981. During that time, Olivet's then president, Donald Morris, told me he believed he could attract $1 million from insurance companies and associations by creating an insurance department and major. When I responded that doing so would be inconsistent with Olivet's liberal arts mission, Morris said that, while he shared my view, he had faculty members with wives and children and it was his obligation to keep food on their tables. The insurance department was formed and is still a part of the college's curriculum.

Unlike Milton, Olivet has survived. One cannot say that it was the new insurance department that saved the day, but Olivet's willingness to venture into more vocational areas clearly was a part of its survival (even though the same willingness was not enough to save Milton). Today Olivet continues to struggle financially but is still in business.

CHAPTER 3

The Declining Demand for Liberal Arts Education

✦

There has, of course, long been a demand for liberal arts colleges and the degrees they award, but it is far from clear that there has ever been any significant demand for the liberal arts education they provide. Henry Adams, for example, reflecting on his four years at Harvard College (1854–1858), where he had been preceded by "generation after generation" of Adamses and other forebears, described attending the college as the "next regular step" after completing Mr. Dixwell's School on Boylston Place in Boston. Although, he said, none of his ancestors "as far as known, had ever done any good" at Harvard, "or thought himself the better for it, custom, social ties, convenience, and, above all, economy, kept each generation in the track. . . . All went there because their friends went there and the College was their ideal of social respect. . . . [T]he College offered chiefly advantages vulgarly called social, rather than mental."[1]

A Brief History

In 1900, the majority of undergraduates at higher education institutions, perhaps as many as 70 percent of them, were pursuing a liberal arts degree.[2] During the first half of the twentieth century, prep schools cranked out students for the Ivy League: Groton for Harvard, Choate for Yale, Lawrenceville for Princeton. The Ivies were largely populated by children of privilege, and the social sorting out often took place in eating clubs, secret societies, and select activities: Hasty Pudding, Fence, Skull and Bones, Tiger, Ivy, the *Crimson,* the *Daily News,* the *Lampoon.* Diversity meant admitting a few boys from the Midwest. If a public high school graduate from Kansas City managed to gain admission to Yale, he could lift himself into the elite East Coast social structures, but only with effort and dedication. The potential payoff, however, was great. Careers on Wall Street beckoned.

While young men at Ivy League colleges were enjoying their leisurely passage to adulthood in the warm glow of privilege, some liberal education rubbed off, at least on some of them. Professors devoted a good bit of their time to teaching, and even if instruction was in the form of annually repeated lectures delivered from tattered notes, many were good lectures. They were the same lectures boys who came before had listened to and boys who would come after would also hear, further strengthening the common experience that bound together these future leaders of our nation. Perhaps some university faculty members were increasingly distracted by the rewards of research and scholarship and the appeal of teaching graduate students, but the commitment of many of them to undergraduate instruction was real. It was not uncommon for professors to guide their young charges outside the classroom as well, as masters of colleges, for example.

There were exceptions, but by and large the Western canon lay at the heart of the undergraduate experience. Teachers knew what mattered, what an educated man should know, and each year they transmitted the wisdom of the canon to their charges. An appreciation of appropriate history, philosophical inquiry, and the "best" culture was comfortably shared, and sometimes even drawn into the social life of young gentlemen, in conversations over sherry and cucumber sandwiches at Porcellian or the Elizabethan Club. While students might have answered, if asked, that they chose the prestigious Ivy experience in order to get a liberal education, and while they actually may have garnered one, what truly attracted most of them was the possibility of taking the next step toward their rightful place in the leadership establishment.

A handful of colleges, a disproportionate number of which were in the Midwest, such as Oberlin and Carleton, were also attracting outstanding students who, even if they were not Ivy legacies, also came from families in which going to college was simply something one did, and who possessed the academic records needed to gain admission to any college or university. Attending a non-Ivy college may not have automatically opened establishment doors, but it did clear the way to go on to the best law, medical, and business schools, as well as premier graduate schools, and their graduates embraced these opportunities.

Why had they rejected the Ivies and "settled"—at least in the view of some of their elders and betters—for something less prestigious? Some high-quality candidates were foreclosed from the Ivies by gender, race, religion, or social-station quotas imposed at the time, or by poverty or distance. Others simply preferred to attend a coeducational college (perhaps because their public high school experience had failed to give them a full appreciation of the magical appeal of the young women at the Seven Sisters colleges).

The liberal arts education delivered at these Midwestern colleges was not unlike that offered by their Ivy counterparts. Some said Midwestern college students were more purposeful in their pursuit of liberal learning, the world not yet being their oyster, and perhaps this was so. In any event, Carleton and Oberlin students, no less than Ivy Leaguers, were looking to their future in selecting their educational program. They, too, may have begun a liberal education during their four college years, but for most of them it was incidental to their postcollege career aspirations.

In the 1960s, Vietnam War protests; sex, drugs, and rock and roll; even anti-intellectualism became reasons to go to college. The focus of student demand shifted from preparing for the future to experimenting now. For many, the perceived advantages of associating with the right crowd were replaced by enthusiasm for associating with the wrong crowd. Long-term aspirations were not forgotten, however, just set aside. Getting high and getting busted were seen as a low risk, not closing any doors; one could stop smoking pot any time. Sometimes this worked out and sometimes it didn't. As remembered by English professor and former president of Wesleyan and Emory Universities, William M. Chace,

> For those like me who immediately followed . . . [the World War II veterans] in the 1950s and early 1960s, the centrality of the humani-

ties to a liberal education was a settled matter. But by the end of the 1960s, everything was up for grabs and nothing was safe from negative and reductive analysis. Every form of anti-authoritarian energy—concerning sexual mores, race relations, the war in Vietnam, mind-altering drugs—was felt across the nation. (I was at Berkeley, the epicenter of all such energies.) Against such ferocious intensities, few elements of the cultural patterns of the preceding decades could stand. The long-term consequences of such a spilling-out of the old contents of what college meant reverberate today.[3]

A longer-lasting change in the demand for a college education also emerged in the 1960s. It began with, for want of a better word, the "democratization" of higher education. Women were admitted to men's colleges, quotas on Jews and African Americans were loosened and then dropped. Minority students began not only to be admitted in larger numbers but to be affirmatively courted.

A college degree replaced a high school diploma as the ticket to a secure future. Millions of Americans, many of whose parents had not gone beyond high school, for whom college had never seemed a viable option, determined to attend. The number of applicants, including veterans with GI Bill money, skyrocketed, and colleges and universities welcomed them. Total undergraduate enrollment in the United States jumped from 2.4 million in 1955 to 7.4 million in 1970, an increase of more than 200 percent. African American enrollment increased by 237 percent.[4]

Many of the "new" students, for whom attending college was not a given, were not applying to college to gain entry into an elite world. They had their own lives. They wanted a better job and more job security and asked, "Will a college degree help me get it?"—a question college-bound "traditional" students had not found it necessary to pose. For traditional students, the answer was as obvious as it had been to Henry Adams: college was simply the "next regular step." For the new students, since college graduates' lifetime earnings substantially exceeded those of persons holding only high school diplomas, the answer to their question was a resounding *yes*.

Even with the vast influx of new students, by the end of the twentieth century the percentage of college students attending liberal arts colleges and universities had fallen below 5 percent.[5] Students and their parents simply wanted a liberal arts degree less or, more precisely, wanted vocational training more. The current fierce competition for admission to the top-rated liberal arts colleges and universities notwithstanding, at less prestigious institutions the annual challenge has become not how to choose which applicants to admit but how to attract *enough* students to fill their dormitories and provide sufficient tuition income to continue operating at current levels.[6] "Will we make our class?" is the annual question or, more precisely, "Can we make our class without admitting unqualified students?"

The main story line for higher education during the past half century is the rise in demand for vocational instruction. The new students asked, "Are the courses I will take practical?" The practicality of courses in business, nursing, or criminal justice was apparent to them; that of literature, philosophy, or sociology was not. Many colleges struggling to attract applicants responded by increasing their vocational offerings, "giving consumers what they want" in the grand tradition of free market competition.[7]

Demand for vocational instruction is, of course, not new. In substantial measure it is the reason the great land-grant universities were created. William Stoner, novelist John Williams's wonderful fictional university professor, went from his family's farm in rural Missouri to the state university because the county agent told his farmer-father about a new college of agriculture at the university. "They got new ideas," the agent said, "ways of doing things they teach you at the University . . . [to deal with land that] gets drier and harder to work every year."[8]

In former Harvard president Derek Bok's view, the growing demand for vocational courses by the new students "came about primarily for two reasons":

> One is the tendency of American employers to demand higher levels of knowledge and skill from those whom they employ. Thus, increasing numbers of young people believe that they must look to college for the competence they need to secure a good job. Many of them are students who would previously have gone directly into the workforce to learn the necessary skills on the job.

The other reason . . . is the marked increase in the number of students who look upon making money and succeeding in one's career as primary motivations for going to college. . . . It is hardly a surprise that these trends have been accompanied by a growing number of students seeking to prepare themselves for a career.

Against this backdrop, can one really blame universities for offering more vocational programs?[9]

In the hedonistic, go-go years at the end of the twentieth century, attitudes and expectations among the traditional students also changed. Previously, the idea that one would spend a good part of one's life working and that, therefore, having a job that is personally rewarding and satisfying is important, had led many to embrace careers with less than maximum earning potential, such as teaching. Increasingly, however, the life one leads and the work one does came to be seen as separate.

Careerism

The career strategy of many graduates now is to get the highest-paying job available and then use the income to support the life they want to lead. Law students aspire to be investment bankers rather than partners in firms. At medical schools, highly paid specialties have taken over from internal (general) medicine. Business schools flourish. Collegians wanting "the good life" have become convinced that money will get it for them.

A recent Harvard graduate explained it this way: "I see my job in [financial] consulting as a chance to develop my personal and interpersonal skills and save some money so that in the future, I will have the tools necessary for truly, not just nominally, making a difference in my life and the lives of others."[10]

The belief that the college a student attends sets the course of his or her life, that "a person must attend a top-ranked university in order to achieve in life," has great currency among applicants and their parents.[11] (Indeed, this belief has even taken hold among parents hoping to get their children into the "best" kindergartens and primary schools.) Gaining admission to a top-rated college or university, where one can secure the most potent career-credential degree, has become even more competitive.

With the encouragement of concerned parents, careerism among students has received a big boost in high schools. Career nights, starting as early as ninth grade, are not exceptional. One junior high in suburban Milwaukee sponsors career programs for their twelve- and thirteen-year-old students. High school guidance counselors frequently encourage their advisees to decide what career they want to pursue before deciding which colleges they will apply to, and then to focus on colleges and universities with vocational programs that match their career choice. Counselors say this gives students a goal for their education. (I recently met a college-bound high school senior whose life ambition is to design computer games, an entirely understandable aspiration for a seventeen-year-old. He has been able to locate a nearby public university that offers a major in computer game design.) More and more, the bromide most collegians heard before 1960—"Don't even think about what you want to major in until the end of your sophomore year"—is getting tossed out the window.

Certification requirements for public school teachers indirectly but significantly contribute to high school seniors' lack of knowledge about and interest in liberal arts colleges. They create a strong incentive for potential high school teachers to pursue a vocational education major. If they take a liberal arts course of study, they will be obliged to spend an additional year or two meeting the course requirements for their teaching certification, a burden and expense most are unwilling—and many unable—to shoulder. A substantial majority of public school teachers obtain their undergraduate and master's of education degrees at state, not private, universities and colleges. They have little or no familiarity with liberal arts colleges, even those located close to the high schools where they teach, and the likelihood that they will suggest that their students investigate liberal arts college options is low. Their own educational experience is passed on to their students. In 2008, 78 percent of all high school seniors planned to attend institutions with enrollments of 5,000 or more.[12]

A former senior official of Stamats, a well-known educational marketing and consulting firm, told me their surveys show that, between

2000 and 2007, the percentage of high school seniors who reported being undecided about their career choice dropped from 21 percent to 6 percent. He added, "I have always viewed 'undecided' as a rough indicator of 'liberal arts susceptible.' The handwriting is on the wall. Liberal arts are not going to pay the bills. The future for small colleges lies in teacher training, business administration, and engineering."[13] His observations are supported by a 2007 study reporting that 92 percent of college-bound students felt preparing for a career was very important, and only 8 percent found the availability of liberal arts education essential in choosing a college.[14]

The importance of choosing a career—or at least planning for choosing a career—before selecting a college is stressed everywhere. For example, Metro Editorial Services, a national media service that distributes editorial content to approximately 10,000 newspapers nationwide, offered its subscribers an article entitled "Tips for Finding the Right College."[15] The advice contained in it most assuredly is not to consider a liberal arts college if you are undecided. Liberal arts and liberal education are ignored.

> CONSIDER A POSSIBLE CAREER PATH. . . . When looking at colleges, kids should look at all of the programs they offer, and make a list of the programs that most interest them. This isn't choosing a career (as many students change majors while in college), but rather doing some preliminary research about what you may want to study. For students who really have no idea what they might want to study, consider applying to a larger state school, as those often offer the most programs of study, meaning a student won't have to transfer once they do decide on a course of study.[16]

It is striking that the advice equates "major" and "career."

In 2006, after a special commission appointed by Secretary of Education Margaret Spellings "to consider how best to improve our system of higher education" completed a year-long study, its fifty-five-page report and recommendations focused on the need for trained workers. It did not even mention liberal education or liberal arts, let alone the need for liberally educated citizens.[17] The Obama administration has also focused on tailoring collegiate training programs to meet vocational needs for such fields as nursing, health information technology, advanced manufacturing, and green jobs.[18]

If all this weren't enough bad news for liberal arts colleges, respected higher education institutions have joined high school counselors and teachers, news media, and the federal government in talking vocationalism up and liberal education down. Georgetown University is a prime example.

Georgetown University describes its undergraduate college, the "oldest and largest school" within the university, as "committed to providing its students with a liberal arts education. . . . Think liberal arts majors can't get a job? Think again. There is no one-to-one correspondence between what you do during college and what you do after college. Your major choice will not restrict certain career options, nor will it guarantee others. . . . Georgetown College aims to produce exceptional communicators, smart interpreters, fast learners, problem solvers [and] creative thinkers, . . . students balanced, well-rounded, and skilled in diverse fields in order to prepare them for a career in whatever area they may choose."[19]

The Georgetown University Center on Education and the Workforce, however, tells a very different story. Its 122-page report entitled *Help Wanted*, released in June 2010, makes the following argument: college degrees have replaced high school degrees as "a virtual must for American workers." Today, Americans without a college education are at risk "of being locked out of the middle [and even the upper] class." People no longer go to work in industries. They go to work in occupations, such as health care, sales, or food and personal services. If higher education fails to focus on occupational training, the report asserts, "it will damage the nation's economic future . . . something we cannot afford."[20]

In a 2009 interview, the Georgetown center's director, Anthony P. Carnevale, contended, "It's very clear that we order society by occupation." Ultimately, he argued, an education system in a market economy such as ours will not survive unless it is aligned with the labor market. This is what career and technical education, such as post-secondary programs in "recreation management," do. And, he said, it will happen naturally in a market economy.[21]

An article in *Inside Higher Ed* reported on Carnevale's findings and what he believes they mean for liberal arts education:

> The lead author [Carnevale] of the [Georgetown Center on Education and the Workforce] report said . . . that the report should also shake up colleges—and challenge most of them to be much more career-oriented than they have been and to overhaul the way they educate students, to much more closely align the curriculum with specific jobs. . . . [Carnevale] said he wants high school students not only to realize the importance of going to college, but also to plan for a career at the time they make their college choices. "It matters a great deal that they go to college and get a credential, but what matters the most now is the occupation that they will pursue," he said.
>
> The key psychological change that is needed, he said, is to move away from "the old model, where you go to college and then go out and find a job" to one in which the college years are explicitly "preparing for an occupation." He said that his recommendations may not apply to the highly competitive college whose graduates can still focus on jobs or graduate education after they finish a bachelor's degree. "But the world isn't like that anymore" for everyone else, he said.
>
> This doesn't mean that community colleges or state universities should eliminate the liberal arts, he said, but that they should counsel students to pick programs based on careers, track the success of various curriculums in preparing students for jobs, and adjust programs to assure that they are focused on jobs. "It's all about alignment," he said.[22]

Carnevale's passion for vocational "alignment" was the apparent cause for a stunning misstatement he made in the interview he gave in 2009. In a chapter he authored in a 2007 book, *Minding the Gap,* he had correctly cited NCES data showing that 1,399,542 bachelor degrees were conferred in 2004, and that 42,106 of them were in "liberal arts and sciences, general studies, and humanities."[23] In the interview, however, he added that all the rest of the bachelor degrees were "essentially occupational or industrial," ignoring the fact that "liberal arts and sciences, general studies, and humanities" is a small, catch-all CIP-code category for general studies, undeclared majors, undecided, and the like.[24] It does not include virtually all liberal arts majors, such as English language and literature or letters; foreign languages, literatures, and linguistics; physical sciences (including general biology, chemistry, geology, and physics); social sciences (including anthropology, economics, geography, political science, and government); philosophy and religious studies; history; psychology; mathematics (including algebra and geometry); theater arts; art history; music history; area, ethnic, cultural, gender, and group studies; and multi- and interdisciplinary studies.[25]

Careerism is now at the heart of the demand for higher education. In response to a survey by noted pollster Daniel Yankelovich, 75 percent of high school seniors and 85 percent of their parents said college is important because it "prepares students to get a better job and/or increases their earning potential. . . . The ultimate goal of college is to get a practical education and secure a first job. . . . Few people believe in the importance of 'learning for learning's sake' anymore."[26] In 2004, 75 percent of the nearly 300,000 entering freshmen responding to the University of California, Los Angeles, Higher Education Research Institute's annual survey gave the same answer.[27] In the 2009 UCLA survey, the year after the recession began, the most cited factor in choosing a school was that its graduates got good jobs. This factor was "very important" to 56.5 percent of all respondents, the highest rate since the question was first asked in 1983.[28]

Yankelovich's survey also revealed that 44 percent of students and 19 percent of their parents could not answer the question, What does a liberal arts education mean? While 14 percent of the students and 27 percent of their parents claimed to be very familiar with liberal arts education, only 3 percent and 2 percent, respectively, understood it to mean to "teach students how to think on their own." The overall impression of liberal arts education among 68 percent of the students and 59 percent of the parents was negative or neutral.[29]

In interviews conducted in the fall of 2008, I asked seven college-bound seniors at a rural high school what they understood liberal arts colleges to be. One said they "were places where they do a lot of art and drawing" and another, that they specialized in "science stuff." The remaining five said they had no idea.[30] Interviews with seniors at a more sophisticated suburban high school revealed their general sense that liberal arts colleges teach "the same courses you take in high school."[31] Only one student indicated she was even considering a liberal arts college. When asked why, she said it was because she was undecided about her career.[32]

Other Factors Dampening Demand

Greater exposure to the world, made possible by the proliferation of Internet and video sources, has had the paradoxical effect of, if not closing minds, at least limiting curiosity. Where once, for example, students attended events involving art, music, theater, and even sports with which they were not familiar, to see if they liked them, young people now can scan images of similar events on their computer or flick across them with their cable TV remote and conclude, on the basis of this microexposure, that they know whether they like them or not. Usually, the response to unfamiliar events is negative. Familiarity, not experimentation, has become the order of the day. This, too, is not good news for liberal arts education.

The ubiquity of the Internet and information technology has also undercut the perceived desirability of a book-centric liberal arts education. If one knows the question one wants to answer, the computer offers a far more efficient way of finding the answer than books do. As one high school student explained, in a book "they go through a lot of details that aren't really needed. Online just gives you what you need, nothing more or less."[33] Books answer questions that have not been asked. High school can be viewed as a collection of questions students are required to answer. Using the Internet is perceived as a way of taking control of your own life, deciding for yourself what you want to know and how you want to learn it.

There has been a general decline in reading, which obviously has an adverse effect on the demand for liberal arts education. Many teens now view attending a liberal arts college, and all the book reading it entails, as being told what you need to know and how you must learn it. David McCullough said to the 2008 graduating class at Boston College, "Learning is not found on a printout."[34]

From 1992 to 2002, the percentage of eighteen- to twenty-four-year-olds who had read a book during the previous year fell by 12 percent, and the percentage of thirteen-year-olds who were daily readers dropped to fewer than 30 percent. Between 1984 and 2004, the percentage of seventeen-year-olds who said they read nothing at all for pleasure doubled and the percentage who read almost every day for fun fell by 30 percent. In 2005, 39 percent of college freshmen and 35 percent of college seniors reported reading nothing for pleasure. In 2006, teens and young adults (ages fifteen to thirty-four) spent less time reading than any other age group.[35]

Years ago, a non-college-graduate said in a Detroit focus group conducted by education consultants James Harvey and Associates, "When things get tough enough, they'll get rid of the trash-can programs like the liberal arts."[36] Things have gotten pretty tough for liberal arts colleges.

Coping with Declining Demand

The actions an individual liberal arts college can take to deal with declining demand are limited. Most liberal arts colleges have very modest financial resources and have already cut expenses to the bone. Significant reductions in spending that will not impair quality are unlikely to be available, with one unfortunate exception. Faculty salaries and benefits, which occupy a prominent place in the expenses of a liberal arts college—typically 40 percent or more of the total annual budget—are always a target for cost cutting. Holding down annual salary increases, often to less than the increase in the cost of living, is probably the rule, not the exception. In times of financial stress, eliminating raises altogether, salary cuts, and layoffs are not uncommon.

An obvious strategy for increasing revenue would be larger annual tuition increases (or reduced financial aid), but the thought of raising tuition more than competing colleges intimidates college administrators, especially during an economic downturn. They receive complaints from parents and students about how outrageously high their tuition is already, and about how large the annual tuition increases have already been. They know that two-thirds of parents decide about a college on the basis of "sticker price," that is, not taking financial aid into account.[37] The fact that tuition increases may be only a marginal outrage, given that tuitions are already outrageous, is small comfort.

Administrators also fear that potential applicants will focus on the percentage increase—worrying, for example, that if other colleges raise their tuition by only 5 percent, a 7 percent increase could turn applicants away in droves. Part of this fear may stem from the critical attention given by state legislators to the percentage tuitions increase at public universities. Budgetary wars in state legislatures, widely reported by the media, are often fought over which agencies are getting the biggest percentage increases (or the smallest percentage cuts). However, while there is little empirical evidence, it may be that potential liberal arts college applicants are less price sensitive than state legislators. Given that they have already swallowed the high-tuition camel, at least some students may not strain at a 7 percent increase gnat.

More aggressive fund-raising is another logical response to declining demand, but most liberal arts colleges are already aggressive fundraisers, with substantial staff and resources committed to development programs. More often than not, there is relatively little further fundraising that can be done.

Attempting to increase demand through product differentiation—creating curriculums or programs that are unique and set a college apart from its competitors—has considerable appeal for liberal arts college faculty and administrators. The problems with this strategy, however, are that there is no assurance uniqueness will have sufficient appeal to attract new applicants, that it will not put off existing applicants, and, even if it is appealing, that it will increase the demand for the college in a timely fashion. Many of the most obvious strategies—for example, eliminating course requirements or block (one course at a time) curriculums—have already been tried and are not unique.

Glamorous new physical facilities, especially sports palaces and dormitories, can attract additional applicants, but they are beyond the means of poor liberal arts colleges struggling simply to maintain their existing, often decrepit, buildings, or they require debt financing the colleges cannot shoulder. In any case, new construction is a long-run strategy that does not meet immediate cash needs.

To meet cash requirements, the only funds immediately available to liberal arts colleges, other than through borrowing (which many colleges have already done too much of), are their endowments. Raiding the unrestricted portion of their endowment, or even invading the restricted portion, is the course many poor colleges are forced to follow in times of severe financial distress. The potentially adverse long-run—and not infrequently, short-run—consequences of such destructive action are apparent, but they may be unavoidable if the situation is desperate.

Finally, the two revenue-increasing strategies followed by most liberal arts colleges when faced with declining demand for their services are admitting more students and adding more vocational programs to broaden their appeal to potential applicants. Both of these approaches merit a closer look.

Increasing Enrollment. Table 3.1 shows the percentage change in enrollment at liberal arts colleges between the years 1986–1987 and 2007–2008. Average enrollment grew significantly in all four tiers of liberal arts colleges but substantially more at those in the lower tiers, doubtless reflecting their urgent need for additional tuition revenue in order to survive. The top-rated colleges enjoyed the luxury of limiting their growth to a more modest rate and, by so doing, protecting their high

Table 3.1 Average undergraduate enrollment

			Percentage change	
Tier	1986–1987	2007–2008	Range	Average
I	1,842	2,029	−21.6% to 154.2%	10.2%
II	1,462	1,642	−31.0% to 188.0%	12.3%
III	1,159	1,414	−70.7% to 364.4%	22.0%
IV	862	1,099	−39.3% to 324.8%	22.4%
All colleges	1,356	1,567	—	15.6%

Note: See Appendix, Table A.1.

ranking by not admitting less-qualified students. Indeed, during this period a few highly rated colleges actually reduced the number of students they admitted, in an effort to improve their *U.S. News and World Report* ranking by becoming more selective.

The range of the percentage changes in enrollment over the twenty-one-year period is quite large, presumably indicating not only differences in admissions strategies among the colleges but also differences in their ability to control their admissions—that is, differences in the number of acceptable applicants or changes in academic programs, or both. We can reasonably assume that, for many colleges, applicants' ability to pay full tuition (or close to it) was a relevant acceptance factor. It is striking that, even though the average enrollment in all four tiers increased significantly, 38 of the 225 colleges saw their enrollments fall, in some cases by a substantial amount.

Increasing Vocationalism. As Table 3.2 shows, there were substantial increases in the numbers of vocational completions at liberal arts colleges between 1986–1987 and 2007–2008. (Completions are degrees granted during an academic year by field of study.)[38]

How did Tier III and IV colleges manage to achieve their substantial enrollment growth? Analysis of their completions data strongly suggests that the key factor was increasing their vocational programs.

Table 3.2   Vocational completions

Percent of vocational completions	Number of colleges	
	1986–1987	2007–2008
0%	51	12
Less than 10%	67	44
10%–20%	36	23
20%–30%	36	28
30%–40%	13	31
40%–50%	10	36
More than 50%	7	51
Total	220[a]	225

Note: See Appendix, Table A.2.

a. 1986–1987 completions data are not available for five of the Tier IV colleges.

Table 3.3 Percentage of liberal arts colleges (by tier) with vocational completions, 1986–1987 and 2007–2008

	Tier I		Tier II		Tier III		Tier IV		All	
	86–87	07–08	86–87	07–08	86–87	07–08	86–87	07–08	86–87	07–08
Less than 20% vocational completions	92%	86%	88%	40%	54%	8%	34%	7%	70%	35%
20% or more vocational completions	8%	14%	12%	60%	46%	92%	66%	93%	30%	65%

Note: See Appendix, Table A.2.

Table 3.3 reveals that, although vocational completions increased at most colleges (including those in prestigious Tier I schools), Tier III and Tier IV colleges had far and away the largest percentages of vocational completions, and the largest increase in that percentage over the twenty-one-year period.

In 1986–1987, more than half of the 225 colleges had more than 90 percent liberal arts completions (as did nearly 80 percent of the Tier I and II colleges). In 2007–2008, the number of colleges with 90 percent or more liberal arts completions had dropped by half (to less than 25 percent of all colleges). Over the same period, the number of colleges with 30 percent or more vocational completions increased from 33 to 118. By 2007–2008, more than half of all colleges (and more than 80 percent of those in Tiers III and IV) had 30 percent or more vocational completions.

The percentage increases in vocational completions, by tier, are shown in Table 3.4. Increases at Tier II colleges were particularly striking. For example, at Luther College they increased from 12.3 percent to 37.0 percent; Muhlenberg College, 0.4 percent to 33.2 percent; Hope College, 18.0 percent to 47.5 percent; and Coe College, 5.6 percent to 43.8 percent.[39] These are colleges with modest financial resources, struggling to compete with the wealthy Tier I institutions. By 2007–2008, 26.8 percent of all Tier II college graduates were vocational majors. (Indeed, 25 percent or more of the 2007–2008 graduates at 133 of the 225 colleges were vocational majors.)

In 2007–2008, liberal arts majors still accounted for more than 95

Table 3.4   Average (per college) percentage of total completions that were vocational in 1986–1987 and 2007–2008

Tier	1986–1987	2007–2008
I	4.2%	10.4%
II	9.4%	26.8%
III	21.0%	44.6%
IV	31.0%	53.6%
All colleges	10.6%	28.7%

Note: See Apendix, Table A.2.

percent of the graduates at nearly half of the Tier I colleges. Five of them—Bard, Holy Cross, Davidson, Kenyon, and Sarah Lawrence— graduated no seniors with vocational majors. In contrast, at 28 of the 43 Tier IV colleges, more than 50 percent of graduating seniors were vocational majors.

Even the 126 Annapolis Group liberal arts colleges—institutions expressly committed to the liberal arts—nearly tripled the percentage of vocational degrees they conferred between 1986–1987 and 2007–2008, from less than 6 percent to more than 17 percent.

David W. Breneman, in his 1994 study of 212 liberal arts colleges, said, "One of the most interesting and distinctive attributes of the liberal arts colleges included in this [Breneman's] study is their commitment to their central educational missions. Unlike many colleges and universities in recent decades, they have refused to shift curricula toward more immediately marketable technological or vocational subjects. In fact, one can almost view these colleges as standard bearers, holding out the promise and the reality of education for education's sake."[40]

Breneman based this commendation on 1988 completions data. However, the more recent data included in this analysis, which are available for 143 of the 212 colleges in his sample, show that the percentage of vocational degrees conferred by almost all of those schools has increased significantly. Whereas 44 of the 143 colleges had awarded 1 percent or fewer of their degrees in vocational fields in 1987, by 2008 that number had fallen to 11. Also in 2008, at 55 of the colleges 25 percent or more of the degrees conferred were vocational; at 14 of the colleges the degrees awarded were more than 50 percent vocational. Over the twenty-one-year period, only 32 of the 143 colleges did not at least double the percentage of their completions that were vocational. Whether or not Breneman was correct in 1994 in praising liberal arts colleges for refusing to shift to "more immediately marketable . . . vocational subjects," the colleges' commitment to surviving has now proven to be an even stronger motivation.

In sum, the demand for vocational education is growing and liberal arts colleges are responding to it. Most have no choice. A few prestigious colleges whose graduates expect to capture good jobs and admission to top professional schools on the basis of the credential their degrees represent, rather than the particular course of study they follow, have been in a position to resist the growing demand for career-based majors. Their huge endowments have relieved them from dependence on tuition revenues and have therefore, in the true but astonishing words of David F. Swensen, Yale University's celebrated chief investment officer, protected them from being "forced to respond to the wishes and needs of the current student body to attract a sufficient number of students to maintain current operations."[41]

Following the 2008 recession, there is reason to expect liberal arts colleges' move toward vocational courses and majors will accelerate. Even though elite Tier I colleges may be able to resist becoming more vocational, they risk becoming marginalized, attracting only students whose sole objective is obtaining a ticket to professional schools. Public universities may seize the opportunity to capture the best and brightest by offering equally desirable tickets. The outlook is not good for private liberal arts colleges.

Ten years ago, Paul Neely wrote that "there may simply be more pure liberal arts colleges than we need, at least as the market defines need."[42] Michael McPherson and Morton Schapiro agreed, writing, "The underlying problem [is] that many are less interested in the [liberal arts college] product than they used to be," and asking "whether anyone should care if this dwindling segment of American postsecondary education were to shrink further."[43] These gloomy observations now sound prescient.

History has repeatedly demonstrated that liberal arts colleges are survivors. The question is, Survivors as what?

CHAPTER 4

Competing

✦

Thomas Carlyle's apt appellation for economics, "the dismal science," could well have been coined by a liberal arts college president. Unhappily, however, as we plunge deeper into the twenty-first century, understanding the economics of higher education is required if we are to understand the current state of liberal arts colleges, the challenges they confront, and why they are having such difficulty meeting them.

General Economic Principles

The United States is a free market economy to a greater degree than most. We believe Adam Smith's "invisible hand" will lead the market to give us higher output, lower prices, and better-quality goods and services. In most areas of economic endeavor, we believe that letting the marketplace—the interplay of the individual interests of sellers and buyers—determine what goods and services are produced, at what price they are sold, and who purchases them is, while imperfect, a much better bet than government planning and regulation.

The fact is, however, there are certain basic conditions that must be met before the invisible hand can feel what it is doing. In some markets free competition does not work very well, and in some it does not work at all and government has no choice but to step in and take control. If, for example, a market includes cheats such as Enron or Bernard Madoff, competition will not work the way we want it to. If a market is occupied by a single entity, a monopolist, most of us are not going to be happy with the way it functions. There are also what might be called unwanted consequences of the free marketplace, as when the invisible hand works well in delivering what individuals want but society at large judges they should not have. Cigarettes are a good example, and there can be little doubt that, absent government intrusion, more crack cocaine would soon be available at lower prices.

In other circumstances the ineptitude of the invisible hand is less obvious. One such circumstance involves what might be called wanted side effects, what economists call "positive externalities."[1] Take, for example, wilderness areas. We could leave their development and operation to the marketplace rather than the National Park Service, and doubtless some areas would be provided to campers, trekkers, backpackers, outdoor sports enthusiasts, and hunters—but not enough. Most would agree that we are all better off because of the existence of public wildlife preserves, seaside reserves, and historic outdoor areas, even when we are not using them and even if we don't use them very much at all. Similarly, if individual consumers were permitted to "purchase" as much or as little military service as they thought they could afford—or wanted more than a new car or a week's vacation at the beach—it is a safe bet the invisible hand would deliver a lot more butter and a lot fewer guns than we need.

Take another example: an informed citizenry is a wanted side effect of education. No doubt the invisible hand would point out plenty of buyers for educational services, it being widely accepted that obtaining an education is the best way to "get ahead." But how much less of such services would be available if state governments did not stick their noses in, provide tax-supported schools, and require everyone to attend them or their private equivalent until they are sixteen years old? Much less. At the higher-education level, without governmental intervention in the form of subsidized state universities, tax exemptions for private institutions and tax deductions for those who contribute to them, Pell Grants, and so on, the invisible hand would not get the job done.

Generally speaking, then, when we ask our economy to produce goods or services with benefits that are as much or more public than private, such as military forces, national parks, orderly financial markets, basic health services, or education—we are rightly unwilling simply to turn the task over to the invisible hand. It is not enough to ask, "Is the market for any particular good or service a free, competitive market?" Free competition, no matter how passionately it is extolled, is a means only, not an end. It does not protect us from the cold, fill our bellies, enhance our understanding, or inspire peace and justice. It is good when it works, bad when it does not—a fact frequently overlooked or ignored by politicians. Conservatives extol unregulated free market competition as always best for the public interest. (A liberal friend of mine says they are like people who learned how to begin spelling *banana* but not how to stop.) Liberals reflexively suspect the free market because it is ruthless, not compassionate, and its rewards are unequally distributed. Both views are wrong.

Every good and service has particular qualities that affect how efficiently the free market will function in delivering them and in fulfilling society's needs. With this in mind, let us turn our attention to the economic characteristics of liberal education services and consider the impact they have on purveyors, particularly liberal arts colleges, and users of those services. At the outset we can observe that liberal arts colleges compete with each other, as well as with private and state universities, for-profit universities, virtual universities, correspondence courses, indeed with all deliverers of postsecondary education services.

The Economic Uniqueness of Liberal Arts Colleges

Liberal arts colleges are, of course, businesses. They sell services. They purchase the materials and labor used to produce those services. Absent an endowment safety net, if there are too few customers or if customers are unwilling to pay a compensatory fee, the colleges will go under. Here, however, the similarities to commercial businesses end. Writing in the *Wall Street Journal*, Stephen Happel, associate dean of the Arizona State University College of Business, said universities "will never be like most businesses for one fundamental reason: their total commitment to academic freedom and rejection of the 'yes-man' mentality."[2] Dean Happel's conclusion is correct, but the reason he gave is not.

A number of unique characteristics of liberal arts education distinguish it from other types of business, and frustrate the efficacy of free market competition.

The Successful Low Bidder. There is a joke in higher education: "We offer services that cost $60,000 for $40,000 and accept $20,000 in full payment." Imagine that a liberal arts college sold automobiles. It had two eighteen-year-old customers and their parents looking at a car on its showroom floor. Both liked the car. One said, "I'll take it" and started to write out a check for $40,000, the list price. The other said, "I can only give you $5,000." The salesman turned to the first customer and said stiffly, "I'm sorry," then smiled at the second customer and said, "This car is yours." If a college were in fact selling cars and this scenario actually transpired, the college's administrators would be adjudged certifiable. Yet selling educational services to the lowest bidders is a routine event in the real world of higher education.[3]

The Sale/Purchase Transaction. Why do colleges do such a foolish thing as selling to the lowest bidder? The answer is that it is not foolish. They confront a circumstance unlike that faced by any other business; they "purchase" students, the key input of their production, in the same transaction in which they sell their education service. Students are not mere customers, each of whose money is as good as the next person's. They are an integral ingredient of the education service liberal arts colleges sell and a key determinant of its quality.

A typical college catalogue says, in essence, "We sell liberal arts education services for $40,000, but we provide discounts (financial aid) of up to 100 percent, that is, $40,000." It could just as well say, "We purchase students and will pay up to $40,000 for a high-quality applicant."

When a college negotiates a discount price (financial aid) with a student, is the college selling its services or buying a student? The answer is, both. Indeed, except for colleges so poor that they have no choice but to admit all applicants, who the applicants are often matters more than how much they can pay. Perhaps the closest analogy in the commercial world of a business that cares deeply about who its customers are is haute couture, but it is a pale analogy. Even the most exclusive purveyors of fashion somehow manage to take the money of customers who have no fashion sense or style.

There is a striking difference between the marketing strategies of liberal arts colleges, on the one hand, and commercial enterprises, on the other. Commercial enterprises (including for-profit education institutions) routinely seek to attract customers and increase their market share through advertisements and promotions that directly compare their products (and their prices) with those of their competitors. A liberal arts college's ability to increase its market share is very limited. Its viewbooks, home pages, and other promotional materials praise the college's qualities, but on a noncomparative basis. Typically, colleges do not get down to the hard competitive question—why you should come to our college rather than the others you are considering—until an admissions officer is pitching the school to an individual student, one on one. Why is this? I suggest it is because the colleges' primary focus in the sale/purchase transaction is on purchasing students, not selling education.

Parenthetically, a little-noticed side effect of discounting tuition with scholarships is that it caps the amount colleges pay to buy students. Imagine that a college with a full-load price (tuition, fees, room, and board) of $50,000 is bidding for a high school senior who is an accomplished cellist, has perfect SAT scores and a 4.0 grade average, has published two novels, won both the $100,000 grand prize in the Siemens Foundation math and science competition (for her biophysics research) and the Boston Marathon, was voted the most outstanding African American high school senior by *Jet* magazine and the best-liked member of the senior class at Phillips Exeter Academy, and whose picture has appeared on the cover of *Time* magazine. Such a student might well be able to command negative tuition—a price in excess of $50,000. Since, however, colleges pay for students by discounting their list price, payment to the super student is capped at free admission, $50,000.[4]

From time to time, payments for student athletes—despite the National College Athletic Association's best efforts—have been lifted above full-load scholarships, for example by the clandestine funneling of clothes, cars, and cash to athletes through the auspices of alumni sports enthusiasts. It is not inconceivable that similar under-the-table payments have been made to nonathlete candidates for admission, but there is little evidence to show this has occurred.

Morehead-Cain Scholarships, which are given by the University of North Carolina and are not clandestine, have provided students with summer employment and job opportunities after graduation, in addition to full-load grants.[5] Many colleges have begun exploring other ways, short of negative tuition, to exceed the full-load cap in bidding for nonathletes—for instance, by providing free airline tickets to potential students and their parents for campus visits. Even without such creative initiatives, putative payments to highly desirable students can be increased simply by raising the cap—that is, by increasing the full-load list price a college charges.

Good Enough. Goods and services of different quality are offered in virtually all commercial markets. Not everyone needs a Mercedes; less-expensive Kias are good enough for many drivers. The fact that some sellers offer goods and services that are good enough, rather than gold plated, makes competitive sense for them and well serves the public interest. Liberal arts colleges, however, do not enjoy this option. The notion of a good-enough education, or one that is good value for the price, does not resonate with top applicants and their parents. They want "the best," but at the lowest possible price.[6]

The Mixed Market. Private colleges and universities are obliged to compete with heavily tax-subsidized public university behemoths. This, of course, is not an entirely unique situation. Sweden, for example, long experimented with a mixed economy in which private and public enterprises competed directly.[7] In the United States, private campgrounds compete to some extent with the National Park Service; private museums in Washington compete with the admission-free Smithsonian Institution. Such competition, however, tends to be less direct than between, say, Macalester College in St. Paul and the University of Minnesota's Twin Cities campus, especially given UMN's undergraduate Honors Program.[8] And it is certainly unlike the circumstance of commercial manufacturing firms for which the government is a customer, not a competitor.

Consumer Ignorance. One of the necessary, but infrequently explicated, requirements of effective marketplace competition, as Tibor Scitovsky incisively pointed out, is some rough parity of knowledge between buyers and sellers.[9] When consumers are ignorant about what they are purchasing, honest commerce is often replaced by scams and swindles, and the wholesome effects of free market competition are lost. When sellers are sophisticated sharpies and buyers are naive and not well informed, buyers soon become victims, as the subprime mortgage scandals have dramatically demonstrated.

By and large, consumers are not very well informed about the services liberal arts colleges sell, and many of the few who do understand liberal arts education either view it unfavorably or consider it a luxury they cannot afford. Almost every other type of higher education appeals to more people than does liberal arts. Indeed, one can make a reasoned argument that liberal arts students are not likely to be able to gauge the quality of the education they receive until after they graduate, and probably not until many years after.

Rankings, such as those published by *Consumer Reports,* and word of mouth, while quite reliable in providing guidance as to the relative quality of automobiles or vacuum cleaners, are much less reliable in the case of colleges, for a host of reasons—not the least being the profound subjectivity involved in choosing a college. One size does not fit all. The likelihood that, if my daughter adores her Honda Civic, your daughter will, too, is far greater than that our daughters will share the same feelings about a college.

Consumer ignorance about liberal arts colleges is exacerbated by the abysmal ignorance of many high school college guidance counselors. And their ignorance is not eliminated by the reams of promotional material published by every liberal arts college.

The Only Modestly Wanted Service. To a significant degree, liberal arts colleges are selling a service that is good for consumers, not one they have a strong desire to acquire—a bit like selling medicine to people who are not sick and don't expect to get sick. Not surprisingly, in their effort to attract applicants colleges mix in as much "sugar" as possible—sports, activities, social life, luxurious dormitories, and so on. There are wide variations among colleges' abilities to sweeten their offerings. Some, thanks to location, can offer skiing or beach sports. Others feature a party-school lifestyle, matriculation into a network of alums that assures business or social success, or the chance to get a degree with little effort. But the appeal to seventeen-year-old applicants of their core offering—a liberal arts education—is ephemeral at best.

Sweetening the Deal. There is some sugar that all colleges can sprinkle to attract students—and that many now do. Colleges can, for example, reduce or eliminate required courses. If two comparable colleges offer the same courses but one requires that they be taken and the other does not, which school will the rational applicant choose? One has to be really enthusiastic about taking classes just because they're good for you to say, "Give me those requirements!"

Even if requirements are retained, other courses and activities expressly designed for popularity can be and frequently are added to the curriculum. In his novel *Beet,* Roger Rosenblatt gives us hilarious examples of such courses (Ethnicity, Gender, and Television Studies; Little People of Color; Bondage Studies; Post-Colonial Women's Sports) and campus organizations (the Sensitivity and Diversity Council, the Robert Bly Man's Manliness Society, the I Am a Woman Center).[10] Actual courses introduced may not be as fribbling as those at Beet College, but their purpose is clearly to appeal to students. Vocational, career-directed courses serve the same purpose.

Grade inflation is another example of something colleges do to attract students. It is said that at one Ivy League university not many years ago, when the percentage of undergraduates graduating with no grade lower than a B reached 90 percent, the administration begged the faculty "to bring back the 'gentleman C.'" When considering two comparable colleges, one that gives high grades and the other low, which is more likely to be chosen, especially by applicants intending to go on to graduate or professional school?

Economic Inefficiency and Perceived Quality. Liberal arts college administrators are bombarded with demands that their college become more efficient—tighten its belt, get lean and mean, be more responsive to consumer demands, apply total quality management (TQM) principles. For the most part, these demands are ignored. More cost-effective ways of delivering educational services—for example, larger classes, greater reliance on adjunct professors, and online instruction—are viewed as being inconsistent with quality. Greater responsiveness to consumer demands, for example, fewer course requirements or more vocational majors, is seen as pandering. In a very real sense, a key indicium of the perceived quality of a liberal arts college is its economic inefficiency.

"Specialness." The faculty and administration of every liberal arts college passionately believe their college is unique and special, and that its specialness matters. Alumni confirm this belief—"Attending our college profoundly changed my life." The fact is, however, that for every liberal arts college there are many colleges that are substantially similar and that equally profoundly change the lives of their students. Moreover, the conviction of specialness impedes collaborative efforts by colleges—efforts that could help them adapt and survive (see Chapter 5).

A Gameable System. There are a number of widely accepted criteria said to measure the excellence of colleges, such as selectivity, student-teacher ratio, percentage of faculty with Ph.D.s, average SAT/ACT scores and high school class ranks of in-coming freshmen. Evidence of the reliability of these claimed excellence indicators is sparse, however, and even if they are reliable predictors, the relevance of the excellence they predict is far from established. Had, for example, Ronald Reagan attended Carleton or Amherst rather than Eureka College, would he have enjoyed a more satisfying, fulfilling, successful life?

Colleges struggle to improve their relative performance on the criteria, a struggle that is encouraged—if not caused—by *U.S. News*'s annual college rankings. Some colleges have chosen simply to dissemble, perhaps by exaggerating their numbers of applicants or inflating the average test scores of their students. Other colleges, reluctant to lie out-right, engage in practices that have no purpose other than inflating criteria performance. For example, since one of the measures of a college's selectivity is the number of applicants it rejects, encouraging applications from high school seniors who have no chance of being admitted, and then denying them, makes a college appear more selective. A more subtle variant of this practice is to make applicants' reporting of SAT and ACT test scores optional. Students with low scores and little likelihood of being accepted are thus encouraged to apply by the opportunity to do so without disclosing their scores.

Optional reporting of test scores has an additional rating-inflating effect. If students with unreported low test scores *are* admitted by the college, eliminating their scores increases the college's average score. In years past, some colleges simply excluded low test scores from their average on the grounds that those scores were irrelevant to the admissions decisions because the low-scoring students were in "special" categories—for example, minority students, athletes, international students, and legacies. *U.S. News,* to its credit, sought to block this gross distortion.

One could write an entire book on the validity of excellence criteria. Are Ph.D.-holders perforce better teachers than those who do not have a Ph.D.? Does alumni giving measure graduate satisfaction or graduate wealth? Do students get a better education when the student-faculty ratio is ten to one than when it is fifteen to one? For our purposes, it is relevant to note that attempting to look good on these criteria is very expensive for colleges, especially because the criteria give applicants the ability to drive up the price they can command for attending (financial aid), thereby further increasing the colleges' operating costs.

Fund Accounting. In fund accounting—the way colleges keep their books—resources are segregated and reported on the basis of their intended use. Commonly reported fund groups are current funds, loan funds, endowment and similar funds, annuity and life-income funds, plant funds, and agency funds.

Sophisticated readers of commercial financial statements—a group frequently found on college boards of trustees—often come a cropper when they confront fund accounting. (Not infrequently, this occurs at the moment they first encounter what are known as quasi-restricted and quasi-endowment funds.) Not unlike the putative premed student who, when he confronted organic chemistry, decided he really wanted to be an English professor, the reaction of many board members from the world of business is to decide they can assess their college without mastering fund accounting. The result is they have an incomplete view of the college's performance, further blurred by the fact that fund accounting is not particularly revelatory to begin with. The simple fact that it is better for a business entity to have more money rather than less money is not well revealed in fund accounting, which segregates resources on the basis of what they are going to be used for, are intended to be used for, might be used for, or will be used for unless things change, in which case they may be used for something else.

The way colleges keep their books is obfuscatory in other ways. For example, if a college's listed tuition is $40,000 and it gives a student a $10,000 financial-aid-grant discount, the college does not enter $30,000 on the revenue side of its ledger. Rather, it records $40,000 in revenue and $10,000 as an unfunded tuition-aid-grant expense. In other words, the college puts on the books revenues it does not receive and expenses it does not pay. This makes no sense (especially when students are admitted on a tuition-free basis).

The purpose of a financial statement is to paint a clear picture of what is actually happening. For many college trustees, fund accounting does not do that job. The net result is to increase the likelihood that important board decisions will be made on the basis of a flawed understanding of the financial situation the college actually confronts.

Felt Obligations. Rightly or wrongly, liberal arts colleges have always felt an obligation to make their costly services available to those too poor to pay for them, a feeling that does not disturb most businesses. Liberal arts colleges have also felt obligated to give their students a broad liberal arts education whether students want it or not, creating a tension with their need to be attractive and appealing to as many applicants as possible, another cross not born by commercial enterprises.

How College Competition Works in Practice

How well does free market competition among liberal arts colleges serve the public interest? The answer is not very well at all. Among other things, it most assuredly does not hold down list prices. Nationally, tuitions and fees have risen 439 percent since 1982, in inflation-adjusted dollars, while median family income has risen only 147 percent.[11]

Unlike commercial firms, liberal arts colleges are not competing to sell as much of their educational services as possible. They are competing to buy the best available students. Like bidders at an auction, the wealthy colleges drive up the price for talented students. Their incentive is not to buy as many students as possible but rather to skim off the cream, to purchase just enough of the best students to fill their lists. Were they to substantially increase the number they purchased, the marginal quality of the students they acquired would decline. Since the quality of the least talented students admitted directly affects the perceived quality of a college, they would risk lowering their reputation by admitting a larger number.

Part of the problem with viewing colleges as competing to sell education is that education is not really what they are selling. They *provide* education, but they *sell* degrees. The quality of the degrees they sell is, in large measure, determined by the quality of the students who receive them.

For vocational institutions, there is a direct measure of the quality of the education that graduates take with them. Graduates who major in accounting, for example, should know how to maintain the books of a potential employer. In contrast, few companies considering hiring a liberal arts college history major care how much history he or she knows. What employers *do* know when they hire a history major with a degree from a prestigious liberal arts college is that they are drawing from a pool of talented young people assembled by the college, which has purchased the best available applicants.

When a company hires graduates of less prestigious colleges, the pool from which they draw is likely to be less talented. Of course, talented persons may—and do—graduate from modest colleges. (Indeed, some extremely talented persons never go to college at all.) The harsh reality remains, however, that an employer (or a graduate or professional school) maximizes the likelihood of obtaining talented young people by shopping for them at the most prestigious colleges. The rich colleges know this and use their wealth to purchase the best and brightest high school graduates. The result is that the net price of attending the richest, most prestigious colleges is often actually lower than the price of attending poorer, less prestigious colleges.

For for-profit colleges, cost-cutting tactics such as larger classes, more online instruction, easier course requirements, and awarding bachelor degrees in three years and vocational certifications in less than three years, make profitable, economic sense. By expressly tailoring their course offerings to student demand, for-profit schools are growing at a far faster rate than their not-for-profit competitors. Between 1980 and 2004, the percentage of all private-college students attending a for-profit college rose from 4 percent to more than 20 percent.[12]

Pricing: Discounting and Discrimination. The fact that there is vigorous competition for top students and yet the list price of colleges (tuition) does not go down seems a paradox. Private college pricing, however, is not paradoxical. It is based on discounting; the higher the tuition, the greater the discount. It is a matter of economic indifference to a college whether its tuition is $30,000 and its average aid grant is $20,000, or its tuition is $40,000 and its average aid grant is $30,000. Either way, the college's net revenue per student is $10,000.

In the same way that buying a $400 suit at a 50-percent-off sale seems somehow a better deal than buying the same suit at a $200 list price, high tuition–high discount pricing enhances the appeal of the deal offered to students. As Thorstein Veblen reminded us in *The Theory of the Leisure Class,* the costliness of a good or service can enhance its value to the consumer.[13] Further, when the quality of a good or service is hard for consumers to judge—which is certainly the case with colleges—consumers understandably tend to put greater reliance on price as their guide.[14] Nonetheless, while parents of prestige-college applicants may be sufficiently sophisticated to focus on discounted net—

rather than list—price, when list tuition prices increase too rapidly it is a source of nagging concern to prestige-college presidents.[15]

Poorer liberal arts colleges lack the resources to provide as costly an education as their wealthy competitors offer. The costliness of the services a college offers does not automatically equate with quality, of course, but there is an unmistakable positive correlation, perceived if not actual. And as we have seen, because wealthy colleges are able to give larger discounts, students attending poorer colleges often pay more for the less costly education they receive. Price competition is pushing us toward a time when concerned parents will say to their children, "You had better study hard and get good grades. We can't afford to send you to a second-rate college."

The fact that reducing tuition is not of concern to the wealthiest schools has the effect of protecting less well-off colleges from pressure to lower their tuitions. As Gordon Winston and David Zimmerman describe it in their excellent study of price competition in higher education, the wealthy, high-cost colleges hold a price umbrella over the less wealthy colleges, shielding them from price competition. "One thing seems sure: that the widespread preoccupation with the fortunes of the wealthiest schools has not been entirely a case of glamour-struck fascination with the rich and famous but, instead, at some level, an appreciation of their role as the 800 pound gorillas whose behavior has inordinate importance for all of higher education."[16]

A rational pricing strategy for a liberal arts college therefore begins with increasing—not reducing—list price and, indeed, colleges have proved to be rational in this regard. In the face of a major recession, both the average published tuition and fees and the total charges at all private baccalaureate colleges were 4.4 percent higher in 2009–2010 than in 2008–2009, even in the face of a 2.1 percent decline in the consumer price index between July 2008 and July 2009.[17]

Rational pricing requires—and this is key—making sure everyone knows the college is prepared to deal. A typical liberal arts college may have nearly as many different pricing deals with its students as it has students. Such discriminatory pricing, selling the same thing to different purchasers at different prices, seems not the American way. It smacks faintly of a corrupt variant of socialism—to each according to his willingness to pay. Nonetheless, it is the well-established, accepted, higher-education way of doing business.

Tuition discounting is fundamentally different from discounting in many other businesses with which we are all familiar. Airlines, for example, charge dozens of different prices for a trip from New York City to Chicago. Each price, however, reflects a different offering: a round-trip, a weekend stay, a purchase made more than two weeks in advance, a departure after 9:00 P.M., and so on. It is possible, indeed likely, that passengers on the same airplane have paid different prices for their tickets, but each price reflects a deal that was available to anyone who met its terms. Airlines are selling different deals at different prices, not discriminating. Private colleges are selling the same bundle of services to students at different prices. They are discriminating.[18]

A Comparison with Public Universities. Liberal arts colleges and public universities are often thought of as higher education institutions that, while obviously singular and unique, confront largely the same economic challenges. The competitive challenges they face, however, are no more alike than those faced by, say, mice and elephants, even though both are mammals.

In his excellent book *Saving Alma Mater: A Rescue Plan for America's Public Universities,* James C. Garland, retired president of Miami University of Ohio, observes:

> In essence . . . state universities are quasi-monopolistic providers of higher education. Their public subsidies [in recent years, about $1 billion annually for the thirteen Ohio, four-year, public universities] give them a price advantage that discourages competitors, making it possible for them to lock up the low end of the market in their state. The product they provide—a four-year college education—is increasingly indispensable, and the purchasers of that product—college students—can either pay the price or abandon their college aspirations.[19]

Liberal arts colleges, in contrast, are most assuredly not monopolists but rather wildly competitive, have no taxpayer-provided subsidies, and the liberal arts education they provide is not perceived as indispensable by most high school seniors.

There are other, obvious differences. State universities are engaged in a volume business. Their scale of operations is huge and diverse. (President Garland describes West Texas A&M University, which has an enrollment of 7,400, as "tiny.")[20] Their pool of potential customers is very large and, while every institution prefers good students to inferior students, whether a state university manages to attract the best students is not central to its success. State university administrators are not free to make critical economic decisions. In most states, the state government controls the universities' tuition charges and there is constant pressure to keep tuitions low (for in-state students).

Public universities "typically charge a flat-rate tuition to all students, with comparatively minimal discounting."[21] Each year, even though the in-state tuition rate is extremely low, state legislators decry proposed tuition increases but never seem to urge coupling them with discounts for poor students. State universities typically have armies of registered lobbyists prowling the halls of the capitol.[22] By keeping list tuition low and limiting discounting, state legislators are maintaining the advantage of the well-to-do (like themselves) at the expense of the poor.

Charging widely varying, unpublished discounted prices to different students, commonplace at liberal arts colleges, would lead to potentially disastrous political consequences were it to be attempted by a public institution. Indeed, the only significant price differential at most state universities is between in-state and out-of-state students. For example, the 2009–2010 freshman tuition at Ohio State University (Columbus) was $8,706 for state residents, $22,278 for nonresidents—a differential of more than 150 percent.[23] At state universities, such huge disparities are the rule, not the exception.

If a public university needs more money—and virtually all of them do—what options are available? It can seek a larger subsidy from its state government, but even in the best economic times this is a tough sell, and in difficult times it is effectively impossible. Indeed, a key reason most state universities need more money is because their beleaguered legislatures are cutting higher-education subsidies.

University administrators can attempt to persuade state legislatures to permit their universities to raise tuition significantly. This strategy, too, is not politically attractive—or viable. Increasing the tuition charged out-of-state students is much less unpalatable politically, but since out-of-staters comprise a relatively small portion of a state university's potential market, the increased revenue-producing potential is limited. Increasing the number of out-of-state students—assuming a university has sufficient appeal to attract them at tuition levels far in excess of the in-state rates in their home state—is not likely to sit well with legislators or taxpayers if the effect is to displace in-state students.

Strong public universities can increase revenues by increasing enrollment, and this is happening. For example, the University of Wisconsin system's board of regents has launched a long-running plan to increase the number of college degree holders in Wisconsin by 30 percent by 2025. That means increasing the number of undergraduate degrees granted each year by the fourteen University of Wisconsin campuses from 26,000 to 33,700.[24]

In 2003 under Garland's leadership, Miami University, the prestige, public, liberal arts university in Ohio, persuaded the state legislature to permit it to raise in-state student tuition to the out-of-state level, a 120 percent increase, and then discount the money back to Ohio students in the form of scholarships of varying amounts—an unquestionable political tour de force.[25] As Garland points out, it was because the university had more applications than spaces, selective admissions, and a high percentage of full-time and out-of-state students that this radical abandonment of fixed tuition worked. It would not, he candidly says, have worked at most public universities.[26]

Now, drawing on his experience at Miami University, Garland has come up with a radical new strategy to increase revenues at all state universities—price discrimination. He proposes that each university raise its tuition and then discount it by giving "scholarships" to in-state students deemed by the state to be worthy—for example, low-income students or those pursuing a course of study desirable for the state's workforce needs, such as engineering. Key elements of his plan are that each university—not state government—determine its own tuition (which doubtless would work out well for Miami University), and that, while the total amount of state subsidy would not be changed, its distribution among state universities would vary depending on how many in-state scholarship students they admitted, scholarship dollars being given to the university by the state.[27] Since fixed tuitions without discounts favor well-to-do students, Garland's plan would permit universities to charge well-to-do students more.

Liberal arts colleges are engaged in massive price discrimination, and it has exacerbated, not solved, their financial problems. Why does Garland believe it will improve the financial well-being of public universities? The answer is because, unlike liberal arts colleges, public universities are selling a service, not buying students. With a few exceptions, for most public universities one potential customer is as good as another. Price discrimination would permit the universities to charge a higher price to well-to-do students who want the universities' services and can afford to pay for them. Liberal arts colleges are in the position of being driven by competition to offer the lowest price to the students they want the most, without regard to how much those students want the colleges' services. While public universities are selling "increasingly indispensable" services to students, liberal arts colleges are buying students whose demand for the liberal arts education the colleges provide is meager at best.

Garland's analysis reveals that the challenges confronting higher education look very different from the viewpoint of public institutions—and doubtless from that of the public generally—than they do to liberal arts colleges. He says, for example, "The majority of private colleges and universities . . . cater mostly to the educational needs of students who can afford a net tuition that is at least twice that charged by public universities. Relatively few of these students would qualify for scholarships in a state-administered scholarship program whose award criteria are primarily based on unmet financial need."[28] This is, however, not correct, at least insofar as flagship state universities (and probably Miami University of Ohio) are concerned. As St. Lawrence University president Daniel Sullivan has pointed out, "In every state in which research has been done, the average family income of undergraduate students in state flagship public institutions is higher than the average family income of students in independent colleges and universities in the same state."[29]

Garland also addresses the possibility that his proposal might lead public universities "to abandon their historic mission of serving the larger needs of society and reshape themselves to satisfy the desires of entering freshmen"—that is, to abandon liberal arts courses in favor of vocational courses directly related to job prospects. Not to worry, he concludes, pointing to the example of private institutions, which he believes "are able to balance successfully academic priorities with the financial necessity of attracting fee-paying students."[30] If only this were true!

Garland enthusiastically describes his proposal as lowering "the barriers that insulate public universities from the beneficial forces of competition."[31] For liberal arts colleges and poor students, competition has been anything but beneficial. Garland's enthusiasm illustrates the fact that how well competition serves society's needs depends on the particular characteristics of the services being sold, and of the marketplace in which they are being offered.

Merit-Based Aid, Need-Based Aid, and Need-Blind Admission. When college administrators talk about discriminatory tuition discounting, they never call it that—it's always "student aid," and they distinguish between "need-based" and "merit-based" aid. Need-based aid is said to be a good thing, making it possible for poorer students to get an education they could not otherwise afford. Merit-based aid, giving discounts to students the college wants, for example, football players, cellists, holders of high test scores, and class valedictorians, is, if not bad, seen as somehow ignoble. In the words of former MIT president Charles M. Vest, "Values of excellence and access come into conflict."[32]

Wealthy colleges proudly proclaim that they practice need-blind admission—that is, that they admit students without regard to their ability to pay. Need-blind admission, however, is another way of saying "We buy the best students no matter how much they cost." Obviously, only the richest schools can indulge in such free spending. Just as the richest bidders come away with the great Monet paintings at Sotheby's annual impressionist auction, so, too, the richest colleges capture the most talented students at the annual admissions auction.

Need-based aid sounds like what charities do: they give whatever they are giving—food, shelter, or medical aid—to those who need it the most. This is *not* what colleges do. First, they decide which potential aid recipients they want the most, and then they pay whatever it costs to get them. Colleges are sometimes described as partial charities because they solicit donations and use them to make gifts to needy persons. True charities, however, make their recipient selection decisions on the basis of recipient need. Financial aid recipients are chosen by colleges on the basis of the colleges' need. Were a college a true charity, it would apply an eleemosynary standard in selecting recipients and give aid to those applicants it determined would benefit the most from it. Such applicants, however, are not necessarily the most talented students; some of them probably are not. Occasionally, a college will admit a few students primarily because they are disadvantaged, but the competitive pressure is always on them to reserve aid for the best students.

Rich colleges get richer not by increasing revenues but by fundraising. Many of the most sought-after students they capture come from privileged backgrounds. They have attended prestigious prep and public high schools, where they received a superior education. Their high test scores and academic distinctions will enhance the reputation of the college they decide to attend. Their parents are likely generous contributors—as they will be, too, after graduation. Their first-choice colleges tend to be the richest colleges; lesser colleges are fallbacks. The result is, the wealth gap between the prestige colleges and their less opulent competitors grows, and pressure increases on the lower-tier colleges to either reduce their standards or become more vocational, or both, in order to attract more applicants.

One could contend that bringing together the best and brightest of America's youth at a handful of elite colleges and universities is an optimal strategy for strengthening our nation's leadership corps. While he was president of Princeton University, Woodrow Wilson did exactly that, telling a meeting of New York City high school teachers, "We want one class of persons to have a liberal education, and we want another class of persons, a very much larger class of necessity in every society, to forgo the privilege of a liberal education and fit themselves to perform specific manual tasks."[33] Even if President Wilson was correct, the question is, who or what decides who belongs to each class? Since my view is that a liberal education is earned, not a privilege given, I favor exposing the maximum number of bright young people to a quality liberal arts education, without regard to their wealth or station. Then let the chips fall where they may as to which of President Wilson's classes each student enters. The public interest is far better served by maximizing the number of young people who receive a quality liberal arts education—not to mention the private interests of those who would not have the opportunity under President Wilson's scheme—and then letting who will become leaders sort itself out after graduation. This requires that the viability of as many quality liberal arts colleges as possible be maintained.

CHAPTER 5

Cooperating

$\cdot\!\!*\!\cdot$

We have seen that competition has not reduced liberal arts college tuitions. It has advantaged well-off colleges and well-to-do students. It has tended to concentrate even more wealth in the hands of the richest colleges, increasing the already severe disparity between rich and poor schools. By fostering high-risk endowment investment strategies, it has made even the richest colleges more vulnerable to recession and other financial reverses. It has caused the shaky financial condition of a majority of liberal arts colleges to become even more unstable.

Competition has not increased the output of liberal arts college education services or, more precisely, not stemmed the decline in output. Enrollment increases that have occurred—primarily at less prestigious colleges—have been more than offset by increases in vocational instruction. Competition has done little—probably nothing—to enhance the quality of liberal arts education, although it has led some colleges to invest in glitzy facilities and faculty workload reductions the colleges cannot afford and the need for which is doubtful at best.

"The rational [pricing] decision for the single school works against the long-term survivability for all the schools in the group," wrote Paul Neely.[1] The tragedy of the commons is at work. In a nutshell, competition has produced such bad results because there is almost no economic course an individual college, acting alone, can follow that does not adversely affect liberal arts colleges as a group.

Cooperating to avoid the adverse consequences of competition has not come not easily to liberal arts colleges. Every liberal arts college is stronger than some but weaker than others. Effective cooperation requires stronger colleges to collaborate with those that are weaker, which many are reluctant to do. Most have been even more reluctant to give up total autonomy in their operations, especially in their curriculums. Liberal arts colleges have, however, made a number of efforts to make common cause.

Consortia

Most liberal arts colleges' consortial activities are targeted at cost reduction or containment, or at providing services too costly for individual members to undertake, and do not intrude on the separateness of individual members. In the past, except for occasional off-campus or study-abroad programs, most college consortia did not involve sharing courses or departments. This may be changing.

In its promotional materials, the five-college Claremont University Consortium (CUC) in California says there are "nearly 100 college consortia in existence throughout the country," an estimate that may understate the true number.[2] There are a wide variety of college consortia. Some are bound together by specific shared problems, others by the commonality of their members, shared vocational interests, or the gender, race, ethnicity, or religion of their students. There are national, regional, single-state, and even single-city groups. Sometimes, informal consortia are formed to deal with a single issue, such as a proposed city ordinance or state regulation.

The Wisconsin Association of Independent Colleges and Universities (WAICU) is a typical state consortium. Its twenty diverse members —church-affiliated and nonsectarian, vocational and liberal arts, colleges and universities, rural and urban, ranging in size from Northland College (700 undergraduates) to Marquette University (8,000 undergraduates and 3,500 graduate and professional students)—are bound together by the facts that they are all private, located in the same state, and obliged to contend with the octopal Wisconsin University System, and the Wisconsin state legislature whose higher-education activities are dominated by the Wisconsin University System. Central to WAICU's mission is obtaining economies through group purchasing of goods and services, such as office supplies, computer software, collection services, insurance, and moving services.[3] Another statewide group, the Maine College Career Consortium, with twenty-four similarly diverse member institutions, including community colleges, limits its mission to searching for employment opportunities for its students and graduates.[4]

Faculty and administrators in the Great Lakes College Association (GLCA) consortium of twelve colleges in Indiana, Michigan, and Ohio meet regularly to share experience, expertise, and knowledge, as do members of the Associated Colleges of the Midwest (ACM) consortium of fourteen colleges in Wisconsin, Minnesota, Iowa, Colorado, and Illinois.[5] Both associations provide off-campus domestic and foreign study programs, some of which are open to students from nonmember colleges. The geographic diversity of members in these consortia makes joint purchasing less feasible, but their substantial similarities—they are almost all Tier I or Tier II colleges—facilitates their administrators and faculty members' working together to address issues and challenges of common concern. From time to time GLCA and ACM meet jointly, but despite their similarities, they have rejected proposals that they merge.

The mission of the Associated Colleges of the South (ACS), sixteen private liberal arts colleges and universities located in twelve southern states, is precisely stated: "to make the case for liberal education and to strengthen academic programs at member institutions."[6] As discussed below, ACS has also been active in pursuing virtual academic department collaborations. The fifty-six members of the Women's College Coalition (WCC), a coalition also devoted to promotion of the liberal arts, are joined together by gender rather than geography. Founded in 1972, WCC's members are private and public, church-affiliated and secular, two- and four-year colleges and universities, including one located in Canada and another in Korea. WCC's goals are to make "the case for women's education, to the media and to the general public"; focus attention on gender equity; promote retention of women in math, science, and engineering; and develop women's leadership.[7]

The Boston Consortium for Higher Education (BCHE), a consortium of fifteen diverse colleges and universities in the Greater Boston area, ranging from the Berklee College of Music to Harvard University, and the OKC Downtown College, a consortium of two public universities, two community colleges, and an open-admissions, associate degree–granting college, all located in downtown Oklahoma City, are both bound together by a common city location. Their functions, however, are very different. BCHE, like the Wisconsin consortium WAICU, focuses on joint cost savings and sharing quality-improvement ideas.[8] OKC members collectively offer both credit and noncredit courses, and the association facilitates access to its members' courses by providing free parking for students.[9]

Three consortia warrant special attention because of the substantial extent to which their members share on-campus courses and facilities. a level of cooperation made possible by the similarity of the members and their geographic proximity. The members of Five Colleges, Inc. (Amherst, Hampshire, Mount Holyoke, and Smith Colleges, and the University of Massachusetts–Amherst), one public and four private institutions, are all located in western Massachusetts, close enough together to share an intercampus, fare-free bus system. They offer open cross-registration, a joint automated library system, joint departments and programs, faculty exchanges, joint faculty appointments, and even shared extracurricular activities, such as open theater auditions. In addition, they collaborate on energy use, rental housing, security, and public safety.[10]

Smith College promotes the Five Colleges consortium. Its students report it is "refreshing to get out of the Smith bubble" and that the Five Colleges system can make the small Smith campus feel like it is much larger.[11] On the other hand, at the June 2009 meeting of the National Association of College and University Business Officers, Mount Holyoke treasurer Mary Jo Maydew spoke about difficulties in "getting colleges with differing missions, cultures and needs to find commonly acceptable solutions."[12] She referred to members' reluctance to collaborate on academic programs, such as significant sharing of majors and departments, saying, "I think there really is a fear that as we do more together, things begin to blur. There's a view that what makes Mount Holyoke Mount Holyoke is the curriculum."[13]

Swarthmore, Haverford, and Bryn Mawr Colleges, all located in the western suburbs of Philadelphia, are also geographically proximate.

They share the Tri-College library system and are lashed together by a dedicated, high-bandwidth Internet network. Students at Haverford and Bryn Mawr, which nearly adjoin each other on the Philadelphia Main Line, can readily take classes at the other college, and 600 to 800 students do so each semester.[14]

The five-college, two-university Claremont University Consortium—Pomona, Scripps, Claremont McKenna, Harvey Mudd, and Pitzer Colleges, and the Claremont Graduate University and Keck Graduate Institute of Applied Life Sciences—are not reluctant to collaborate on academic programs. Each year, CUC students collectively take roughly 6,000 courses at a campus other than their home campus, about 16 percent of the total courses taken. Members also share a common library system (Libraries of The Claremont Colleges), student health and counseling services, chaplains, a central bookstore, physical plant and facilities support, and staff and services for payroll and accounting, information technology, human resources, real estate, risk management, and employee benefits. CUC describes itself as "a unique model for American higher education," adding that "cooperation among colleges appears to be the wave of the future in higher education, and Claremont is already on the crest of the wave."[15]

There is no doubt that CUC is unique, but as a model for U.S. higher education, it is problematic for two reasons. First, all of the CUC members are located within a square mile, a short bicycle ride from each other. More important, all member institutions except the first, Pomona College, were created as a part of the consortium in the first instance. In 1925, when CUC (then known as The Claremont Colleges) was established, only Pomona College existed. The other four colleges and two universities were founded over the next seventy-two years, coming into existence not as independent institutions but as a part of the consortium. They are analogous to the different colleges that make up an English university, distinct but part of a whole. Each of the five colleges—no less than Mount Holyoke—has a unique personality: Pomona is a comprehensive liberal arts college; Scripps is a women's college; Claremont McKenna, originally a men's college, now coeducational, emphasizes economics, government, and international relations; Harvey Mudd offers the bachelor of science degree; and Pitzer, with majors in both the sciences and the humanities, encourages social responsibility and self-direction.

Another form of liberal arts college collaboration virtually certain to become more prominent in the coming years is virtual departments. As we have seen, full-scale, for-profit, online, primarily vocational universities are already the fastest-growing segment of higher education. Now, not-for-profit universities are beginning to convert academic departments into virtual collaborations, often in disciplines not taught at many universities and colleges. Sunoikisis, for example, is a national, virtual classics department, begun by the Associated Colleges of the South in 1995 with backing by the Mellon Foundation. Sunoikisis now operates under the aegis of Harvard University's Center for Hellenic Studies in Washington, D.C. There are presently thirteen participating colleges and universities.[16] ACS has also experimented with virtual departments of modern languages and art.[17]

The goal of the Virtual Geography Department Project being organized by the Geography Department of the University of Colorado (Boulder) is to interlink the curriculums of college and university geography departments nationally and internationally, offering high-quality curriculum materials and classroom and laboratory modules that can be used across the Internet by geography students and faculty at any college or university in the world.[18] Such virtual departments are already common in Europe.

The Consortium of Liberal Arts Colleges (CLAC), organized in 1984 under the leadership of then-president of Oberlin College Frederick Starr, includes sixty-two members, almost all of which are Tier I or II colleges. While CLAC focuses on uses of computing and related technologies in the service of the liberal arts mission, movement by it or its members into virtual course and department creation seems a virtual certainty.[19] The National Institute for Technology in Liberal Education, also backed by the Mellon Foundation, seeks to "advance liberal education in the digital age," integrating "technology into teaching and learning."[20]

In 2006, forty lower-ranked, not-for-profit "small and midsized colleges . . . formed a consortium to share online courses and raise money to create more of them." The dean of one of the member colleges described their group, the Online Consortium of Independent Colleges and Universities (OCICU), as "a very cost-effective way to grow our program and serve our students."[21] Today, ten of the eighty-one members of OCICU provide 824 online courses to members.[22]

Mergers, Acquisitions, and For-Profit Colleges

In a sense, a merger is the ultimate collaboration. For a merger of two colleges to be successful, geographic proximity is almost mandatory. In David Breneman's words, "Why would anybody want to merge ... unless they're close enough that they can actually make meaningful savings by selling some buildings and integrating the faculty and administration?"[23]

Whatever economies or other advantages might be realized by the combining of two financially sound liberal arts colleges have never overcome every college's commitment to its own uniqueness and independence. Even if colleges were not fiercely independent and certain of the worth of their own specialness, acquiring a financially distressed competitor would not be likely to appeal to the board of trustees of a not-for-profit college, especially if it is itself struggling. (One of my predecessors at Beloit wanted to acquire a failing college located thirty-five miles away. The board rejected his proposal. One trustee suggested it would make much more sense to buy a commercial business that makes money, as, he noted, NYU Law School had done when it purchased the C. F. Mueller Company, the well-known maker of macaroni, spaghetti, and egg noodles.[24]) The likelihood that acquiring a failing college would generate cost savings or attract more or better-quality applicants, let alone increase revenues, is remote.

In 2008, Woodbury College in Montpelier, Vermont, sought to merge with Champlain College, a vocational college in Burlington, Vermont, that offered many of its courses online. Woodbury, classified by *U.S. News* as a Baccalaureate College, had begun offering baccalaureate degrees in 2000, but the change had failed to revitalize the college.[25] By 2007, Woodbury's enrollment had fallen to ninety-nine students, many of them part-time, most of them women, a large percentage of them over forty years old, and all of them taking online courses. That year, the college accepted all but one of its twenty-three applicants, only four of whom were men. Eleven women enrolled. Clearly, Woodbury's days were numbered.[26]

In the end, however, Woodbury sold its assets—primarily a building—to Community College of Vermont (CCV), one of five Vermont state colleges, which already had a "learning center" with 600 students in Montpelier.[27]

There is a group of higher education institutions eager to buy up struggling liberal arts colleges—for-profit colleges and universities. Consider the following acquisitions of two Iowa colleges in 2008.

Mount St. Clare College was a small, financially struggling, Catholic liberal arts college located in Clinton, Iowa, on the Mississippi River twenty-five miles north of the Quad Cities. *U.S. News* ranked it in Tier IV of the best liberal arts colleges. In 2002, the college had 443 full-time and 117 part-time students, a substantial number of whom were pursuing vocational majors, including 18 percent in elementary education and 20 percent in business administration and accounting.[28] At the end of 2002, Mount St. Clare College changed its name to Franciscan University and began offering master's degrees in vocational subjects.[29]

The next year, the number of students fell to 401 full- and 78 part-time, and the percentage of elementary education and business administration and accounting majors increased to 26 and 28 percent, respectively. Enrollment continued to drop in the following years, to 388 full- and 70 part-time students in 2004, and to 373 full- and 53 part-time in 2005. Between 2002 and 2005, total enrollment had fallen nearly 25 percent. It was not surprising, therefore, when, in 2005, Franciscan University was sold. The buyer was Bridgepoint Education, a San Diego corporation operating a for-profit, online university. Bridgepoint renamed the college Ashford University.[30]

In 2006, *U.S. News* continued to report the college (now Ashford University) as a Tier IV liberal arts college. It did not, however, report Ashford's enrollment or most popular majors, noting that Ashford had not completed the *U.S. News* questionnaire. The next year, 2007, Ashford was gone from the *U.S. News* rankings. It reappeared in 2008, however, reclassified as a Baccalaureate College with 3,449 full- and 36 part-time students, 67 percent of whom were majoring in education; business; parks, recreation, leisure, and fitness studies; and visual and performing arts. No indication was given as to the number of students who were taking classes exclusively online, although, given the small size of the Mount St. Clare/Franciscan/Ashford classroom facilities, it is safe to assume most of them were not on campus.

In September 2007, Bridgepoint acquired a second educational institution, the Colorado School of Professional Psychology, located in Colorado Springs, which offered master's and Ph.D. programs in psychology, and renamed it the University of the Rockies. That same year, Bridgepoint reported sales of $85.7 million and 2,800 employees.

Bridgepoint was listed on the New York Stock Exchange in 2009. It described itself as a leading provider of postsecondary education services focused on associate's, bachelor's, master's, and doctoral programs in business, education, psychology, social sciences, and health sciences. In its press releases, it stressed its "regionally accredited academic institutions—Ashford University and the University of the Rockies—that deliver their programs online as well as at the two traditional campuses," and that Ashford University offers "a range of student activities and athletics."[31] Ashford's fourteen sports teams continued to be known as the Saints.[32]

In May 2009, at its semi-annual commencement, Ashford University graduated 1,702 students (awarding 25 associate, 1,275 bachelor, and 402 master's degrees). More than 90 percent of them earned their degrees online. Bridgepoint reported that "the majority of the company's campus-based revenues are derived from federal financial aid" and that more than 95 percent of its 30,000 registered students were "exclusively enrolled online." "Ashford," it added, "provides our traditional and online students the ability to connect with the history and traditions of a brick and mortar campus, while enjoying the flexibility of an online learning experience," and it said the fact that both Ashford and University of the Rockies were accredited (by the Higher Learning Commission of the North Central Association [NCA]) "provides assurance to prospective students that Bridgepoint's institutions have been found to meet the commission's stated requirements and criteria."[33]

Things did not go well for Waldorf College either. Located in Forest

City, a town of 4,500 in north-central Iowa, Waldorf was classified by
U.S. News as a Baccalaureate College. Its endowment never exceeded
$10 million, and the college survived because of annual gifts, totaling
$3 million to $4 million, most of which came from a handful of very
loyal supporters (one of whom typically provided up to $2 million a
year). The college depended on tuition revenues but had only slightly
more than 600 full-time students in its best year (see Table 5.1).[34] In
each of the seven years from 2002 to 2008, between 77 and 92 percent
of Waldorf's students were pursuing vocational majors.[35]

On the eve of its 2008 commencement exercises, Waldorf's president, Dick Hanson, issued a guardedly optimistic statement, noting
that while the graduating class was large (by Waldorf's standards), the
sophomore and junior classes were small and the college had yet to see
the "enrollment explosion" it had hoped for after it became a four-year
institution in 2003.[36] The size of the incoming first-year class would be
key, he said, adding that Waldorf would continue to stress student involvement in campus life through athletics, music, and theater, and
would consider adding tennis, cross-country, track, and bowling, as
part of an effort to increase enrollment. A few days later, however, on
April 28, Waldorf announced it was eliminating the equivalent of fourteen full-time positions, including some faculty jobs. President Hanson
said the college had been borrowing money "to make ends meet" and

Table 5.1   Waldorf College enrollment

Year	Full-time	Part-time
2003	542	100
2004	463	84
2005	484	108
2006	546	83
2007	568	81
2008	611	59
Average	536	86

Note: Data from *America's Best Colleges*, 2003–2008 eds. (New York: U.S. News and World
Report, Inc.).

that its debt was relatively high. "If we had 750 students, we would not be here today," he told those at the announcement.

In mid-August, President Hanson acknowledged that the hoped-for large freshman enrollment had not occurred. "We're going to continue focusing on how to attract more students," he said, while ominously noting that "recessions aren't the best friend to small, private colleges." A few days later, he reported an additional round of budget cuts: phasing out Waldorf's computer information systems major; discontinuing its art minor, English-as-a-second-language program, and Spanish courses; leaving unfilled a faculty position in its History Department; and "adjusting faculty credit loads" in music. President Hanson characterized the budget cuts as painful but said he remained optimistic about the college's future.

In February 2009, Waldorf's director of brand and marketing announced, "Waldorf is pursuing a collaborative relationship with another institution," an "industry leader in online instruction." Three days later the college signed a "non-binding letter of intent to partner" with Columbia Southern University (CSU), a for-profit, Alabama-based, exclusively online university with more than 16,000 students. The agreement was conditioned on Waldorf's obtaining approval from the NCA's Higher Learning Commission, that is, on its retaining its regional accreditation. In April, sale of the college's assets to Columbia Southern was formally approved by the college's governing body, the Waldorf Lutheran College Association, which instructed the board of regents to continue under a collaborative relationship with CSU prior to the formal transfer of assets. NCA certification was obtained, the purchase agreement was formally signed on May 6, and new vocational majors—international management, criminal justice administration, fire science administration, sports management, and organizational leadership—were announced.

Reflecting on the events leading up to the sale of Waldorf to a for-profit institution, President Hanson told the online news publication *Inside Higher Ed,* "You are going to be seeing a lot more of this from colleges like us. . . . We had been living on the backs of our donors and suddenly those dollars were not available. . . . I went to our bond underwriter and told him to put out the word that we were looking for a partner. He said, 'What kind of partner?' and I said, 'Any kind of partner.'" Robert Mayes, Jr., president and cofounder of CSU, said in the same article that acquiring an accredited college "should speed the way for. . . . [Columbia Southern] University to enter nursing and education programs more broadly than it can now," and opined that online students want to feel some connection to a place, to a campus. "Even if they never come, they feel a connection," he said.[37]

President Hanson was correct. Bailouts, like those of Mount St. Clare and Waldorf College, are likely to happen with increasing frequency. For-profit institutions—exclusively vocational (except to the minimum extent required to maintain accreditation), entirely or primarily online, frequently publicly traded and accountable to their shareholders to show a profit—are growing like weeds. (*Business Week* reported that Apollo Group, the NYSE-traded company that owns the University of Phoenix, had annual sales in 2008 of $3.3 billion and net income of $517 million.[38]) For-profit higher education is big business and growing bigger.

The experiences of Mount St. Clare and Waldorf are illustrative, not unique. The College of Santa Fe (New Mexico), for example, also confronted declining enrollment and unmanageable debt. It was borrowing and using restricted endowment funds to meet operating expenses. In 2009, it declared a financial exigency, eliminated tenure, terminated its faculty members, and rehired a small portion of them at low wages.

The year before, the college had floundered about in search of a merger solution—perhaps being acquired by public New Mexico Highlands University, perhaps a partnership of some sort with for-profit Laureate Education.[39] The acquisition by New Mexico Highlands fell through, however, because the state legislature would not approve it, and the partnership notion—if indeed Laureate ever truly intended to partner with a failing, not-for-profit college—quickly gave way to a proposed outright purchase of the college's assets. College of Santa Fe, founded in the state capital in 1859, was unique because its continued existence was perceived as important by the Santa Fe city council, the state legislature, and New Mexico's governor, Bill Richardson.

In the end, the college was purchased by the City of Santa Fe and leased by the city to Laureate with an option to purchase. In June 2010, Laureate announced that the college's name would be changed to the Santa Fe University of Art and Design.

Dana and Midland Lutheran Colleges, both affiliated with the Evangelical Lutheran Churches of America and located near Omaha, Nebraska, about twenty-five miles apart from each other, also struggled with declining enrollment and strangling debt. They would have been well advised to merge and, indeed, a wealthy major donor announced in 2006 that he would cease donating to both colleges until they began merger talks. They did not heed his wise advice (although professors from the colleges did meet and discuss some sort of collaboration short of a merger).[40]

Ultimately, Dana College agreed to sell its assets to a new for-profit company, formed by a former Laureate employee. The deal fell through in 2010, however, when the Higher Learning Commission refused to extend accreditation to the for-profit purchaser. Dana has had to wind up its affairs, and about 350 of its students have transferred to Midland Lutheran—in effect, a merger by default.

According to court documents, Daniel Webster College in Nashua, New Hampshire, had accumulated debt of $23 million and needed to find a buyer or it would be forced to close its doors (and lose its accreditation). For-profit ITT Educational Services bought the college in 2009 for $29.3 million and, shortly thereafter, fired the college's president along with sixty other employees, including several department heads.[41]

Their motive being profit, companies like Bridgepoint, CSU, Laureate, and ITT are not constrained in the use to which they can put the colleges they acquire. When they purchase a failing liberal arts college, the for-profits get a physical campus to complement their online operations, sports teams with which students can identify, legitimizing accreditation, and, most important, federal student financial aid dollars. The bulk of for-profit school revenues are derived from federal loans and grants. According to the *New York Times,* with less than 10 percent of the nation's college students, for-profits took in $26.5 billion in federal money in 2009, up from $4.6 billion in 2000.[42] The federal administration estimates that by the 2011–2012 school year, more than

$10 billion in Pell Grants alone will be going to students at for-profit schools, more than to students at their public counterparts.[43] Accreditation is required for a college to receive federal funding. That is why, when the Higher Learning Commission refused to accredit Dana College's for-profit purchaser, the purchase agreement fell through.

There is a striking similarity between liberal arts colleges and for-profit colleges: their overarching commitment to teaching and instruction, as opposed to research and scholarship. The fundamental differences between them, however, are profound. Students attend for-profits to be instructed in specific vocational skills. The for-profits view their students as customers and attempt to tailor and deliver courses that are as consumer-pleasing as possible. Liberal arts college students do not have such singular, focused, instructional goals, and it is more difficult for the colleges to maximize the consumer appeal of their course offerings. It is far easier for them to contrive attractive ancillary services, such as sporting events or good-looking campuses, features for-profits lack (but can gain by acquiring a liberal arts college). Generally, liberal arts colleges seek to maximize the appeal of their courses by providing more alternatives. For-profits seek to give students exactly what they want.[44]

At some point in the movement from liberal arts to vocational courses that liberal arts colleges are making to survive, the logic of being a four-year institution offering only four-year baccalaureate degrees falls apart. If, for example, students want to become law enforcement officers, and the courses needed to obtain certification for law enforcement employment require one and a quarter years to complete, why should they keep on trucking for another two and three-quarters years, studying subject matter that has little or nothing to do with law enforcement? If they want to study history, philosophy, or biology, they can do so at a later time, after getting a job. (The fact that they probably will not do so is unlikely to enter into their planning calculus.)

It makes sense for a college already heavily invested in vocational programs, including a law enforcement major, to start offering a one-and-a-quarter-year law enforcement program and certification. Doing so, however, fits uncomfortably with a bachelor-degree focus. How will instructors in the law enforcement program be compensated? What about tenure? Will sufficient student demand remain to support the English lit department? It makes compelling economic sense for such colleges to cut back on—or abandon—liberal arts and add more vocational programs of varying lengths and with varying completion requirements. Doing so can relieve the economic crisis in which many Tier III and IV colleges (and even some Tier I and II colleges) find themselves. The alternative is to sell out to a for-profit college or university. When this happens, the employment days of English lit professors are numbered.

National Associations: The Annapolis Group

There are many national higher education organizations—consortia of a sort, but more accurately, trade associations. Many are headquartered in Washington, D.C., where they interact with and lobby federal agencies and Congress. One of them, the 900-member National Association of Independent Colleges and Universities, is expressly focused on the needs of private institutions. The Council of Independent Colleges (CIC), with more than 600 member schools and nearly 70 associations as affiliate members, represents small and midsize, independent liberal arts, comprehensive, four-year, two-year, and international colleges. It has paid particular attention to assisting its members in making their case for the education they provide.

Other associations focus on various aspects of college and university operations, such as business management (NACUBO), admissions (American Association of Collegiate Registrars and Admissions Officers [AACRAO]), fund-raising and marketing (Council for Advancement and Support of Education [CASE]), trustees and senior administrators (Association of Governing Boards [AGB]), and, of course, teaching and tenure (American Association of University Professors [AAUP]). The National Survey of Student Engagement (NSSE) conducts surveys designed to provide assessment and diagnostic tools for improving the quality of undergraduate education. Colleges and universities are designated participants rather than members, but NSSE functions much like a special interest association.

In 1993, the first national organization solely concerned with the needs of liberal arts colleges was founded. That organization, the Annapolis Group, "provides a forum" where the presidents and academic deans of its 125 members can meet semi-annually "to share best practices, seek higher levels of excellence, and advance the cause of liberal arts education on a national scale."[45] In 2000 the group member sponsored the publication of *Distinctively American,* a collection of writings about the qualities and strengths of liberal arts colleges.[46]

The Annapolis Group has no executive director; its leadership rotates among its members. It has devoted itself to discussing common problems, not to acting on them. Its one major tactical initiative did not occur until 2007, when some of its members agreed, at least in principle, to challenge "the perverse incentives of the rankings of *U.S. News & World Report,*" which fuel the destructive competition fire.[47]

The Annapolis Group was not the first to challenge *U.S. News.* In 1995, Reed College, a group member, refused to provide the data required by *U.S. News* to compute Reed's ranking. *U.S. News* retaliated by dropping Reed from Tier II to Tier IV in the next year's rankings.[48] Thereafter, however, *U.S. News* restored Reed to Tier II (even though the college steadfastly continued to refuse to participate in the rankings survey), collecting data on Reed from other sources or creating data by undisclosed means.

In 2007, after it had decided to drop reliance on SAT scores in its admissions process, Sarah Lawrence College was still asked by *U.S. News* to provide SAT score data for its applicants. Sarah Lawrence refused. The next year *U.S. News,* after threatening to fabricate SAT data for Sarah Lawrence, dropped the college, which had been ranked in Tier I the preceding year, to a new category: "Unranked Schools."[49]

Clearly, collective action was required if opposition to the powerful *U.S. News* rankings was to be effective. At their June 2007 meeting, more than fifty of the Annapolis Group college presidents announced they would not participate in rating liberal arts colleges as a part of the so-called reputational survey conducted each year by *U.S. News.*[50] This seemed daring, since each college's reputational score accounts for 25 percent of its *U.S. News* ranking. The Annapolis Group, however, was not the leader in this initiative. A month earlier, a letter signed by representatives of more than sixty college and university members of the Educational Conservancy, a group concerned with improving the college admissions process, had urged college presidents to refuse to participate in the reputational survey.[51]

The Annapolis Group presidents' June 2007 announcement was followed by a September 7, 2007, letter signed by representatives of nineteen of the twenty-five top-rated liberal arts colleges (all but one, Annapolis Group members), pledging not to use rankings in their colleges' promotional materials but conspicuously saying nothing about cooperating with *U.S. News* in constructing the rankings.[52] And there the rebellion ended, with a whimper, not a bang. Nothing happened. *U.S. News* continues to publish its college rankings, seemingly unimpeded. Perhaps a few of the presidents refrained from cooperating; perhaps *U.S. News* devised a method for replacing their survey responses. Only *U.S. News* knows.

In May 2010, a *Washington Post* story was headlined "Some Colleges Are Opting Out of Magazine's Annual Survey."[53] The annual survey referred to was the one by *U.S. News*. Many of the colleges involved were Annapolis Group members. In fact, the headline was not correct. As the *Post* reported, the colleges were *not* opting out of the *U.S. News* survey. Rather, they were abandoning the practice of sending coffee-table books, CDs and DVDs, brochures, and other glitzy promotional materials to administrators at other colleges in an effort to skew the scores given their colleges by those administrators when they completed the *U.S. News* annual "reputational survey."[54] But this collaborative action, too, can hardly be characterized as boldly standing up to *U.S. News*.

The Overlap Group

By far the most significant and successful tactical, cooperative effort by private colleges and universities was carried out in the most sensitive operational area, tuition discounting, and lasted for more than a quarter century.

Under the 1890 Sherman Antitrust Act, conduct that unreasonably restrains trade is illegal.[55] Certain conduct, including price fixing, has been found by the Supreme Court to be so pernicious in effect and to-tally without redeeming virtue as to be "per se" illegal. That is, once a price fixing agreement is proven, a court will listen to no justifica-tions, excuses, or claims of reasonableness. Individual participants are subject to a fine or imprisonment.[56] Despite this menacing prospect, an Ivy League coalition, the predecessor of the much-publicized Overlap Group, was formed. Its history is informative.

In the 1950s, a group of Ivy League universities met to consider the problem of bidding wars for star athletes and agreed to stop the prac-tice. The agreement held and was broadened to include limiting schol-arship aid discounts for all students. In 1958, some of America's most successful universities and colleges, no less alert to the advantages of pricing agreements than were the captains of industry, formed the fa-mous (or infamous) Overlap Group, a consortium of the eight Ivy League universities, plus MIT, Tufts University, and thirteen wealthy, Eastern liberal arts colleges—Amherst, Barnard, Bowdoin, Bryn Mawr, Colby, Middlebury, Mount Holyoke, Smith, Trinity, Vassar, Wellesley, and Williams Colleges, and Wesleyan University. There were a few other, similar groups scattered across the nation, but it was the Overlap Group that caught the attention of the Justice Department, and for that reason it is the group about which the most is known.

Prior to 1991, when the Justice Department mobilized against it, the Overlap Group had been meeting for thirty-two years and agreeing on the tuition discount to which each student admitted to more than one of the group's schools was entitled. The Justice Department issued warnings about this practice as early as 1987–1988. At Yale, adminis-trators were told they could not discuss financial aid arrangements, prospectively, with other universities. This word came from Yale's pres-ident, Benno Schmidt, himself a distinguished lawyer, and was based on warnings he was getting from federal officials.[57]

Nonetheless, the Overlap Group's agreement continued in effect. Its purpose, in the eyes of its participants, was noble. As then president of MIT Charles M. Vest opined, years later, the Overlap Group was "a fair and powerful tool in advancing talented under-represented minorities in American society."[58] He believed that by agreeing to give discounts only on the basis of need and not on merit, the group prevented institutional resources from being "consumed in bidding wars for affluent students, absorbing revenues that could be used instead to offer better aid packages to high-need students and/or to offer admission and aid to larger numbers of high-need students."[59]

U.S. Attorney General Richard Thornburgh's answer to President Vest was succinct: "Students and their families are entitled to the full benefits of price competition when they choose a college," and they should not be denied "the right to compare prices and discounts among schools, just as they would in shopping for any other service or commodity."[60]

Neither President Vest nor Attorney General Thornburgh, however, was entirely correct. Contrary to Vest's argument, in the absence of the agreement, there was nothing to stop individual Overlap Group members from independently determining discounts solely on the basis of need, except their distrust of each other—their suspicion (probably well founded) that their competitors would not do the same. Indeed, MIT's lawyers conceded at trial that, absent an agreement, colleges (presumably including MIT) would in fact engage in bidding wars for desirable students, many (if not most) of whom had little or no need.[61] Thornburgh's contention that college applicants should be able to shop "just as they would . . . for any other service or commodity" ignored the obvious fact that higher education services are not the same as any other service or commodity. Tuition discounts do not reflect how much each student wants a college, but rather how much a college wants each student.

Another way to look at the Overlap Group's agreement is as an effort to avoid negative tuition. Negative tuition, paying students to attend, has long been a reality at top graduate schools (like MIT). It is masked to some extent by requiring graduate students to serve as teaching assistants so that payments to them can be styled as salary for teaching duties. The fact remains, however, that top graduate students are paid for attending and, as Gordon Winston and David Zimmerman have gently suggested, it may be only a matter of time before negative tuitions reach the undergraduate level.[62]

The way the Overlap Group case ultimately came out is not very instructive. The eight Ivies caved immediately and agreed to stop agreeing on discounts. Tufts and the thirteen liberal arts colleges disappeared from the scene. MIT was the only institution that did not give up. It litigated in federal court, lost, appealed, won a new trial, and only then agreed to stop agreeing on discounts—not surprisingly, since there was no longer anyone left for MIT to agree with.

The Overlap Group stressed it "made no common decisions about what tuition to charge or how much aid to provide" but rather made "a common assessment" of each applicant's need, perhaps because this sounded more like beneficent concern than crass price fixing.[63] In large measure, however, it was a distinction without a difference.

For the agreement to be effective, there were a number of requirements. First, the list prices of agreeing colleges had to be roughly the same. If College A's full-load list price was $20,000 and College B's was $10,000, a student admitted by both who could afford to pay only $10,000 would get $10,000 in aid from College A but nothing from College B. This fact alone would make College A seem a better deal. If the difference in list price between Colleges A and B was relatively small, however, the difference between the agreed-to need and the amount of aid offered a student by each member would be small, and would presumably be overlooked by both the colleges and the student. In fact, the list-price tuitions at the Overlap Group colleges were very similar: in 1991, $20,000 or slightly more.[64]

Second, for a successful agreement there had to be rough parity in the perceived quality of participating colleges. Equal amounts of aid offered by unequal colleges would not provide equal inducements to attend. Further, if College A were seen as far superior to College B, some of B's applicants would not have bothered to apply to College A, knowing they would probably not be admitted. The fewer common applicants there were, the less utility there would be in the agreement. While the Overlap Group colleges were distinctive, all of them were perceived as top-quality institutions.

Third, Overlap Group members had to agree to provide no discounts at all to no-need, wealthy applicants.

In an interesting paper written in 1994, economist Dennis Carlton (MIT's expert witness in the Overlap Group litigation) and two colleagues stated that the group's purpose was "to concentrate their scarce financial resources on needy students while leaving their total revenues unchanged," whereas the government claimed it was "to limit the amount of discounting off of list price and thereby raise the schools' revenues."[65] In other words, the group focused on what members had to pay students, and the government, on what students had to pay members, a dichotomy that does not exist in ordinary commercial price-fixing agreements in which sellers seek to maximize profits and purchasers are fungible.

Carlton and his colleagues, noting at the time they wrote their paper that there were inadequate data available to do an analysis based on data from before and after the termination of the Overlap Group's activities, constructed an elaborate regression analysis to examine whether the total revenues of the members (or the average price paid per student) was raised by the agreement. The sample they used was 225 private and public colleges and universities, including the 23 Overlap Group members. They found "no statistically significant evidence that the Overlap conduct raised revenues or, equivalently, average price. If anything, the results indicate that Overlap schools charged lower average prices, though the results are not statistically significant."[66]

Carlton and his fellow economists pointed out that the "economic content of the antitrust laws is simple—prevent inefficiency." "The general hostility that most economists (including us) have toward cooperative price setting in the profit-maximizing sector should not lead to a knee-jerk condemnation of a practice that raises equity concerns and few if any efficiency concerns and would never arise in the profit-maximizing sector."[67] They concluded:

> First, in the absence of an average price effect, the behavior [of Overlap Group schools] does not raise the traditional antitrust concern of economic efficiency. Second, collective action was likely necessary to achieve the goals of Overlap and . . . empirical analysis . . . indicates that Overlap was successful in increasing access of the poor to Overlap schools. Third, despite the hostility of the antitrust laws toward collective price behavior, the law should allow a Rule of Reason defense of collective action to certain non-profits based on social purposes, when, as here, there are no price effects. . . . Any sensible

antitrust policy must involve some balancing of harms and benefits to all affected consumers. Such balancing here shows no net efficiency effect.[68]

To put it less elegantly, the only "positive" effect of barring the Overlap agreement was increasing the probability that rich kids would get bigger discounts. Carlton and his colleagues argued not that the Overlap Group did not restrain competition, but rather that the restraint it imposed was reasonable and in the public interest. Their analysis also said, in effect, even if we accept the government's view that colleges, like for-profit commercial businesses, seek to acquire more wealth by selling their services at higher prices, that didn't happen here.

The government's premise, however, was wrong. Colleges acquire more wealth by becoming more prestigious, and purchasing the best students is an essential part of doing this. As the endowment wealth of the Overlap Group members has skyrocketed, the average price paid by their students—including well-to-do students—has fallen. Whether well-credentialed but poor students are less likely to be admitted to Harvard or Yale today than they were during the Overlap era is hard to know, but they are certainly less likely to receive sufficient financial aid to make it possible for them to accept their admission.

It is sometimes suggested that not-for-profit colleges are quasi-charities, that is, that the discounts they give are charitable distributions. As we have noted, the difficulty with this suggestion is that merit-based distributions do not go to the needy. Still, it is interesting to pursue the quasi-charity notion a bit further.

Suppose that, instead of one national Red Cross, there were hundreds of independent mini–Red Crosses and that we applied the antitrust laws to them and insisted they compete and refrain from cooperatively coordinating in making their distributions. The result would be that some recipients would receive money from several of the mini–Red Crosses, more than they needed, and others would be left out when the money ran out, even though their need was great. This would be absurd. Obviously we would not simply permit the mini–Red Crosses to cooperate but would *insist* they do so to ensure the widest possible distributions to the greatest number of recipients with the greatest need.

This is not to advocate treating liberal arts colleges as charities. They aren't. But it is to suggest that treating nonprofit colleges as profit-seeking enterprises, and subjecting their efforts to provide financial aid to needy students to the competition-promoting antitrust laws, makes no sense whatsoever.

The impact of the Overlap Group decision depends on the wealth of a college. The less wealthy a college, the more it must rely on tuition revenues. One can envisage a continuum running from the wealthiest to the poorest college. As one moves along it, the funds available to purchase students decline and the need for tuition revenues to meet operating expenses increases. The poorest colleges cannot afford to buy students. Colleges at the midpoint of the continuum can give aid to poor students only if they earn tuition revenues from full-pay students. Nine months into the recession, Morton Schapiro, then president of Williams College, put it succinctly: "You can't say someone should be need-blind unless they have the resources to fund it. It sounds immoral to replace really talented low-income kids with less talented richer kids, but unless you're a Williams or Amherst, the alternative is the quality of the education declines for everyone."[69] This is exactly the competitive—as opposed to cooperative—outcome President Vest feared.

It is a great irony that Major League Baseball, an association of for-profit teams, has enjoyed an exemption from the antitrust laws since 1922, when the Supreme Court, in an opinion authored by Justice Oliver Wendell Holmes, bizarrely held that baseball games "are purely state affairs" and therefore not covered by the antitrust laws (which apply only to interstate commerce).[70] Baseball's antitrust exemption permits the insertion of so-called reserve clauses into player contracts. The reserve system is simply an agreement between team owners not to raid the player rosters of their rivals. The parallel to an agreement between colleges not to raid each others' applicant rosters is self-evident. It is hard to see how an agreement between the Boston Red Sox and the New York Yankees is less interstate than one between, say, Wellesley and Barnard Colleges.

I have discussed the Overlap Group decision at such length because I believe the time is right to revisit it. There are sound legal as well as public-policy reasons why its prohibition of joint action by educational institutions should be eliminated. Among the potential collaborative actions liberal arts colleges could take, one that could have the most immediate, significant, affirmative effect on their economic health would be to pursue elimination of the Overlap Group precedent, thereby preventing institutional aid resources from being, in Charles Vest's words, "consumed in bidding wars for affluent students, absorbing revenues that could be used instead to offer better aid packages to high-need students and/or admission and aid to larger numbers of high-need students."[71]

CHAPTER 6

Recruiting Students

✦

Promoting the general value of a liberal arts college education has largely been left to the Annapolis Group and occasional forums like the Pew Foundation Roundtable of liberal arts college presidents. The efforts have been scant and not very effective. Realistically, it would be too much to expect a college to tell a prospective student, "We don't care which college you attend so long as it is a liberal arts college." Each individual college devotes substantial resources to promoting demand for its own offerings.

In promoting the value of the unique educational experience they offer, all liberal arts colleges face a daunting obstacle. In the minds of most citizens, higher education and universities are nearly synonymous. Media attention to universities is constant. When the 2008 presidential candidates' debates took place, the University of Mississippi was in the news. When President Obama gave commencement addresses, Notre Dame University and Michigan State University were on the front pages. When he announced that stem cell research would be accelerated, the University of Wisconsin received national attention.

Nobel Prize announcements, research discoveries, distinguished visitors, student demonstrations and riots, marching bands, rock concerts, shows, art exhibits, and special events increase the name recognition for the big public and private universities. And all of this is accompanied by daily reporting on the universities' sports teams. Their football and basketball games are televised nationally. On the rare occasion when a liberal arts college has gotten national sports coverage, for example when Davidson College's basketball team became one of sixty-four teams to make it into March Madness or Colorado College's hockey team reached the Frozen Four, the college was noticed in the press, but only until its team was beaten by a university team.

The impact of this drumbeat of national media attention on the universities' admissions and fund-raising cannot be overestimated. It stimulates their obtaining federal and private research grants. And with their hundreds of thousands of alumni, university fund-raising campaigns are powerful engines. Even tax-supported state universities have private foundations that raise billions of dollars.

While the most prestigious liberal arts colleges may be described as "national," it is because they draw their small classes of students from around the nation, not because they attract national attention. Liberal arts colleges go largely unnoticed by the media.[1] Self-promotion does not come naturally to liberal arts colleges. The story of the liberal arts education they offer goes largely untold. Eva Brann, the former dean of St. John's College (Annapolis), said, "Liberal education has its concrete seat in institutional communities, and it is they, severally, who have to achieve a brief, clear, persuasive language about themselves."[2] Brann might have added "because no one else will," and she probably should also have said "collectively," rather than "severally." The "several" efforts to promote the value of liberal arts education have not proven effective.

As the concerns of high school seniors have changed over time, the story liberal arts college promoters have told has also changed. Sixty years ago, a liberal arts college president might have noted that his college was a good place to meet your future spouse, pointing to the large percentage of students who married classmates immediately after graduation. He might have stressed that the high quality of his college's kindergarten and primary teacher education programs ensured female students a good job after graduation, possibly adding that the jobs would provide needed income until graduates married and started a family. Today, the challenge confronting each liberal arts college is to find a way to attract high school seniors and parents to a kind of education most of them know nothing about and are not predisposed to learn about, and a type of college they have never visited.

Liberal arts college administrators perceive, doubtless correctly, that the value of life-long enrichment a liberal education provides, and the high quality of teaching their colleges offer, are tough to sell to ill-informed, wealth-seeking, "what's in it for me?" seventeen-year-olds and their nervous parents. Every college has therefore carefully tailored a recruiting case, "the pitch," the "sell" seen in viewbooks and online solicitations and carried to high schools by the college's recruiters.

Current versions of the recruiting case begin with jobs and income. As we have noted, far and away the single greatest concern of high school seniors and their parents is getting a good job after graduation. This is an apparent weakness of liberal arts colleges, because their courses do not relate directly to employment. Recruiting cases address this problem with statistics showing the higher life incomes baccalaureate degree-holders achieve. This is true, of course, but for postsecondary education generally, not specifically for a liberal arts education. Further, there is some question as to how true it still is. The claimed $1 million difference between the average lifetime earnings of college and high school graduates (a claim usually attributed to the College Board) may actually be less than $300,000 when tuition costs are deducted and lifetime earnings are discounted to their present value.[3]

Recruiting cases seek to detail how a liberal arts education will provide the skills graduates need to succeed in the workplace, another challenge for recruiters because, unlike vocational programs, the liberal arts are not directly tied to career opportunities. The cornerstone of this aspect of the recruiting case is almost always "critical thinking," described as a fundamental skill that will well serve graduates not only in the workplace but in all of life. "Critical thinking," Jane Smiley wryly observed in her novel *Moo,* "is to a liberal education as faith is to religion."[4] There are few college presidents and admissions officers who do not routinely feature "critical thinking" in their public utterances.

But what exactly is critical thinking? How does it differ from plain good thinking? Whatever critical thinking may be, why is it more likely to be learned by studying English literature or philosophy than business management? Why would one suppose that English literature or philosophy professors are more likely to inculcate critical thinking in their students than business administration professors? To be blunt, why would one expect English literature or philosophy professors to *be* critical thinkers? The recruiting case neither asks nor answers these questions.

A liberal arts education is said to be the best way to develop oral and written communications skills, and it is certainly true that it can facilitate the development of those skills. But, is it more likely to do so than a career-based, vocational education, or, for that matter, than the education that comes from being in the workplace? Recruiting cases do not answer these questions. Nor do they offer convincing evidence that liberally educated persons are more effective communicators or, even if they are, that it is because they are liberally educated.

A newer element in some versions of the recruiting case runs as follows: As is well known, most young men and women will have several careers during their lifetime. A course of study involving several disciplines, as a liberal arts education does, is particularly good preparation for a life likely to include several careers. This contention comes close to being a non sequitur. Consider the following multicareer life scenario.

Jobs were tight when John graduated from college, so he began selling encyclopedias door to door. After a year and a half, he and a friend, both cycling enthusiasts, pooled their resources, including the small inheritance John had received from his grandfather, and opened a bicycle shop in Golden, Colorado. They actually manufactured high-end mountain bikes, as well as selling and servicing all makes. Their shop managed to survive for six years. By then, John was married and had one child and another on the way. No longer comfortable with the uncertain income the bike shop generated, he took a marketing position with a major national outdoor sporting goods manufacturer. He attended graduate business school at night and, after four years, earned an MBA.

Once John had his graduate degree, his employer promoted him to a midlevel financial analyst position. Through contacts he made over the next several years, John received an offer to become an assistant vice president with a nationally respected investment banking firm, which he accepted, and moved with his family to New York City. In his new position, he specialized in making deals involving communications companies, an industry he came to love. In the last ten years of his professional career, he was the senior sales VP for a large broadcasting and cable television company.

How studying English literature, philosophy, French, and geology best prepared John for his career journey is an unanswered question.

A relatively recent addition to the recruiting case for liberal arts, added by some colleges in an attempt to resist pressures to increase their vocational offerings, is a liberal arts–vocational straddle. Liberal arts departments, so the claim goes, are actually vocational because they support or lead to careers. Biology, for example, is described as premed, political science as prelaw, and economics as prebusiness. It is not clear how persuasive this relatively untested pitch will prove to be.

Study abroad is featured in the recruiting case made for many liberal arts colleges. It is true that we live in a global world and it behooves colleges to internationalize their curriculums. Further, foreign travel is a meaningful, often life-changing, experience. But consider the following typical liberal arts college promotion: "Our college recognizes the importance of international education by encouraging all students to spend a semester abroad." Restating this promotion from the point of view of a potential student's parents can yield the following reaction: "You have told us that our daughter's spending twenty-six months at your college over the next four years at a cost of $200,000 is a sound investment, but now you say she should spend more than three of those months somewhere else. Are you trying to cut your costs by giving her less, or do you believe twenty-six months on campus is more than she needs?"

In an effort to attract students, some liberal arts colleges have reduced and even eliminated course requirements. "Study only what you like best" is a college recruiter's dream argument. To the extent that colleges eliminate requirements, however, they turn over liberal-education curriculum design to students who are not yet liberally educated, and they create the strong probability that their education will be less broad, less liberal. Maria Montessori's maxim, Follow the child, may make sense in kindergarten, but not at a liberal arts college—unless, of course, the college's education philosophy is that students will find liberal education on their own, in which case why should they spend $200,000 for twenty-six months of college?

To gain admittance to graduate and professional schools, under-graduates need a high grade-point average, especially now that so many graduate schools are evaluating applicants' grades on grids that do not differentiate among GPAs on the basis of the difficulty of courses taken. Colleges do not explicitly include grade inflation in their recruiting cases, but everyone knows it is going on. Easy grading has real consumer appeal. Grade inflation, however, cheapens the value of a liberal arts degree and signals to students that a liberal arts education is simply a part of the credential-seeking game. Further, since everyone is doing it, it doesn't work very well.

Princeton University has made an effort to retard galloping grade inflation. In 2002–2003, A's accounted for 47.9 percent of Princeton undergraduates' grades. The next year, the Princeton faculty adopted a policy setting an institutionwide expectation for the percentage of A grades (less than 35 percent for undergraduate courses), and providing guidelines on the meaning of letter grades. In 2008–2009, A's fell below 40 percent for the first time following the policy's adoption.[5]

Other universities and colleges do not appear to be following Princeton's lead, however, and the result at Princeton has been an unpopular policy of dubious success. In the words of a Princeton junior: "There are tons of really great schools with really smart kids applying for the same jobs. People intuitively take a GPA to be a representation of your academic ability and act accordingly. The assumption that a recruiter who is screening applications is going to treat a Princeton student differently based on a letter [from Princeton explaining its tougher grading policy] is naïve."[6]

Liberal arts college recruiting cases reflect the fact that the art of persuasion is not always artfully practiced in the academy (as anyone who has attended a faculty meeting can attest). Indeed, in scholarly writing, overt efforts to persuade are often viewed with suspicion. It is not surprising, therefore, that liberal arts college recruiting cases are not very persuasive. As a national survey in 1997 showed, overall, high school juniors and seniors, and their parents, believe the majority of the goals of higher education can be achieved with any curriculum, especially "writing and oral skills," "professional school preparation," "exposure to the business world," "critical thinking," "problem solving," "computer literacy," "strong work habits," and "time management." The only goals of higher education seen as being uniquely provided by liberal education are "developing an appreciation for culture," and "basic skills in sciences, arts, humanities and social sciences," goals survey participants generally rated as less important.[7]

On balance, liberal arts college recruiting cases probably do no harm but little good. They do not discourage students predisposed to attend a liberal arts college, nor those whose choice depends primarily on extrinsic factors such as a college's closeness to their home, where their parents went, or where their friends are going. The recruiting cases are not, however, well calculated to attract students who possess the raw intellectual firepower to be outstanding students and to become leaders, but who have no such predisposition or connections. Nor are they likely to persuade parents not already committed to liberal arts education. They do not directly address the fair question, "Will my child's attending a private liberal arts college yield a better return on my investment than her attending a far less expensive public university?" (And I have long suspected that some parents believe attending a national liberal arts college increases the likelihood that their child will move away from home after graduation, something many of them do not want.)

College-bound high school students with little or no experience with liberal education have significant personal concerns that are not well addressed by recruiting cases. "Will I like being at a liberal arts college with many students whose life experience is entirely different from mine?" "None of my friends ever went to one." "Will my friends and neighbors think I'm 'fronting?'" "The courses sound to me a lot like those in high school, and I really haven't enjoyed my high school classes all that much."

For most students and parents, subject matter and education are conflated; subject matter is what one learns. The nub of the problem for admissions officers is how to explain that liberal arts education *is useful because what is studied is not.*

Because they are perceived (correctly) as salespersons, admissions officers are not well positioned to be credible in addressing the question of what is useful, any more than a General Mills salesperson can be credibly persuasive in explaining why eating Wheaties for breakfast will make one a better basketball player. But athletes like Michael Jordan or Kevin Garnett can be. They are prequalified to speak both knowledgeably and objectively. Business leaders, such as those interviewed by Professor Goldstein, are similarly well situated to make the case for liberal arts education. They would be telling it like it is, not just making a sales pitch. Unlike Michael or Kevin, however, they are rarely called on to do so.

Henry Adams and his classmates at Mr. Dixwell's school were implicitly exposed to the value of a liberal arts education from the day they were born. The exposure came from their community, trusted family and friends, not from sales pitches by admissions officers. Doubtless there are still some applicants to liberal arts colleges who have had such exposure. The overwhelming majority of high school seniors, however, are not exposed to liberal arts education and will never hear even the flawed recruiting case, let alone testimonials from successful leaders in business, culture, and politics.

When I began thinking about this book, I believed what was needed was to sharpen recruiting cases, eliminate their internal inconsistencies, make them more direct and candid, and rework them to make sense to young people who are not, by virtue of their life circumstance, presold on liberal arts. This is still a good idea, but it will not reverse the decline in demand for liberal arts colleges. Society as a whole is putting greater and greater emphasis on vocational goals and aspirations, and losing patience with the "useless" scholarship of liberal arts. If the greater community that informs the views, goals, and aspirations of all of us is unaware of, or does not believe in, the value of a liberal arts college education, seventeen-year-olds and their parents will not be persuaded by any recruiting case, no matter how adroitly it is constructed.

CHAPTER 7

Liberal Arts Teachers: A Profile

The core element of the special value of liberal arts colleges is excellent teaching. In reflecting on this fact, I found myself thinking about what is unique about the liberal arts college teaching experience, and why I find many liberal arts college professors inspiring.

One evening, while I was visiting with a professor in my office, the telephone rang. It was a friend calling to tell me a joke. I laughed at the joke and said good-bye. When I hung up, the professor asked, "Why did whoever was on the phone call you?"

"To tell me a joke," I said.

"I know he told you a joke, but why did he call?" the professor asked.

Aside from lawyers, librarians, and trolls who live under bridges, few groups carry stronger stereotypes than college professors. They are commonly perceived to be eccentric, impractical, liberal, effete, intellectual eggheads. "What is it," Arthur Schlesinger asked, "the sense they give of collective unreality? collective complacency? collective pomposity? collective futility? And their jokes are so bad! Yet individually they are most agreeable, admirable, rewarding people. Why does the academic environment, as distinct from the academic discipline, seem to bring out the worst in otherwise decent individuals?"[1] Former U.S. attorney general John Mitchell captured a popular sense of academics when he observed, "They don't know anything." (In fairness, Mitchell went on to say, "Nor do these stupid bastards who are running our educational institutions.")[2]

In fact, college teachers are no more likely to be eccentric than are investment bankers or accountants. They possess the practicality imposed on those who must make do with modest incomes. They tend to be conservative and cautious, not daring or unpredictable, and uncomfortable with change.

College teachers live in a borderless ghetto with other members of the college teaching profession. They may serve on local school or church boards, PTAs or town councils, but they are likely to spend most of their time with their own kind, both where they live and teach (especially at residential colleges in rural settings) and at the learned association meetings they attend. Just as living in a small town often breeds conservatism, so does the parochialism of their lives. Even if they travel widely, wherever they go they meet others like them. Their neighborhood is nationwide (not unlike the national "neighborhoods" of wealthy residents of Grosse Pointe or the Hamptons). They are unlikely to interface socially with a diversity of persons, except to the extent they are studying them. They are eager to be perceived as individualistic, but as an anthropologist once observed to me about the faculty at her liberal arts college, "I have never seen a group of individualists who are more alike."

Because they teach about worldly events, social-scientist college teachers are often expected to be worldly themselves. This expectation is no more well founded than expecting a baseball player to be knowledgeable about finance because he has a bank account. The same observation applies to the popular assumptions that all English professors are good writers and all economists know how to make money.

Do college teachers come naturally to teaching, or are they the product of their environment? Probably both. Obviously they tend to be drawn from the ranks of persons who enjoyed being college students and were good at it. (Persons who were good at their collegiate studies but did not especially enjoy them are more likely to become lawyers or doctors.) Equally clearly, however, something deep within each college teacher drew her or him to the academic life.

James Redfield, a classicist at the University of Chicago, amusingly observed that prisons, mental hospitals, and colleges are all places where people are kept for a while with the understanding that, when they have done well enough, they will be allowed again to go out into the world. . . . [I]n all such institutions . . . the inmate who enjoys the institution too much will not profit from it. . . . The prisoner who is at home in prison becomes an old lag, and the mental patient who is at home in the hospital becomes incurable. . . . [At colleges, however,] those who do very well as students can, if they wish, stay on and join the faculty. . . . It is as if the prisoners who did best become the guards and warden, the mental patients who did best become the doctors and nurses.[3]

Often, when they were students, college teachers came under the influence of an outstanding professor who became their mentor and urged them to go on to graduate school. Professors, not surprisingly, frequently urge their students to become what they are. It is less common, for example, for a chemistry professor to encourage a student to go to medical school. (There is a student joke that, if you want to get good grades in chemistry because you plan to go to medical school, you had better not let your chemistry professor learn about your plan.)

A seminal event in the life of college teachers is the decision to attend graduate school. Once there, they are submerged in and indoctrinated by a pervasive academic culture that values research and publication over teaching. The most successful traversing of the graduate school road leads to an appointment at a large research university.

Do newly matriculated graduate students realize what they are getting themselves into? To a surprisingly substantial degree, given their tender age, the answer is yes. They know the odds are high they will end up as college teachers, not university research scholars. (Indeed, having been impressed by their own undergraduate professors and wanting to emulate them, this is the goal some of them seek.) They know that, by following this course, they will never make a lot of money. New college teachers make a life-shaping social contract, trading the possibility of worldly gain for a particular lifestyle: to be paid (however inadequately) for what they like to do best, to have three months in the summer to do their own research and a sabbatical every seven years, and to be able to spend the rest of their life at their beloved college or one very much like it. This social contract toughens them.

For nonacademics who graduate from college or professional school, the future is an exciting unknown, the potential seemingly limitless. Who knows where their careers will take them, what fields they may move into or out of, where they will live, how much they will earn, how far they will travel, where they will be in twenty years? For most, a defining moment at the onset of middle age is the slow-dawning realization that the world is not their oyster, that their options are limited and becoming more so; that life may not get any better.

In contrast, while graduate students may not fully appreciate what it will be like to teach Introductory Microeconomics or Shakespeare's Tragedies for the twentieth time, they do have a clear sense of the limits of the path they have chosen. They recognize that if they are successful in their first college teaching position and earn tenure, they will probably never move from there. They choose the academic life knowingly, willingly, and with a certainty not found in most of their nonacademic contemporaries. Some of the discoveries of middle age will not be part of their life voyage. They already know. Perhaps they are guided by an aversion to risk, but I believe committing to a life of teaching takes courage.

The impact the graduate school experience has on college teachers is substantial. There often is no precisely fixed term for completing a Ph.D. degree. That it may take many years is acceptable and accepted. Unlike law students, who study for three years, take the bar exam, and get out, whatever sense of urgency besets graduate students comes largely from outside their academic work: needing to pay off student loans, getting married, starting a family.

When they are in college, students for the most part study textbooks and treatises, the scholarly work of others. In graduate school they are charged more and more with doing their own independent scholarly work. Their work now must be unique; work duplicative of that done by others will not be accepted. Each year it becomes harder to find something new on which to base a doctoral thesis. In the quest for originality, Ph.D. candidates are driven toward minutiae, remoteness, replowing old fields but with a different blade cant, knowing (to quote the old saw) "more and more about less and less." It is the metaphor of a thousand monkeys at a thousand typewriters in reverse; the more monkeys typing, the less likely they are to produce a work of value.

Ever-increasing pressure toward greater specialization, greater narrowness, often commented on in the public press, is inherent in the system. But the more specialized graduate students become in their academic training, the less well-prepared they are to teach at a liberal arts college.

I learned that a famous university professor and scholar whose writing I greatly admired was spending a semester as a visiting scholar at a university near my home, and I arranged to meet him in a classroom on a Saturday morning. When I walked into the classroom, he was slumped at the desk in the front of the room, his head down, obviously in a state of distress. After we exchanged introductions, I said, "Professor, you seem very disturbed."

"I am," he said. "It's the seminar I'm being required to teach."
"Ah," I said, "the straw that breaks the camel's back?"
"No," he replied, "it is the only course I am teaching."
"I don't understand," I said.
"I'm a professor," he exclaimed angrily, "not a teacher!"

"Professors in the leading graduate programs are actively propagating themselves," writes David Kirp, who teaches at the University of California, Berkeley. "They discourage their best students from considering careers in liberal arts colleges, instead preparing them for positions in research universities—that, after all, is where academic reputations are made."[4] If worse comes to worst, however, and a graduate student is obliged to accept a teaching position at a liberal arts college, he or she still will recruit future graduate students for universities, thereby renewing and replenishing the academic life cycle. "On a campus mainly devoted to research and graduate school teaching," said Andrew Delbanco of Columbia University, "those of us who focus on college teaching sometimes feel like Jonah in the belly of the whale."[5]

While the faculty at American research universities are doing their research and scholarly writing, they leave much of the undergraduate teaching to graduate student assistants. Teaching assistants are given little or no training in how to be a good teacher. True, they can observe their graduate school professors' teaching styles, but those styles tend to be adapted to teaching highly motivated, cream-of-the-crop, twenty-five-year-old graduate students, not a mixed bag of eighteen-year-olds with at best uncertain motivation. Occasional, sporadic graduate school efforts to encourage the development of teaching skills notwithstanding, most graduate students will begin to learn these skills by working for minimum wages as teaching assistants so their mentors, whom they admire, won't have to teach.

Most rewards and recognitions given to graduate students are for research and publication, not teaching. A few students will go on to scholarly careers at research universities, but most will devote their lives to teaching. Many will view a teaching position at a liberal arts college as failure, a view reinforced by their graduate schools. Letters of recommendation written by graduate school deans for new Ph.D. holders applying for liberal arts college positions are frequently paradigms of subtle denigration: "perfect for the position for which he is applying" or "in her work as a teaching assistant she has shown an outstanding facility." Medical students, in contrast, whatever doubts and anxieties they may feel, leave medical school with a sense that they are as well prepared as possible for the life course they have chosen, and with pride in having "made it."

When new Ph.D. holders arrive at their first liberal arts college teaching position, there often is no formal mechanism in place for on-the-job training. They may be assigned a mentor who may or may not be generous in giving advice, but neither the mentor nor other faculty colleagues are likely to sit in on classes taught by neophyte teachers, critique their syllabi and classroom performance, or guide their development. No one did it for them. New college teachers are largely on their own, to sink or swim until, at the end of seven years under the tenure system, they have either learned how to swim or are permanently banished from the pool.

New teachers' well-founded self-doubt about their teaching competence may never be lost. Formal performance evaluations rarely occur more frequently than annually. Student feedback is a more reliable in-dicator of popularity than of teaching skill. The success of a college teacher's students after they graduate may be a measure of teaching competence but cannot be seen until well into the teacher's career.

From day one, young doctors and lawyers get a steady stream of feedback on how well they are doing. Do their patients recover? Are their cases won or lost? Colleagues at a hospital or in a law firm see their work on a daily basis and can and do advise them on how to improve their professional skills. In contrast, in some convoluted way, some faculty members see advising a colleague how to teach as an in-trusion, almost a violation of academic freedom.

In addition to fostering self-doubt, the way college teachers are trained—or rather, obliged to self-train—can make them proprietary about the teaching skills they acquire. They have done it on their own, the hard way. Let others do the same. Some senior professors may be generous in sharing their knowledge about how to teach, but others will be too busy to devote time to such a collegial undertaking.

The tenure system's inflexible, ruthless, up-or-out requirement at the end of the year following the sixth-year evaluation has a corrosive effect on young professors. A professor who has been denied tenure is seen as damaged goods and is unlikely to land a teaching position at another college or university, or at least a position with job security that pays more than subsistence wages. The pressure to succeed in at-taining the tenure grail can be almost unbearable.

To make matters worse, there are few clear guidelines for what is ex-pected of a successful college teacher, no dependable, sure signposts to tenure. Should they focus on becoming star classroom performers ad-mired by students, or will that breed resentment among their depart-mental colleagues? Should they devote every spare moment to publish-ing scholarly articles, or will that be seen as shirking their teaching obligations? If they publish in general-audience magazines and news-papers, will they be disrespected as mere popularizers? Should they give time to being good academic community citizens, doing commit-tee work and serving on advisory panels, or will that be perceived as pandering, or as avoiding the hard work of teaching?

It is immediately apparent at any liberal arts college that well-respected faculty members make different contributions—to teaching, to scholarship, to community service—and that what brought success to one faculty member is not the same as what worked for another. Realization of this fact makes it difficult for a new teacher to determine how best to proceed. Times may have changed, and what worked for their mentors or department chairs may not work for them. Young assistant professors run scared. Postures and facades to conceal self-doubt, to convey a false sense of self-confidence and assurance may be developed.

Anxiety created by the tenure-track maze can leave other psychological scars. Will successful tenure recipients resolve to work less hard, never to go through "that" again? Will they seek to ensure that nothing changes, that all who come after them will be obliged to endure the same tortuous journey? One thing seems clear: the anxiety serves no useful purpose. There is no reason to believe the mere fact of surviving the tenure-track journey better qualifies assistant professors as teachers.

Much is made in the popular press of the fact that professors spend only a few hours in the classroom each week, and even if they devote two hours to preparation for every classroom hour, they are still seen as having a less than thirty-hour workweek. Nothing could be further from the truth. Good teachers often spend many hours preparing for each class, particularly when they are teaching a course for the first time. (For new teachers, every course is taught for the first time.) Added to these long hours are countless other duties: counseling students; grading papers; committee assignments; new faculty searches; professional association meetings; preparation of papers and reports; and endless, niggling, administrative details. At many liberal arts colleges, secretarial support is inadequate. For lowly assistant professors it is sometimes nonexistent.

Summer is supposed to be a time for research and scholarship, but it is the rare college teacher who does not need a portion of that time for recuperation, and then it is time to start course preparation for the fall semester. The grueling pressure of assistant professors' first seven years is relentless. Like the Red Queen, they must run to hold their place, to keep from falling back.

Sabbaticals are redemption. Typically, every seven years a tenured professor is awarded a half-year at full pay or a full year at half pay, often subsidized with grants, with no teaching or other college obligations. Sabbaticals are intended to be used for scholarly activities, but on the teacher's own schedule, free from daily pressures. They can involve exciting travel, perhaps to do research overseas. A teacher's first sabbatical, which generally comes the year after tenure is achieved, is a major life event. Only tenured faculty members are entitled to sabbaticals. For untenured instructors there is no respite.

All institutions, enterprises, and communities tend to look inward, not outward. The academy is no exception. It has its own agenda, its own pace, its own rhetoric. College professors understand the separateness and uniqueness of their world. Having chosen to set themselves apart, away from much of the hurly-burly of the outer world, they develop special survival skills, albeit skills not readily transferable to other work environments.

The grove of academe is branded not the "real world," and it is cloistered. Within its confines, however, professors are knowing and mature. A common joke is that academic disputes are especially intense because the stakes are so small. So it may seem from the outside, but within a liberal arts college the stakes are never small and the combatants are battle hardened and skillful. Who is to say that the issues of academia matter less?

College teachers are sensitive to the fact (or myth, it does not matter) that they are not toughened by their career. They tend to believe—probably rightly, at least to some extent—that if they leave the friendly confines of the grove they are vulnerable to being taken advantage of, or to being made to look foolish. They read the *New York Times* and bloggers' opinions and know the popular mistrust the tenure system engenders, and they are told by the *Chronicle of Higher Education* that a majority of college and university presidents oppose it. They are suspicious of colleagues who develop outside agendas, as consultants, entrepreneurs, or political activists. Outsiders who are supportive of the academy may be appreciated, but they are never fully trusted and accepted; they will never understand what it has taken to become a professor.

In the world outside the academy, the typical career path is from specialization to generalization. Young people start their careers working at a particular task. As they move up the ladder of success, they broaden their scope, develop new areas of expertise, and strive to integrate all they have learned. Generalists, men and women of wisdom whose life experiences qualify them to comment meaningfully and usefully on a wide variety of subjects, occupy the pinnacle of success. The value of their insights derives from their understanding of the human condition and life's lessons; not from mastery of a particular subject.

For academics, the pressure to specialize never abates. The most successful are frequently the most specialized, publishing articles on the narrowest topics in the most narrowly specialized journals. Disciplines develop specialized languages that outsiders, no matter how bright and interested, have difficulty understanding. Communication becomes an in-group activity.

While interviewing a candidate for an assistant professorship in the history department, I asked about her Ph.D. thesis (on nativism in Philadelphia in the early nineteenth century). It was beautifully written, and I said, only half facetiously, "You write so gracefully. Aren't you afraid you will be attacked for being a mere popularizer, not scholarly?"

"Yes," she replied, entirely seriously.

"Then why don't you make your writing more obscure, more academic?" I asked.

"I've tried; believe me I've tried," she sighed, "but I just can't do it."

Writing in the *International Herald Tribune,* University of Texas historian Richard Pells observed that American academics write "miserably" and asked why. His answer was that they do it on purpose, for two motives:

> The first is fear.
>
> Graduate students and assistant professors are terrified of unemployment. They know that members of hiring and promotion committees like to clone themselves. So academic neophytes adopt an

esoteric language designed to please their mentors, and the scholarly experts who recommend or reject a manuscript for publication. They learn to use trendy post-modernist words like "discourse" and "contextualize," and to mention everything ever written about their subject. I have often heard my younger colleagues refer to their first work as a "tenure book" which will get them a secure job, but is not designed to be a means of communicating with the outside world.

The second is snobbery.

Academics are distrustful of best sellers. They reject the idea that a widely read book might be good. They suspect that to write a popular book, an academic must be superficial and willing to settle for sound bites. There is no harsher epithet in a scholar's vocabulary than to call a book "journalistic."[6]

The consequence of academics' writing only for each other, Pells concludes, is "that American scholars are increasingly isolated from the public, with little impact on social issues or cultural trends." Americans, he says, are learning their history from Steven Spielberg and James Cameron.[7]

Liberal arts colleges are characterized as intellectual communities. Perhaps so, but it depends on how one defines intellectuals. If they are persons who enjoy debating any topic—social, political, or cultural—and who are not deterred by the facts that their knowledge is limited and that of the other debaters far greater, the characterization is not correct. College teachers tend to stand back until a topic is raised about which they are expert, at which point they declaim enthusiastically. Their colleagues whose expertise is in other areas listen respectfully and wait for their area of expertise to come up so they can take the floor. College teachers are, by and large, the wrong people to invite to a dinner or cocktail party if the host's objective is animated conversation. (Lawyers are better bets as invitees to such events because of their willingness to speak out on topics about which they know absolutely nothing. Indeed, lawyers seem affirmatively to search out such topics.)

The well-known tendency of college teachers to form a committee at the drop of a hat for every issue that arises, no matter how insignificant—perhaps reflecting a reluctance to take the heat for decisions made—is facilitated by a general resistance to change at liberal arts colleges. College teachers are disinclined to stop doing things they way they have always been done. The fact that it may take a committee years to reach a decision that an individual could make in days (or hours or minutes) makes no difference because it really does not matter whether the decision is ever made. Because problem identification and analysis, not problem solving, are the basic skills required of professors—and a sense of urgency or of the centrality of timeliness is not—this is probably not surprising.

The propensity for forming committees creates an enormous amount of burdensome, unnecessary work for faculty members. Recognizing that committees are often extraordinarily ineffective in making needed decisions and accomplishing important tasks, academics have created a rhetorical justification for them. Committees, they say, ensure that the faculty will "take ownership" of a decision, plan, or project. It is not clear what this means.

College teachers' professional lives are most directly affected by the quality of their students and their departmental colleagues. Partners in the banking department of a law firm see clearly that they will be advantaged if the firm's litigation department grows in size, reputation, and influence. The additional clients it attracts may bring with them new banking business, but even if they don't, the firm's profitability will increase and along with it, the share of profits paid to the banking-department partners. In contrast, if the strength of one academic department at a college grows, for example because of an increase in the number of majors, necessitating additional faculty, resentment in other departments is more likely than celebration.

There is one last essential element of the environment in which college teachers work and it is, of course, students. When I practiced law, I saw myself in combat with the other side. It was the battle of litigation—being stretched and challenged to the limit—that excited me. Undergraduate teaching seemed to me like doing intellectual battle with students who, no matter how bright, lacked the experience to outflank the professor; at least they could not do so very often. The professor knows going in that he will be the winner, I reasoned. Litigation, I thought, is to teaching as playing tournament tennis is to giving tennis lessons. Giving lessons is a nice thing but it must get old fast, unless the instructor feeds on a false sense of self-worth from always being the victor.

I could not have been more wrong. The best college teachers find their greatest satisfaction in seeing their students learn, not in triumphing over them in the classroom. The satisfaction is neither ethereal nor abstract. For most liberal arts college students, a professor will be included in the small group of the most important people in the student's life. They know it, their professors know it, and it is a very satisfying and fulfilling relationship for both.

The concept of "mentor" has a particularly deep and profound meaning for students and teachers. There may not be many Mr. Chipses left at liberal arts colleges, but there are still many mentors. Their satisfaction in focusing and enhancing the lives of young men and women remains sweet, vivid, and satisfying "I touched this young life and it was good," is an experience nonteachers enjoy infrequently—if at all—in their work life. For many college professors it is the norm, not the exception.

The longer college teachers teach, the more they can see the fruits of their handiwork, and the more fruits of their handiwork there are to see. This is especially so when a teacher's efforts are reflected by returning graduates (or by their matriculating children). The law case won, the conflict resolved, the business deal closed, or, for that matter, the letter complimenting an article in an obscure academic journal, can be rewarding, but it pales in comparison to the returning alum who says, "I came to the class reunion to see you, Professor. You changed my life. Thank you."

CHAPTER 8

Employing and Deploying Faculty
for Teaching Excellence

✦

John Wyatt died on June 27, 2008. For twenty-five years he had taught Greek, Latin, classics, and comparative literature at Beloit College. Shortly after he died, a former student created a Web site in his memory. In the month after it was created, more than 2,500 persons, most of them former students, visited the site. Many of them left remembrances of John as a teacher and a friend:

"John deeply touched everyone he met."

"He found the moment to believe in each one of us."

"He was curious about your life and remembered everything you ever said."

"He sent our minds racing, set a great bonfire of curiosity and glee that something so compelling was out there waiting for us, if only we would take the challenge."

"Many years after I graduated from Beloit, I asked John to speak at a special dinner of our company's executives and he agreed. He stood up after dessert and said something along the lines of, 'Each of us is going to die one day, and how we choose to live our life with the knowledge of how precious and finite life really is will determine whether we can say that we lived a good life. It is not just about what you accomplish in the office, what you have achieved materially, but the force of who you are as a person, the love you have for and from your family and friends, your good deeds.' He then taught our sales people how Plato might handle a difficult situation, and our creative people how Aristotle might have spent a lifetime editing just one paragraph (and still not have got it right)."

John Wyatt is an example of the best in liberal arts college teaching. There are many, many others. While a student at Lake Forest College, for example, Guggenheim Foundation director Richard Armstrong was "deeply influenced" by art history professor Franz Schulze (1952– 1991), whose classes, he said, were "electrifying." For Tara Zahra, an assistant professor at the University of Chicago, Swarthmore College history professor Pieter Judson is "the model of the scholar, teacher, and human being I strive to be . . . [and] still the first person who reads my academic work." A former student who studied with Pomona College professor of English Martha Andresen (1972–2006) said Andresen helped "blur the line between academia and life, and for that I will always be grateful."

For a college to fail to take every possible action to ensure teaching excellence is, bluntly stated, to give up on liberal arts education. How can a college make sure that its faculty will include men and women like John Wyatt, Franz Schulze, Pieter Judson, and Martha Andresen?

Hiring

Sometimes, it seems, there is a sense among liberal arts college faculties that new assistant professors' strengths and weaknesses will become apparent soon enough after they begin teaching, so it doesn't matter if the hiring process is a little casual. It is true that gauging the teaching potential of new hires—fresh out of graduate school and never having held a teaching position—is difficult. There is not a lot of information to go on.

One would think that, in selecting a new assistant professor, looking at whether candidates are liberally educated would be the first-cut test. Typical hiring procedures, however, such as putting ads in trade publications and on Web sites asking candidates to furnish information about their qualifications to teach a single specialty, twenty-minute interviews at professional meetings where specialists gather, or observing a candidate teach a fifty-minute class to students chosen because they are majoring in the candidate's area of specialization, are not well calculated to expose the extent of a candidate's liberal education. Certainly nothing that happened to a candidate in graduate school provides assurance that he or she is liberally educated.

The passive approach to recruiting—see who applies and then pick the best of the bunch—which characterizes much hiring by liberal arts colleges, does little to ensure that the best possible candidates are identified. The way to find excellent teachers (and administrators) is to look for them, not to wait for them to find you by dropping in at association-meeting receptions or responding to your advertisement. Networking is the key, talking to friends and friends of friends. Businesses understand this and colleges should, too. Similarly, once potential candidates are identified, each must be checked out, not simply by calling the references indicated on a résumé but, again, by networking. Who do you know who knows the candidate, or who knows someone who knows the candidate?[1]

Reading a résumé is not enough. First, it may not be true. Second, it can play into the increasingly worrisome practice of credentializing. Despite the current tight job market, the number of newly minted Ph.D.s continues to increase. Between 1985–1986 and 2007–2008, the number of doctorates conferred in disciplines relevant to the liberal arts increased 58 percent.[2] This puts colleges in the enviable position of having a large pool of candidates to choose from. That advantage can be lost, however, if a first cut is made on the basis of the ranking of the university from which a candidate graduated, or the nonteaching awards or recognitions a candidate has received.

There is no automatic assurance that a top-ten research-university graduate is more liberally educated or more likely to become an excellent teacher than one from a less prestigious institution, or that winning a thesis prize is a reliable indicator of potential teaching skill. The efforts and aptitudes required to gain admission to and earn a Ph.D. from a highly rated university are not closely correlated, if at all, with good teaching. (Indeed, a respectable argument can be made that they are counterindications.) A sense of a candidate's teaching potential as gauged by experienced professors who are themselves good teachers, after a conversation with the candidate, is more reliable.

Conversation is the best way—if not the only way—to judge whether a candidate is liberally educated. This, of course, takes time, more time than some faculty members have been willing to give. Next to their own teaching, however, time spent assessing the liberal education and teaching potential of candidates is the single most important expenditure of faculty members' time, far more important than almost every committee.

The common practice of requiring teaching-position finalists to teach a class is a good one, but giving decisive weight to the response of the students is not. Students can judge whether they enjoyed a class or liked a candidate. But , while being likable and making a class pleasant are good things, neither equates with the capacity to liberally educate.

It is, incidentally, far from clear that holding a Ph.D. facilitates teaching excellence, yet possession of one is table stakes for faculty hires at most liberal arts colleges. One hundred years ago, William James warned:

> America is . . . as a nation rapidly drifting towards a state of things in which no man of science or letters will be accounted respectable unless some kind of badge or diploma is stamped upon him and in which bare personality will be a mark of outcast estate. . . . [I]s not our growing tendency to appoint no instructors who are not also doctors an instance of pure sham? Will any one pretend for a moment that a doctor's degree is a guarantee that its possessor will be successful as a teacher? . . . The truth is that the Doctor-Monopoly in teaching, which is becoming so rooted in American custom, can show no serious grounds whatsoever for itself in reason. As it actually prevails and grows in vogue among us, it is due to childish motives exclusively. In reality it is but a sham, a bauble, a dodge, whereby to decorate the catalogues of schools and colleges.[3]

When a college has an opportunity to hire an exceptional teacher who lacks the Ph.D. credential—perhaps a former judge, a newspaper editor, or an artist—the opportunity should be seized.

Hiring to fill a specific vacancy, the most common practice, risks missing an excellent teacher. Obviously a chemist cannot be hired to replace a retiring historian, but if a French Revolution expert is the strongest candidate to replace a retiring professor of modern European history, changing course offerings should at least be seriously considered. Unlike vocational instruction, liberal arts education is not subject-matter specific.

Flexibility is especially important in hiring minority faculty. For example, the likelihood is remote that a minority group member, highly qualified and desiring to teach organic chemistry at your liberal arts college, will happen to be available the very year old Charlie decides to retire from the chemistry department. But such a candidate may be available at another time and, even though the timing does not fit perfectly into the staffing requirements of the chemistry department, grabbing that candidate before he or she goes somewhere else can make good sense.

Further, while there may be no minority organic chemist available, there may be an outstanding astronomer or sociologist who could advance the liberal arts excellence of the college as well as add diversity to its faculty. When Branch Rickey set out to hire Major League Baseball's first black player, he did not search for a third baseman but rather for the best player he could find, and then played him where he fit in— at third base. Incidentally, in hiring Jackie Robinson, Rickey gave full consideration to Robinson's personal, as well as athletic, qualifications. The parallel to giving full consideration to liberal "educatedness," as well as academic qualifications, in hiring teachers is apt.

Hiring minority teachers has been strikingly slow. At many liberal arts colleges, the number of minority students has increased dramatically but minority representation on the faculty remains token. Further, the few minority professors are sometimes relegated to "special" or "appropriate" teaching slots, such as black studies or Spanish. College teachers have shown themselves to be more adept at discussing minority underrepresentation than at doing something about it.

If diversity in the student body is desirable for a liberal education, as almost all colleges proclaim, so too is faculty diversity. A college with 20 percent minority students and an all-white faculty makes no sense and is surely pedagogically unsound. What lessons do students—majority as well as minority—draw from such a mix? It should go without saying that colleges need to practice what they preach. Some of them still do not.

Training

Most of us have a well-developed—and probably well-founded—suspicion of normal schools, teachers colleges, and education departments that train primary- and secondary-school teachers. We observe that the quality of teachers they train is often not good. Their training seems to include inordinate amounts of purposeless busywork, and state certification requirements create a "train to the test" environment. The idea of subjecting new assistant professors to similar training seems appalling. One would think their time would be better spent studying the liberal arts subjects they will teach rather than teaching methods.

Nonetheless, while some individuals have a greater aptitude and motivation to teach undergraduates than others, teaching is still a learned skill. There are useful teaching techniques to be mastered, and the fact that they are badly taught in primary- and secondary-teacher preparation venues is a reason to do it well at the undergraduate level, not a reason not to do it at all.

The sink-or-swim method of training assistant professors is surely not the best way to produce excellent teachers (or, for that matter, swimmers). Pairing each new assistant professor with a skilled mentor from the faculty is a common, good practice. Regular lectures, visiting experts, discussion groups, and classroom visits should also be part of the teaching training program. Encouraging faculty to take pride in the program, and making it a part of the culture of the college, will ease any resistance, especially if financial rewards are given to senior faculty members who participate as teaching instructors and mentors.

Top-down directives from the administration to expand teacher training may well encounter faculty resistance. The faculty as a whole needs to buy into the importance of the undertaking. This is more likely to occur if faculty members develop enthusiasm for improving their own teaching skills. Here again, the success of the program requires that contributions by the participating senior professors be fully recognized and financially rewarded.

A striking but little commented on similarity between nonprofit liberal arts colleges and for-profit universities is the centrality of teaching to the educational mission. Both sell only one service—instruction—and therefore take seriously the need to maintain the quality of the instruction they provide. In a 2006 paper on the for-profit University of Phoenix, David Breneman reported on the extensive teacher training it requires for its instructors:

> The selection of practitioner faculty is carefully done, with a review of credentials and an extensive orientation and training program. Preservice faculty are assigned an experienced faculty mentor and must take 10 workshops covering the following topics: Adult Learning Theory; Facilitation Techniques; Learning Team Management; Grading, Evaluation, and Feedback; Classroom Assessment; Human Equity; Copyrights and Copy "Wrongs"; Administration, Organization, and Orientation; Internet Training; and Electronic Library. Only about 30 to 40 percent of all eligible applicants are approved to teach at UOP.[4]

The University of Phoenix, unimpeded by tenure, also does not hesitate to terminate nonperforming instructors who receive consistently low evaluations.[5]

Assessment

If students who major in vocational disciplines get good jobs in the fields in which they major, it may reasonably be concluded that their professors did a good job preparing them. Were the objective of a liberal arts college to get its students into graduate or professional schools, their gaining admission to top schools would be a fair measure of their professors' excellence. Were the college's objective the transmission of information, students' test results could reveal their professors' skill. The difficulty, of course, is that liberal arts colleges' "products are the lives of our students."[6] The colleges' objectives are inculcating in students an enthusiasm for learning and a desire to understand. Success in these realms is observable, but not readily quantifiable.

Too often, what is known about a young professor's teaching skills is largely anecdotal, based on passing comments by students or passing impressions of the professor garnered by other faculty members. Some kind of systematic monitoring and evaluating of each new teacher's progress is necessary. Teaching reviews by senior faculty members who are good teachers, conducted semi-annually from the time new professors are hired until they come up for tenure and focused on helping them improve their skills as well as assessing their progress, will doubtless seem excessive to some. The objective of teaching excellence is so important to the future of liberal arts colleges, however, that such a review system makes sense. Ultimately, however, the observations of experienced faculty members are the key to reliable assessments of teaching quality.

It is a mistake, in my view, to assess professors' publications as a separate element of their contributions to a liberal arts college. If research and scholarship enhance the professors' teaching, that fact will be revealed by assessing their teaching. The assertion here is not that enthusiasm or support for scholarship by professors is misplaced, but rather that teaching excellence, not publication, is paramount at liberal arts colleges.

The more time and effort professors devote to teaching (including, but not limited to, staying current in their disciplines), the less time they have available for research and writing for publication. This reality squares uncomfortably with the objectives of so-called research colleges that require scholarly production before tenure is granted. Research colleges style themselves as mini-universities. At universities, however, it is research and scholarship—not teaching excellence—that generates grants, enhances the universities' reputations, and secures their professors' positions. None of this is to say, however, that joint student-faculty research is not to be encouraged. Numerous studies have shown that it is an especially effective teaching tool.[7]

Deployment

Instructional needs of colleges change over time. Some departments grow in importance, others contract, are merged, or disappear. But changes in faculty deployment are glacially slow and rarely made on the basis of careful, forward-looking needs assessment. It is too much to expect a faculty member to say, "My department needs one less professor and yours needs one more." Saying the opposite can be uncomfortable, too, putting the speaker in a potentially adversarial posture with his or her colleagues. The result is that, except when programs or departments are discontinued or in times of financial exigency when changes in faculty deployment can be undertaken, reallocation rarely occurs, no matter how much it is needed.[8] Times of financial crisis are the worst times to make careful deployment decisions.

Redeployment is most comfortably achieved within departments and at times when a faculty member is retiring. If each year only a handful of students have had an interest in studying German, when the college's German professor retires, replacing him or her with a Chinese- or Arabic-language professor can probably be accomplished relatively smoothly and with little or no interdepartmental friction. If student interest in geography has flagged, the departure of the geography department's only member can open the bidding among other departments for an additional position.

While taking advantage of retirements and shifts in student demand can relieve the stress of redeployment, it puts the college in the position of reacting, rather than planning for future instructional needs. Further, student demand is not a guide to what courses and majors will contribute most to their liberal education. Hard, forward-looking deployment decisions need to be made on an ongoing basis about which departments should expand or contract, or be combined, split, added, or eliminated. A faculty committee can provide essential guidance, but a decision made on the basis of the committee's vote can be influenced, if not controlled, by complex interpersonal and interdepartmental factors rather than what is in the best interest of the college as a whole. Ultimately, the one who makes the decision needs to stand apart from the faculty—presumably the academic dean, provost, or president—and be willing and able to take the heat that redeployment decisions can generate.

Compensation

The first thing most firms and agencies try to save money is holding down workers' salary increases. They are frequently frustrated, however, by pressure from unions. At most liberal arts colleges such pressure is less strong and more easily resisted. As a result, faculty salary increases are often already reduced because of other perceived needs, lag behind those at other employment venues, and languish below cost-of-living increases. Since far and away the most valuable resource of a college is its faculty, shorting faculty salaries is foolish.

Parenthetically, a reluctance to grant salary increases for college administrators is far less apparent. Perhaps, in making budget decisions, the corporate executives on college boards identify faculty with their workers and administrators with themselves. An article in the *Chronicle of Higher Education* in November 2009 opined that the "increase in salaries [of private college presidents] can partially be attributed to the trustees who set the president's compensation and come to the table with corporate backgrounds." The article quotes Raymond D. Cotton, a Washington lawyer who specializes in presidential contracts, as saying trustees "have brought their business ideas with them, including things like bonuses and pay-for-performance."[9]

Some observers have suggested that when the salary of an institution's president exceeds three times that of senior faculty members, a disruptive disequilibrium is created. If they are correct, the disruption is already ubiquitous. A survey of the 2007–2008 compensation of university and college presidents done by the *Chronicle of Higher Education* included 132 liberal arts colleges, all but 3 of which (129 colleges) are analyzed in this book.[10] The annual American Association of University Professors faculty salary survey for 2007–2008 (also reported by the *Chronicle*) provided the average salaries of full professors at 110 of the 129 colleges.[11] At only 8 of those 110 colleges did the president receive compensation in an amount less than three times the average salary of the college's full professors (and 4 of those 8 presidents were clergymen who received no monetary compensation at all from the church-related colleges they led). The compensation of the remaining 102 presidents (93 percent) was more than three times greater than the average salary of their full professors. In fact, 51 of them received more than four times as much as their full professors, and 9 of them received more than five times as much as full professors (including the president of DePauw University (fourteen times as much as full professors);

Franklin and Marshall College (ten times); Gettysburg College (nine times); and Hartwick College, St. Lawrence University, and Westminster College (Pa.) (all eight times). The compensation of 27 of the 110 presidents exceeded $500,000 per year, including 2 presidents who received more than $1 million. The enrollment at the liberal arts colleges the 110 presidents led ranged from 750 to 4,300 students, with the majority having fewer than 2,000 students.

When a college puts faculty salaries at the bottom of its spending list, it reveals something about how it values teachers' services and, inevitably, how its teachers value themselves. I am aware of no established rule for what faculty salaries ought to be, or of a useful comparison (for example, no less than auto mechanics). It really does not matter, however, because liberal arts college professors' salaries are so low that all that is needed for the moment is to get them up as rapidly as possible.

There are, however, some useful salary guidelines. First, faculty salaries should increase, at the very least, no less rapidly than those of administrators. Second, salaries of senior faculty should increase, at the very least, no less rapidly than starting salaries for assistant professors. Third, teaching excellence should be rewarded by salary increases, not bonuses or prizes, which are sporadic, capricious, and often cynically designed to portray the institution as more generous than it in fact is. Fourth, special effort should be given to encouraging donors to earmark gifts for faculty salaries. Fifth, increases in faculty support—equipment, secretarial service, conferences, and so forth—should be in addition to, not in lieu of, salary increases. If colleges, in their budgeting process, follow the dictate that increasing faculty salaries is a paramount objective, additional guidelines (and support for teaching excellence) will be found.

The National Survey of Student Engagement, an association of more than 700 colleges and universities, was created

> to address . . . [the problem] that not enough colleges seem to *want* to get better at the task of teaching and learning.

The reason for this is that there are few incentives in the system to do so. In many industries, *competition* motivates innovation and improvement. The way the professionals who work in industry are trained and rewarded is a second source. But in higher education, issues of effectiveness play a small role in students' decisions about where to go to college. The faculty are trained to believe that good teaching is simply a matter of staying current with the content of the field. So, the market is highly imperfect, and the faculty don't compensate for these deficiencies.[12]

This problem, serious for all higher education institutions, is potentially disastrous for liberal arts colleges.

CHAPTER 9

Tenure

.✦.

One need not be an opponent of tenure to recognize that, once granted, it provides no further incentive for teaching excellence and can provide a safe haven for nonexcellence. Says prolific commentor Richard A. Posner, "In effect what tenure guarantees is that you won't be replaced—even by a better candidate!"[1] Further, tenure can be—and often is—awarded to merely "good" teachers, which is not a good thing. As my former law partner (and dean of Harvard Law School) Erwin Griswold often observed, "The good is the enemy of the excellent."

Some years ago, I wrote an article for an educational journal about the partnership track for young lawyers in large law firms. The partnership track was then almost identical to the tenure track, but substantial changes were brewing at law firms. The article reported on the changes, noting that it behooved academic institutions to pay attention to them and consider their implications for colleges and universities. When the editor called to say that the journal would not accept the article, I asked why it was being rejected. "Because," the editor told me, "your article does not take a position for or against tenure."

"But my piece is purely factual and reports on law firm partnership— not tenure—tracks," I said.

"We require that a position be taken in all articles dealing with tenure," the editor said.

"If I add an opinion for or against tenure, will you publish the article?" I asked.

"Yes," the editor said, "either one."

"That makes no sense," I said.

"Tenure is a hot-button issue," the editor replied, "and we want to keep it that way."

The editor appears to have succeeded. As Richard Chait has observed, "Tenure has become the academy's version of the abortion issue—a controversy marked by passion, polemics, and hardened convictions."[2]

History

Modern tenure, as embodied in policies of the American Association of University Professors, was a university—not a college—creation. While the AAUP crystallized its tenure policies in its 1940 *Statement of Principles on Academic Freedom and Tenure,* the policy's origin was a 1915 report by a committee made up of fifteen university professors drawn from the physical and social sciences, the humanities, and the law (Harvard Law School professor, and later dean, Roscoe Pound). No liberal arts college professors were included.

At issue, said the 1915 committee, was how to safeguard "a proper measure of academic freedom [for teachers] in American universities," in particular: freedom of inquiry and research, freedom of teaching, and freedom of extramural utterance and action. Tenure was perceived as central to academic freedom because, the committee said: "It is not, in our opinion, desirable that men should be drawn into this [academic teaching] profession by the magnitude of the economic rewards which it offers; but it is for this reason the more needful that men of high gift and character should be drawn into it by the assurance of an honorable and *secure* position."[3]

If greater economic rewards for faculty members had been a realistic possibility, it seems unlikely that the committee would have found them undesirable. One cannot but assume that the committee was making the best of the realities it encountered, and that assurance of a secure position was offered university professors in lieu of "economic rewards."

The committee made three "practical proposals," the third of which was "to render the profession more attractive to men of high ability and strong personality by insuring the dignity, the independence, and the reasonable security of tenure, of the professorial office."[4] The idea that better pay, commensurate with the high ability and training of professors, would also make the profession more attractive was not mentioned.

Even though university professors are officially hired by trustees, the committee stressed that professors "are not in any proper sense the employees" of the trustees. Once appointed, "the scholar has professional functions to perform in which the appointing authorities have neither competency nor moral right to intervene. The responsibility of the university teacher is primarily to the public itself and to the judgment of his own profession," not to his employer.[5] The report continues:

> [It is] inadmissible that the power of determining when departures from the requirements of the scientific spirit and method have occurred, should be vested in bodies not composed of members of the academic profession. Such bodies necessarily lack full competency to judge of those requirements; their intervention can never be exempt from suspicion that it is dictated by other motives than zeal for the integrity of science; and it is, in any case, unsuitable to the dignity of a great profession that the initial responsibility for the maintenance of its professional standards should not be in the hands of its own members.[6]

The committee, it said, was not suggesting "academic freedom implies that individual teachers should be exempt from all restraints." Such restraints as are necessary, however, "should in the main . . . be self-imposed, or enforced by the *public opinion of the profession*." Discipline or dismissal actions, the committee flatly asserted, "cannot be safely taken by bodies not composed of members of the academic profession."[7]

Perhaps had the committee been drafting its report today, after all we have gone through with the defalcations of financial institutions, the banking industry, and others, it would have been less cavalier in asserting the efficacy of self-regulation. It is striking that the committee saw so clearly the flaws in permitting the trustees and administration to discipline faculty, but completely ignored obvious concerns implicit in permitting any group to discipline itself. Will faculty members involved in disciplining a colleague face retribution from him, or from his friends and supporters? Will they risk creating a precedent for discipline that could adversely affect their self-interest? Questions such as these haunt any system of self-regulation.

The committee's really quite extraordinary assertions were, it said, analogous to the proper relationship between federal judges and the president, in that the president appoints judges but cannot fire or discipline them.[8] (Perhaps the reason the committee included Dean Pound in its membership was to make this analogy.)

The committee's case would have been stronger and more persuasive had it expressly conceded the risks inherent in self-regulation, but argued that those risks were outweighed by the lack of competence of any group except an academic committee to make correct decisions about the abilities of a scholar or teacher. Indeed, the committee seemed to hold in low esteem not only university trustees and administrators but all men other than university professors:

> The tendency of modern democracy is for men to think alike, to feel alike, and to speak alike. Any departure from the conventional standards is apt to be regarded with suspicion. Public opinion is at once the chief safeguard of a democracy, and the chief menace to the real liberty of the individual. It almost seems as if the danger of despotism cannot be wholly averted under any form of government. In a political autocracy there is no effective public opinion, and all are subject to the tyranny of the ruler; in a democracy there is political freedom, but there is likely to be a tyranny of public opinion.[9]

Trustees, however, are not in competition with faculty. Trustees' actions are generally taken in what they perceive to be the best interests of the institution. The actions may be wrong, misguided, or impose a burden on faculty members, but they are rarely self-interested attempts to enhance personal wealth, prestige, or power. Faculty management of tenure, in contrast, is potentially highly self-interested, enabling professors, for example, to block tenure for an unpopular (or too popular) department member, to enhance their own departmental standing, or strengthen the prestige of their personal research interests. Such manifestations of ordinary human weakness have been consistently ignored by AAUP principles and policies.

Since rewards at universities for research and publication exceed those for teaching excellence, and given the composition of the 1915 committee, it is not surprising that the "complete and unlimited freedom to pursue inquiry and publish its results" was perceived as being of paramount importance. Such freedom, the committee said, "is the breath in the nostrils of all scientific activity."[10]

With respect to freedom of utterance in the classroom, the committee opined, "No man can be a successful teacher unless he enjoys the respect of his students, and their confidence in his intellectual integrity." After all, even "the average student is a discerning observer, who soon takes the measure of his instructor[!]."[11] The committee, however, identified one required limitation on unfettered freedom of utterance in the classroom, "namely, the instruction of immature students. In many of our American colleges, and especially in the first two years of the course, the student's character is not yet fully formed, his mind is still relatively immature." For this reason, the committee said, teachers should provide an "intellectual awakening" for young students, but it should "be brought about with patience, considerateness and pedagogical wisdom."[12] (One cannot help wondering if the implication of this last assertion is that, in teaching graduate students, impatience, inconsiderateness, and pedagogical incompetence are tolerable.)

The committee's assumption that job security facilitates higher quality scholarship and teaching is at odds with a fundamental premise of free enterprise, that rewards follow risk taking. AAUP has argued that "free enterprise is as essential to intellectual as to economic progress."[13] But tenure, by eliminating risk taking, is antithetical to free enterprise. Tenure-track teachers can reasonably be expected to work hard to maximize the likelihood of receiving tenure. After tenure is achieved, however, it is no longer a goad but rather a shield against the risk of adverse consequences from not doing one's best.

Over the decades, AAUP has polished the case for tenure, avoiding at least some of the sweeping, unsupported assertions that characterized the 1915 *Declaration of Principles*, becoming much more "politically correct" in its articulations, and refining the initial recommendation of tenure after no more than ten years to a mandatory requirement that, if a tenure track is in place, tenure be granted or denied in no more than seven years and, if denied, that the unsuccessful candidate be terminated.[14] But after nearly a century, the underlying premise that tenure is a precondition for academic freedom remains unchanged.

Analysis

In the popular press, tenure is controversial, seen by many as an undeserved life-long sinecure, a system that rewards, rather than protects against, laziness and incompetence. The claimed essentialness of tenure to preserving academic freedom, relied on by tenure supporters, is less than fully persuasive. Instances where it can reasonably be said that, but for tenure, a faculty member would have been fired are rare. According to a 1994 study published by the *Chronicle of Higher Education,* only "about 50 tenured professors nationwide are dismissed each year for cause," and most of those cases involved misconduct, not incompetence.[15] A study reported in the *Wall Street Journal* in 2005 estimated that 50 to 75 professors out of 280,000 lose their tenure each year.[16]

John Kenneth Galbraith's fictional Harvard professor of advanced psychometrics, Angus Maxwell McCrimmon, amusingly explained tenure to a graduate student this way:

Tenure was originally invented to protect radical professors, those who challenged the accepted order. But we don't have such people anymore at the universities, and the reason *is* tenure. When the time comes to grant it nowadays, the radicals get screened out. That's its principal function. It's a very good system, really—keeps academic life at a decent level of tranquility. . . . [Waiting until one has tenure to show one's liberal tendencies is] the only sensible course. But by then conformity will be a habit. You'll no longer be a threat to the peace and comfort of our ivied walls. The system really works. . . .

[Tenure is] the first step to senility. It usually comes very soon thereafter.[17]

Academic freedom can be guaranteed without tenure, at least at private institutions, with such contractual stipulations as, "No professor will be terminated, demoted, or disciplined for expressing a controversial or unpopular view."[18] Hampshire College, for example, promises its faculty academic freedom without a tenure track. And while its policies clearly assume tenure is the best protection of academic freedom, the AAUP does not require a tenure system.[19]

At universities, tenure-track hires are increasingly being replaced by untenured adjunct faculty. Between 1988 and 2004, the percentage of U.S. college and university teachers who were tenured dropped from 40 to 28 percent, and the percentage who were not on a tenure track rose from less than 13 to 51 percent.[20] Whether or not it is true at universities that tenure will soon become a thing of the past, this seems unlikely to happen at liberal arts colleges, at least so long as salaries remain low. Without being offered substantially higher salaries, potential new hires at liberal arts colleges are likely to demand tenure. If the glut of unemployed recent Ph.D. holders continues to grow, however, such demands may become difficult to make.

Tenure imposes substantial burdens on an institution by obliging it to make long-term employment decisions on the basis of short-term information, and by imposing a substantial cost on the institution for each wrong long-term employment decision it makes. The latter burden is a one-way street. If, by awarding tenure, the institution makes the right decision, the recipient may receive other, more attractive offers and leave. If the institution makes the wrong decision when it awards tenure, the recipient will remain at the institution until retirement. With the elimination of mandatory retirement, this can be a very long time.

The smaller the institution, the greater the institutional burden of an ill-advised tenure award. In a two- or three-person department, not uncommon at liberal arts colleges, the burden can be disastrous. Similarly, the poorer the institution, the less likely it is to have the financial resources to compensate for a wrong tenure decision by hiring an additional teacher. For many liberal arts colleges, hiring an additional faculty member in one department means that a needed addition to a different department will not be possible. The bottom line is, the economic risk of tenure falls most heavily on small colleges.

Tenure is ruthless. A faculty member denied tenure at one college is unlikely to get it somewhere else. The conservative economist Armen Alchian observed that "firing a person is an unpleasant task, but in a profit-seeking business it is even more unpleasant not to fire them." Denying tenure is analogously unpleasant.[21] But in nonprofit liberal arts colleges, *not* denying tenure (that is, not firing a poorly performing teacher) is less unpleasant. Whatever the merits or demerits of the tenure system, so long as liberal arts colleges remain nonprofit and substantially subsidized by nontuition income, this situation is not likely to be eliminated. This does not mean, however, that the manner in which the tenure decision is made cannot be significantly improved.

Improving the Tenure Process

At present, there are typically three formal points of evaluation in the progress toward tenure: at the second, fourth, and sixth years. The information on which the second-year evaluation is made is largely drawn from the first year and discounted as "too soon to tell." The fourth-year review is more substantial, but too often the hard message, "You are in trouble and unless you improve you will not get tenure," is not delivered with clarity. The decision to deny tenure is put off to the sixth-year review—the eleventh hour, when it is too late to change anything.

Tenure denial is a wrenching experience not only for the teacher denied but also for the persons making the denial decision. The human response is to try to avoid making it. Doubts are resolved in favor of granting tenure. Weaknesses are underweighted and strengths are overweighted to reach the "grant" decision. Nonteaching contributions by the candidate are used to justify granting tenure to a candidate whose teaching is less than first-class.

There is some truth in the perception common among liberal arts college faculty members that tenure will be granted to any candidate who succeeds in navigating six years without a serious blemish on his or her record. Indeed, some see tenure as an entitlement. For them, tenure is a reward for not failing, not for succeeding. The "acceptable" or "pretty good," not the excellent, are rewarded, and an acceptable or pretty good, but not excellent, teacher takes possession of one of the college's limited number of teaching positions for the next twenty-five to thirty-five years.

Two steps should be taken to substantially ameliorate this problem. First, tenure reviews should be annual (if not more frequent), not biannual. Words of support, encouragement, appreciation, and praise can be given at any or all of the reviews. Harder messages must also be given:

Year 1: "You need to work on A, B, and C."

Year 2: "We are still concerned about B and C."

Year 3: "Your failure to improve B and C is becoming a serious concern."

Year 4: "You have not made any progress on C. If you don't do better, tenure is unlikely."

Year 5: "If C does not improve in the next six months, you will not receive tenure. In addition [if appropriate], we do not believe you will be able to solve your C problem on a timely basis and strongly recommend you resign before the tenure decision is made."

Second, each tenure review should be blunt and candid. No one likes delivering hard messages, but failing to do so ill serves both the tenure candidate and the college. The hard message in Year 5 ("We don't think you will receive tenure and urge you to resign before the tenure decision must be made") is especially important in this regard, and should at least be foretold in the Year 4 review.

Because tenured faculty at liberal arts colleges move to other institutions relatively infrequently, each tenure decision is central to the future teaching excellence of a college. While tenure messages should always be delivered humanely, they must be made forthrightly.

CHAPTER 10

Curriculums

∗

Teaching excellence is the focus of an earlier chapter of this book because it is centrally important to the success of a liberal arts college education and college faculties tend to give it insufficient attention. I include this separate chapter on curriculums because, in contrast, course distribution and major requirements tend to attract obsessive and excessive faculty attention, even though they are not centrally important to a liberal education.

Most liberal arts college curriculums have distribution and major requirements, but not all. The Great Books curriculum at St. John's College, for example, is a four-year, all-required course of study.[1] Most colleges have distribution requirements in three areas (humanities, social sciences, and physical sciences), but some require taking courses in four, five, six, or even more areas. Middlebury College students must take courses in seven of eight categories and four cultures-and-civilization areas.[2] Some colleges require courses (or proficiency demonstrations) in a foreign language or physical education, or both.

College curriculums often require specified core courses, or course types, such as quantitative reasoning or intensive writing. Williams College's Exploring Diversity Initiative requires students to take at least one designated exploring-diversity course, and Carleton College requires one course from its Recognition and Affirmation of Difference set (courses concerned with gender, sexual orientation, class, race, culture, religion, or ethnicity).[3] Taking a Dynamics of Difference and Power course at Pomona College is not a requirement, but it is an "aspiration."[4]

The fact is, however, the curriculum game plan is far less important to educational success than the skill and commitment of the individual teachers who implement it. Lewis Lapham says, "Awaken the student to the light in his or her own mind, and the rest of it doesn't matter— neither the curriculum nor the number of seats in the football stadium, neither the names of the American presidents nor the list of English kings."[5] Former Williams College president Francis Oakley took note of "the intensely serious and frequently quite wearing debates" about curriculum "into which the faculties of . . . [selective] colleges fling themselves, generation after generation, with seemingly undiminished ardor" and gently suggested:

> It may be . . . [that] we would do well to focus our energies less on persistently inconclusive wrangling about the overall *content* of our curriculum than on the way in which we characteristically frame our courses and the manner in which we teach them. . . . Despite my own long-standing preoccupation with the overall content of the curriculum, then, and despite the obsessive amount of public attention focused on it of late, I conclude that as we at the liberal arts colleges assess the undergraduate course of study today we would do well to direct our attention elsewhere.[6]

When graduates reflect on their college years, it is professors they remember, especially those who became their mentors and left lasting impressions on their lives. An optimum liberal arts curriculum would simply require students to take courses with the college's finest teachers, regardless of discipline or course content. Making the best possible use of the particular talents of faculty members is a sound curricular goal.

Historically, as Michael Bastedo has succinctly noted, curriculum wars have been fought on three battlegrounds: prescription versus election, stability versus growth, and conservation versus innovation.[7] From the Calvinist tradition of the eighteenth century to the famous Yale Report of 1828, Harvard's "Red Book," the Great Books curriculum, Robert Hutchins, Allan Bloom, and Martha Nussbaum, the troops and armaments deployed have shifted, but the battlefield has remained unchanged. The courses chosen for inclusion in college curriculums ebb and flow with changes in technology, social attitudes, and issues, but there is nothing notably new under the curricular sun. Doubtless this explains why curriculum claims are often so well crafted, polished, sophisticated. They have been made before.

Faculty curriculum debates usually focus on the details of electives and distribution requirements, not on how courses are taught (although sometimes the details are surrogates for other issues, such as resource allocation or political philosophy). The debates can be involving, stimulating, thought provoking, often passionate, and frequently confrontational. One cannot help wondering, however, how there can be general agreement that a first-class liberal education can be obtained at colleges with widely disparate course requirements and, at the same time, that minute details of curriculum requirements are worth fighting about.

There can be political as well as personal reasons why curriculum debates are fierce. While faculty members may sincerely believe one cannot be liberally educated without having taken certain courses, the fact is, members of departments with curricular prominence enjoy personal prominence in their academic community. Opinionated champions of a particular curriculum are often advocating the importance of knowing what they know. All curriculum champions bring profoundly subjective judgments to their cause, no matter how artfully they cloak them in claimed fundamental, albeit perhaps ineffable, truths.

Classical, general education, core, and Great Books curriculums have the advantage that, once established, they maintain themselves without great debate, except, perhaps, for an occasional tweaking, such as a book deletion or addition here, a minor subject-matter shift there.[8] (Long-time St. John's College faculty members—tutors—do remember that Aeschylus's *Prometheus Bound* was replaced by Aristophanes' *The Birds,* and that Justinian was dropped from the college's Great Books curriculum, although not precisely when these fine tunings transpired.[9]) A "no requirements" regimen minimizes debate but does not entirely avoid it. The curriculum decision simply shifts to what courses will be offered.

A college faculty can avoid debating its curriculum but not deciding on it. Like it or not, it is an inescapable fact that when students' studies are divided into four courses per semester, and the work schedule of faculty members is arranged according to teaching two or three courses per semester, you are talking curriculum. One way or another, there is going to be a curriculum at every college, even if it is no more than a statement of no requirements coupled with a list of courses offered. Although curriculum debates can be mind-numbingly grinding and counterproductive, curriculum design cannot be totally ignored. Faculty members need to be on the same page, to share a common strategy so that their own efforts support and reinforce the efforts of the others. Collegial faculty involvement in curriculum design may in fact enhance members' sense of community and shared purpose.

A further, inescapable fact is that someone has to decide what courses students take, and the decision will be made by either faculty members or students. Life experience teaches that students, like the rest of us, instinctively turn to what is known and familiar. In a speech to the Beloit College community, Clint McCown, a talented fiction writer and teacher, said that the best, most interesting, and most memorable college course he took when he was an undergraduate was astronomy, a course that, but for his college's science requirements, he would never have taken.

Brown University and others that follow a no-requirements strategy are in effect turning the keys to the institution over to the inmates.

Most Americans assume students go to college to learn "something," a possibly unspecified but nonetheless specific something. That is how it was in grade school and high school, and how it will be in graduate or professional school. How could college be different? If a collegian is majoring in sociology, it stands to reason he or she is in college to learn sociology. Even for those who understand that liberal arts colleges seek to provide a broad education, this is perceived to mean students are learning a variety of "somethings."

Liberal arts colleges, however, are purveyors of an attitude toward learning and knowing, not of specified knowledge. This is why medical schools happily admit history majors, law schools accept English majors, and corporations hire political science majors. The quality of liberal arts college graduates admired by professional schools and in the commercial world is not what, but how, they have learned.

To be an effective vehicle for liberal education, an undergraduate course of study cannot be free from doubt, not impossible to expand or revise, and not exclusively belief-based. Even with these limitations, the aspects of nature, the universe, and human experience on which a liberal arts curriculum can be constructed are virtually limitless. Other than special considerations affecting their majors, so long as students are exposed to a range of diverse, well-taught courses, the mix is not crucial. Students can gain a passion for learning from almost any set of courses if they are well taught, even from a hodgepodge of specialized courses. (Even a student who pursues a purely classical curriculum can be expected to acquire sufficient intellectual capability and interest to read the newspapers, look at a blog or two, and find out what is going on.)

Within each well-taught class, it does not matter whether the instructor's slant is traditional or modernist, conservative or liberal, politically correct or incorrect, so long as it is fully revealed to the students. Just as students cannot be exposed to every aspect of knowledge in four years, they cannot experience every intellectual and ideological take on knowledge. They can (and should), however, receive the clear understanding that what they are getting is not all there is.

Within departments, the logic of the series of courses required of majors is a continuing source of debate. Given that majors are being minted as infant experts in the area in which their department members teach, this is probably inevitable, especially when the faculty members are trying in good conscience to shape their budding scholars to meet graduate school requirements. But the more major requirements they impose, the narrower the resulting education. If all departments reduced their major requirements, liberal education would be facilitated. Graduate and professional schools—not to mention entering the workplace—will give students all the depth they need. Liberal arts colleges should collaborate to resist graduate schools' increasing undergraduate course requirements for admission.

Too many majors mark the way toward career-based education, especially in the social and physical sciences. Some universities, for example, offer literally dozens of undergraduate economics majors, each directed to a specific career path and each leading away from breadth.

Liberal arts colleges are to some extent insulated from this practice by the relatively small size of their faculties, but they are not immune.

On the other side of the coin, a much-used cost-containment strategy with curricular implications is combining departments, for example, anthropology and sociology, art and art history, philosophy and religion. Reducing, or failing to increase, the number of teachers in the merged departments is a common by-product (or cause) of such combinations. While there is nothing inherently wrong with multidiscipline departments, and while they may partake of the positive liberal arts qualities of interdisciplinary learning, combining departments can have unintended adverse consequences on the breadth and quality of instruction and should only be carried out after careful analysis.

Exposure to fundamental questions to which the human mind has been directed lays the keel for the ship that will carry students on their liberal-education life voyage. Entry- and intermediate-level courses are key to this exposure. Cross- and interdisciplinary courses are challenging to prepare, and in a departmentalized environment, rewards and recognition for teaching them are sometimes slow in coming. Interdisciplinary courses are, however, inherently pro-liberal education.

An intriguing cross-curriculum experiment is suggested by a mathematics course Beloit College professor David Ellis has offered for some years. It is based on six questions:

What does this statement mean?
Why is it true?
Does it relate to any other statements I know?
What consequences does it have?
Is a more general statement true?
What is really going on?[10]

Expanding Ellis's mathematics course to a collegewide Six Questions Day, a day on which a few minutes were devoted in every class, no matter what the discipline or subject matter, to considering the applicability of the six questions, would illustrate for students the interrelatedness and commonality of learning and knowledge, without putting an undue burden on faculty. (And it might put some meat on the bones of the abstruse concept of "critical thinking.")

Parenthetically, there is, in my view, one curriculum content imperative: history. None of us can live safely in the world without the ability to identify the risks and dangers a course of conduct poses. To take only one example, before one assumes that an invading army from the West will be greeted in Iraq or Afghanistan as liberators, the safety of the world demands that leaders have some understanding of the thousand-year history of such invasions. Global security is put at risk by leaders ignorant of, or who chose to ignore, history.

These are practical realities, not theoretical ones. At stake is not whether mastering the Western tradition and canon should take precedence over training world citizens, or whether we risk slavishly following Santayana's bromide. Gaining a clear sense of how what has gone before affects the present and is likely to affect the future should be a part of every collegian's academic experience. Yet, as historian David McCullough has said, "We, in our time, are raising a new generation of Americans who, to an alarming degree, are historically illiterate."[11]

It is obviously not possible for students to do more than scratch the surface of what humankind has experienced, no matter how many of their college courses are devoted to history. It is, however, possible and imperative for citizens, especially leaders (which many liberal arts college students will become), to be aware of the impact of the past on the present, and to be able to ask the right questions in assessing the potential consequences of conduct.

Finally, the fact that curriculums have marketing significance as tools for attracting students and enthusing donors is a good reason to keep college presidents and other administrators out of the curriculum design process. A good rule for the faculty members to follow might be: Listen respectfully to outsiders' views on curriculum, but keep a weather eye out for the reasons they are being espoused. For that matter, this might also be a good rule for them to follow *within* their faculty councils.

CHAPTER 11

At the Brink

✦

Today, a few public voices are still raised in support of liberal arts education. For example, while quipping that when "the going gets tough, the tough take accounting" and observing that students feel they "have to study something that will lead directly to a job," *New York Times* columnist David Brooks nonetheless "stand[s] up for the history, English and art classes, even in the face of today's economic realities, . . . the rich veins of emotional knowledge that are the subjects of the humanities."[1] Wesleyan University president Michael Roth optimistically adds that if we "educate individuals broadly so that they are capable of moving from one problem to another with confidence, capable of moving from one opportunity to another with courage . . . [and] understand the value of freedom and the virtue of compassion, . . . we will have plenty of defenders of the liberal arts."[2]

The handful of voices supporting the liberal arts are, however, being drowned out by the economic forces driving colleges to vocationalism, and by the rising chorus of advocates for the abandonment of liberal arts education.

As readers have doubtless deduced by now, I am firmly convinced that liberal arts education and the manner in which liberal arts colleges deliver it continue to be of great value not only to the recipients but also to society as a whole. The evidence that both are slipping away is overwhelming. Sadly, David Breneman's optimism that liberal arts colleges would be able to resist the pressure to turn more and more to vocational majors and courses has proved to be misplaced.[3]

Between the academic years 1986–1987 and 2007–2008, the percentage of graduates at the 225 liberal arts colleges examined in this book who majored in vocational disciplines increased from 10.6 percent to 27.8 percent. When the 51 prestigious Tier I colleges are excluded, vocational majors at the remaining 174 colleges increased from 15.2 to 31.3 percent. There is no evidence that the movement away from liberal arts education to vocational instruction is temporary, or that it is cyclical and, over time, will reverse itself. To the contrary, it appears to be an accelerating trend. The demand for vocational instruction is skyrocketing.

What young persons want (or are willing) to spend time learning has long been in a state of change, probably since the dawn of humankind. What we now think of as liberal arts education—broad, general, nonvocational, informed by the past—is a point on a continuum of learning that began with fire building, hunting, and crop cultivation. No thinking person would quarrel with the view expressed by Elia Kazan's father, that a college education should be "use-eh-full," but at this point on the continuum, what *is* useful to learn, know, and understand? Just as the trivium and quadrivium, the classical curriculum, and the gentleman's education no longer frame what is taught, the time for liberal arts education now appears to be passing away, a change driven by shifting societal norms and values.

There may have been a time, long ago, when the line between "liberal" and "vocational" was not bright. For example, more than two thousand years ago Vitruvius, the father of Western architecture, stated that the vocational instruction required for an architect was a "liberal education," including history, philosophy, life sciences, physics, astronomy, music, and art. "The function of the architect," he said, "requires a training in all the departments of learning."[4]

Did the divide between liberal and vocational first become clear in Europe during the Dark Ages or in the time of the guild system? Who is to say? Without doubt, however, in modern times the demarcation was radically sharpened in this country by the arrival of the "new" students in the years following the end of World War II. The Carnegie Foundation's bright-line classifications were reportorial, not causal, but they may have intensified the divide.

Liberal arts colleges have done virtually nothing to reverse the current movement away from the education they offer. For the most part, convinced of their individual specialness, the colleges have persisted in going it alone. Their leaders have been distracted by day-to-day problems—the endless need to find financing, to maintain and burnish their separate reputations, to keep order on their campuses. Endless, too, are the stresses of having donors to court, trustees to guide, alumni to satisfy, community officials to negotiate with, faculty members to placate, and student issues to resolve. Liberal arts colleges' long history of scraping by, overcoming obstacles, and surviving has created the confidence—unhappily, no longer well founded—that one way or another, they will get through this rough patch, too.

Even as their nets pull in huge hauls, commercial fishermen are aware that they risk depleting the fishing grounds on which the entire fleet must depend. Liberal arts college presidents and deans, in contrast, have seemed all but oblivious to the fact that the efforts their colleges make to improve their own circumstances adversely affect the collective interests of all of them. Their colleges, like the fishing fleets, confront the tragedy of the commons.[5]

Leaders of liberal arts institutions complain heatedly about *U.S. News*'s rankings, a brooding omnipresence. There *is* an elephant in the liberal arts parlor, but it is not *U.S. News*. Nor is it endowment size, recession, financial aid, high tuitions, rising costs, or deteriorating plants. It is declining demand for the liberal arts college education, and this is something no college, acting alone, can do anything about. An individual college can try to slow its slide away from liberal arts by cutting costs or increasing financial aid, but such efforts are like putting a finger in the hole in the dike.

Of all the problems a college (or, for that matter, a business) can face, falling demand for what it sells is the most intractable. Because the only thing liberal arts colleges sell is liberal arts education, they are not at a crossroad; they are at the brink. All liberal arts colleges—not just the poorest—are threatened with sliding over the brink. The threats they face, however, are not the same. Impoverished colleges, especially those in Tiers III and IV, are at the brink of being forced to close their doors, sell out to for-profits, or completely abandon liberal arts. Wealthy Tier I colleges face becoming mere credential generators—isolated, marginalized remnants of economic privilege, no longer exemplars of liberal arts education. The gravest threat may be to the middle group, particularly the Tier II colleges, which, despite inadequate endowments, struggle to remain small and true to their liberal arts mission, and to keep up with Tier I. These colleges also suffer the most in the competition with tax-supported, low-tuition, public universities, with which the colleges are obliged to compete for students whose means are modest and who know little or nothing about them.

Declining demand poses another threat to all liberal arts colleges in the key area of their operations: excellent teaching. As student demand for liberal arts education dwindles, so, too, will the colleges' demand for men and women to teach liberal arts courses. It may be that college graduates will persist in pursuing Ph.D.s and preparing themselves for liberal arts teaching careers. It may be that the fact that fewer and fewer teaching positions are available will not influence their career plans. It may be that they, like artists who confront the odds-on probability of an impecunious life in a cheerless garret, will persevere. I doubt it.

What can be done to pull liberal arts colleges back from the brink? Some have proposed remedies, but the proposals are, for the most part, wishy-washy, foolish, or both. For example, after calling for "bold action before the liberal arts college sector becomes too small to be relevant and influential," two professors proposed (1) urging private philanthropic foundations to "step up to the plate and assume the vital leadership role" by convening a series of meetings "to discuss the future of the liberal arts college with the goal of recommending specific actions to update and strengthen these institutions," and (2) the establishment of a "competitive funding program encouraging liberal arts colleges to design innovative and entrepreneurial educational programs."[6]

A University of Chicago professor says what is needed is for society to stand up to capitalism before it succeeds in "retooling . . . American education into an adjunct of business, . . . bringing education to heel by forcing it to meet its [business's] criteria for 'success.'"[7] The president of the American Association of Colleges and Universities has exactly the opposite idea. She thinks the way "to reclaim our commitment to the aims of liberal education" is through "the creation of a new partnership between the academy and leaders in the business and civic communities."[8]

Perhaps the most discouraging proposal comes from the Council of Independent Colleges. After a series of no fewer than twenty-one roundtable discussions, the council came to the insipid conclusion that what is needed is a "stronger case" for "the forms of education offered by," and the "characteristics of mission and purpose" of, "small to medium-sized, teaching-oriented, private colleges and universities," a case that recognizes that "students and legislators may not be influenced by the same stories[!]."[9]

Twenty years ago, Williams College president Francis Oakley did not even suggest a rescue strategy, but instead flatly asserted that less-selective colleges were going to be forced to abandon liberal arts and move to vocationalism, that "small face-to-face residential communities" would become even more an exception to the norm, and that the burden of preserving those desirable communities would fall squarely on the few selective liberal arts colleges that remain.[10]

Two years later David Breneman, in his book *Liberal Arts Colleges,* urged that "all groups and individuals who believe strongly in the value of this type of higher education, and want to see it survive and flourish," must "continue to invest private and public resources in it."[11] Perhaps understandably, the chronic impecunious state of liberal arts colleges has caused leaders like Breneman to conclude that if the colleges had more money, that would solve their problems. Lack of funds, however, is a symptom, not the cause.

Individual liberal arts colleges can convene conferences, solicit foundation support for new programs, add a few more students, increase their student/faculty ratio, add a vocational major or two, experiment with nontraditional students or nontraditional course delivery on or off campus, add a master's degree program, spruce up their dormitories, sharpen their recruiting pitch, or fiddle with their curriculums, but such actions are at best palliatives. No matter how much such measures may relieve immediate economic distress, the declining-demand elephant will still be in the parlor.

One constructive action individual colleges can take that is not a palliative is to work aggressively to improve the teaching excellence of their faculties. Better teaching may not increase demand, but if a sense develops that the teaching is just as good at a $7,500-tuition state university as it is at a $40,000-tuition private liberal arts college, demand will suffer even more.

Collective action on behalf of liberal arts education is the colleges' only hope for ousting the declining-demand elephant, and it is a slim one. It is disheartening that so few college presidents have recognized the fact that the tragedy of the commons is at work, even though Paul Neely spelled it out for them ten years ago in *Distinctively American,* a book the college presidents themselves produced.[12]

It is also disheartening that there is no existing entity ready, willing, and able to take the laboring oar in organizing collective action. The national higher education associations, even those devoted exclusively to private institutions, like the National Association of Independent Colleges and Universities and the Council of Independent Colleges, have other fish to fry. The Annapolis Group—which has no real organizational structure, no executive director, and a rotating leadership system, and which could not manage to stand up to *U.S. News* even a little bit—has proved itself toothless.

There have been some constructive collective undertakings by groups of liberal arts colleges that could—and probably should—be broadened. Collaborative efforts by existing consortia could be expanded, and new consortia created. College groups will continue to make more extensive use of the Internet to share courses and majors, and this makes good sense. Seeking to eliminate the Overlap Group precedent that prohibits joint financial need determinations represents a particularly attractive collective project because it can be undertaken by a relatively small group of colleges. However, while each of these undertakings has the potential to improve the colleges' economic health, all of them are directed at saving costs, not enhancing demand.

A sensible observation that does directly relate to enhancing demand comes from former Denison University and Sarah Lawrence College president Michele T. Myers. Myers has called for "substantial improvement of the elementary and secondary education system, broader education of high school counselors, a keener understanding in society that our world is not just a technical world, but one in which to make a decent living and have a rewarding life, one needs imagination and thinking skills that go beyond purely vocational training."[13]

Myers gets it. High school counselors and primary and secondary schools directly influence how high school students and their parents perceive the value of a liberal education, and hence their demand for it. But she does not go far enough. Who influences the perceptions of counselors and primary and secondary teachers? Neighbors, friends, relatives, clergy, leaders—the entire community. To successfully persuade high school seniors of the value of a liberal arts education, the entire community, that is, society as a whole, must be persuaded.

Seeking to induce society as a whole to take notice of the tiny corner of higher education occupied by liberal arts colleges and, even more, to take favorable notice, would be a daunting project for the colleges to take on. It would take years to accomplish, require strong leadership, and be expensive. Nothing in the record of liberal arts colleges suggests they are capable of accomplishing something of this scope. But were they to get their collective act together and try, one optimistic fact in their favor is that they would likely have a great deal of support from their alumni, an impressive group.

Perhaps ironically, the liberal arts college graduates who would be particularly helpful are business leaders. The business executives' testimonials to the value of a liberal education gathered by Professor Warren Goldstein are impressive.[14] We know that business majors are very popular and that students (and their parents) are focused on getting a good job and making a good income. Could liberal arts colleges generate support from business leaders?

After a quick look, I collected a list of thirty-nine liberal arts college graduates who are current or former corporate CEOs and presidents of companies in finance (American Express, Bank of New York, Bank One, Barclays Capital, Dreyfus, Morgan Stanley, Sovereign Bank, Wachovia, and the World Bank); the media (America Online, CBS, Gannett, Knight-Ridder, Meredith, NBC, National Public Radio, Ogilvy & Mather, Time Warner, Walt Disney Company); insurance (Prudential, Travelers); manufacturing (Colgate-Palmolive, General Mills, Hallmark, Honeywell, Johnson & Johnson, Miller Brewing, Playtex, Procter & Gamble, Sara Lee, Snapple, Starkist Seafood, Texas Instruments); retail (Abercrombie & Fitch, Burger King, L.L. Bean, Saks Fifth Avenue); and shipping and transportation (American Express, Union Pacific); not to mention the heads of the Federal Reserve Board of Governors, the U.S. Internal Revenue Service, and the Securities Exchange Commission.

This is an impressive list. It would be presumptuous to assume what any of these executives would say about his or her undergraduate experience, or that they would want to assist in focusing favorable attention on liberal arts college education, but the way to find out would be to ask them.

Another area of particular interest to college-age students and their parents is entrepreneurship. Are there liberal arts college graduates who have founded businesses and other enterprises? Again, quick research reveals there are many, including the founders of such diverse entities as Angie's List, Ben and Jerry's, ESPN, Hard Rock Cafe, Home Depot, House of Blues, Intel, Kohlberg Kravis Roberts, Netflix, Subway, TGI Friday's, and YouTube, in addition to entrepreneurs such as Martha Stewart, Yoko Ono, Justin Hall (the first blogger), and the inventor of the game Trivial Pursuit.

Former *Newsweek* editor Jon Meacham (a Sewanee graduate) wrote one column extolling the value of a liberal arts education. Would he write more? Would *The Nation*'s emeritus publisher, Victor Navasky (Swarthmore College), publish a series on liberal arts colleges addressed to liberals, and would *American Spectator* publisher Alfred Regnery (Beloit College) do the same for conservatives? What about articles in the *New Yorker* by its columnist Louis Menand (Pomona College), pieces written by Doris Kearns Goodwin (Colby College), or documentaries by Ken Burns (Hampshire College)? And what might an array of reporters like Paul Duke, Roger Mudd, Cokie Roberts, Diane Sawyer, Garrick Utley, and Bob Woodruff, and diverse commentators such as Dave Barry, Michael Beschloss, Bryant Gumbel, Molly Ivins, Chris Matthews, Daniel Pinkwater, Andy Rooney, Barbara Walters, and George Will—all liberal arts college graduates—be willing to contribute to bringing liberal arts colleges to the public consciousness?

Sinclair Lewis attended Oberlin College and hated it, so he put an unfavorable reference to Oberlin in all of his novels. I don't know how

E. L. Doctorow, Jonathan Franzen, Annie Proulx, Tom Robbins, Philip Roth, and Tom Wolfe feel about their liberal arts college experiences, but they might, if asked, be inclined to write favorably about them.

What would Ron Reagan say about his father's time at Eureka College, President Obama about his at Occidental College, Kofi Annan about his at Macalester College, Justice Clarence Thomas about the College of the Holy Cross, Woodrow Wilson Center for Scholars president and former U.S. representative Lee Hamilton about DePauw University, Senator Richard Lugar about Denison University, New England Patriots coach Bill Belichick about Wesleyan University, or former secretary of state Madeleine Albright about Wellesley College?

Would soprano Dawn Upshaw (Illinois Wesleyan) give concerts, Edward Albee (Trinity) mount a play, actress Jane Alexander (Sarah Lawrence) present evenings of readings, and Chevy Chase (Bard) put on comedy shows, all in honor of liberal arts colleges?

There are many, many well-known and well-respected public figures of all sorts, including scholars, scientists, educators, and religious and military leaders, who graduated from liberal arts colleges. By their lives, these men and women already give witness to the value of a liberal arts education. They are a huge, untapped resource.

Without an effective national liberal arts college association in place, and without leaders who can focus beyond the immediate needs of their own colleges, it seems unlikely that mobilizing a massive, long-term effort to bring the value of liberal arts college education to the public's mind could be accomplished. Nonetheless, I continue to cling to the immortal words of Yogi Berra, "It ain't over 'til it's over."

Saving liberal arts colleges is not an all-or-nothing undertaking. No doubt some of them cannot be saved. But even if the result of a concerted effort to increase interest in and demand for liberal arts colleges were that 50 colleges, rather than 25, were able to retain their full liberal arts mission, or that 200, rather than 100, were able to continue graduating more liberal arts majors than vocational majors, the effort would be worthwhile.

Epilogue:
A Fable

✦

In the make-believe country of Nomohighered, colleges and universities have given up selling educational services and are now leasing automobiles. In every market, there are at least two dealerships, Private Auto, Inc., and the State Public Car Company. Both offer two car models, a high-end, liberal arts, LA model and a stripped-down, vocational, V model. The LA model is much more luxurious, but both models provide reliable basic service.

A potential customer enters Private Auto, Inc.

"Good morning. I'd like to buy a car."

"I'm sorry, sir. Our cars are available only on a lease basis."

"Well, all right, I'll try one for six months."

"I'm sorry again, sir. Our shortest lease period is four years."

"I can't believe this! How much is the lease fee?"

"$40,000 for our high-end LA model."

"$10,000 per year for four years?"

"I'm afraid not, sir. It's $40,000 per year. And of course we reserve the right to increase the rate each year during the lease period."

"But this car isn't even for me. It's for my seventeen-year-old son. Don't you have something cheaper, something more basic?"

"Surely you don't want anything but the best money can buy for your boy, sir."

"Of course not, but if I lease one of your cars, I won't have enough left to pay the mortgage on our ski chalet in Sun Valley, which is very important to us. The family that skis together stays together."

"I'm sorry, sir."

"Well, how much is your stripped-down V model?"

"Also $40,000 per year, sir."

"Good Lord! Why would anyone lease it?"

"Instant gratification, sir. Your boy will derive an immediate payoff from your leasing a V model for him. After driving it for four years, he will be able to get a job that pays $10,000 a year more than he would have gotten otherwise. With any luck at all, he will stay that amount ahead of the pack for the rest of his life, a tidy gain of $400,000 over a forty-year work career. Not a bad return on a $160,000 investment, wouldn't you agree, sir?"

"What about the LA model?"

"It is a bit more problematic and there are no guarantees, but the payoff could be two or three times greater, and perhaps many, many times greater."

"Well, all right. I'll roll the dice and lease one of your LA models for my boy."

"I'm afraid it's not quite that simple, sir. First, he will have to prove he's worthy. Here's an application form for him to complete. Be sure he is particularly careful completing the financial qualifications portion."

"That does it! I'm going to another Private Auto dealership!"

"You won't find their policies are any different from ours, sir."

"I don't care!"

"If you feel that strongly about it, sir, before you leave I'd like you to talk to our director of leasing, Mr. Admissions. Oh, Mr. Admissions, could you come over here for a moment, please?"

[*Mr. Admissions*] "What seems to be the problem?"

[*Customer*] "$40,000 per year is too damned much money. That's the problem!"

"Many of our customers feel that way. Perhaps we can work out a deal. $40,000 is only our list price. I'll let you in on a little secret. Our average price, after certain discounts, is only $26,000."

"That's still too much!"

"Well, if you fall into what we refer to as our Financially Challenged Class, we are prepared to make additional price concessions. How much was your taxable income last year? How big is your mortgage on the Sun Valley ski chalet? Are you and your wife on a prudent budget?"

"It's none of your business!"

"An entirely understandable position. Here is what we'll do. Your boy seems a likely lad—attended one of the best prep schools and that sort of thing. If he does very well on the Select Auto Transactions (SAT) test, we will let him have an LA model for $10,000 per year. How does that sound?"

"Better, but now you've really made me angry. You have some nerve trying to get me to pay $40,000. You must have one helluva markup."

"*Au contraire.* We lose money even at $40,000. Actually, our sticker price covers only about 75 percent of our total cost."

"Why don't you get more efficient and put in strict cost-containment policies like any rational businessman would do?"

"Ah, there's the rub. We are not in a regular business. Let me explain. You said yourself you want nothing but the best for your boy. Correct?"

"Correct."

"But if you were going to buy a conventional automobile, you wouldn't say that. You would want a car for your boy that's good enough; a good buy for the money. You might buy him a Ford or a Chevy, but not a Rolls Royce or Lamborghini."

"True."

"On the other hand, if you were buying medical care for your boy, would you be shopping for a good buy? Suppose a doctor told you he could save your boy's arm for $40,000 but said his 'best buy' would be to cut it off for $10,000, and he assured you your boy could get along very nicely with only one arm. Would you go for the best buy?"

"That's absurd. Of course not!"

"Unhappily for us, most of our customers feel the same way. They demand champagne but are only willing to pay for beer. If we don't cut our price below cost, we won't get any leases."

"What an insane business. Let me ask you this: if you are only covering 75 percent of your costs at $40,000, why on earth would you cut your price to me to $10,000?"

"We didn't used to. All of the Private Auto dealerships had agreed to cut their prices only for poor, truly financially challenged customers."

"Why on earth did you agree to do that?"

"With all the criticism we've been receiving, I'm beginning to wonder myself. I'm afraid the answer sounds rather Pollyanna-ish, but we thought it was the right thing to do; in the public interest and all that."

"Then why are you offering me such a big discount? I'm not needy."

"Competition, sir."

"I don't see how you can keep giving such big discounts."

"You're right, of course. No two ways about it—sooner or later we are going to have to slash quality or go out of business, although we have managed to temporarily improve our financial situation somewhat by cutting out most of the discounts for the poor."

"What will happen if you go out of business?"

"That, of course, is the genius of competition. When enough Private Auto companies go out of business, those that remain will be able to raise their prices to profitable levels again. It will also radically reduce the number of cars we lease, which, I'm afraid, is what the marketplace wants."

"I'm not sure that would be such a good result."

"I couldn't agree more! Well, enough of this philosophical chitchat. Do we have a deal at $10,000?"

"I'm going to do some comparison shopping at State Public Car Company. Maybe I'll see you later. Good-bye."

The scene at the State Public Car dealership is somewhat different.

[*Customer*] "I don't want any fancy sales pitch. Just answer this question. Do you lease LA model cars?"

"Yes."

"How much?"

"Do you live in this state?"

"Yes."

"Then the answer is \$7,000 per year."

"For four years?"

"Maybe for five or six years."

"Why so long?"

"At our prices, there are so many people who want both our LA and V models that we don't have enough to go around, so we are starting to have to ration them."

"It's still a better deal than I can get from Private Auto. I'll take one of your LA models for my boy."

"I was sure you would. You look like someone who knows the value of a dollar, or of a ski chalet in Sun Valley."

"How much would I have to pay if I didn't live in this state?"

"\$40,000 per year."

"Does \$7,000 per year cover your costs?"

"Far from it."

"Can I ask you one more question?"

"Of course."

"How can you afford to charge me so little?"

"You are subsidized by your fellow state taxpayers."

"Why would they do that for me?"

"Well to be blunt about it, they think you are either a very poor farmer or the unemployed head of a single-parent family."

"Why in heavens name do they think that?"

"Beats me."

Appendix:
Data on the 225 Colleges

All of the data contained in the following eight tables come from the Integrated Postsecondary Education Data System (IPEDS) of the U.S. Department of Education's National Center for Education Statistics (see http://nces.ed.gov/ipeds/datacenter) and are for the academic year 2007–2008, the most recent year for which complete data were available at the time the analysis in the book was done. Additional 1986–1987 data are presented in Tables A.1 and A.2. (It is noteworthy that the 2008–2009 data will be quite different from those for 2007–2008, since the start of the 2008 market collapse and recession coincided with the start of that academic year.)

Each table provides data for the 225 private, not-for-profit colleges included in this study. The schools are divided into four tiers: there are 51 colleges in Tier I, 68 in Tier II, 63 in Tier III, and 43 in Tier IV. The tiers are based on the rankings of the "Best Liberal Arts Colleges" (Tier I being the highest and Tier IV the lowest) listed by *U.S. News and World Report* in *America's Best Colleges,* 2009 edition.

U.S. News's 2009 list of best liberal arts colleges includes 265 colleges. Twenty-seven of them are public institutions and are not included in this study. An additional 13 are unranked for various reasons and are also excluded here, with one exception: Sarah Lawrence College, ranked in Tier I by *U.S. News* in prior years, is included. One ranked college, Hillsdale College (Tier II), which is not required to file with NCES because it does not accept federal funds, and chooses not to, is also excluded.

The Carnegie Foundation lists 374 arts and sciences (A&S) institutions. All of the colleges analyzed in this book are included in the Carnegie A&S classification. When public institutions, for-profit schools, and private universities are excluded, the Carnegie A&S list is substantially the same as that used in this study. Carnegie does not provide rankings.

Table A.1, "Colleges and enrollments," includes the location of each college and its undergraduate enrollments in 1986–1987 and 2007–2008. It also notes which colleges are members of the Annapolis Group. (Annapolis Group members are singled out because, by their membership, they have indicated their commitment to liberal arts education.)

Table A.2, "Completions," provides completions data for the academic years 1986–1987, the earliest year for which comparable IPEDS data are available, and 2007–2008. Completions are degrees conferred. They are reported by the major department of each degree recipient. For Table A.2, completions were collected into two groups, arts and sciences, and vocational, using Classification of Instructional Programs (CIP) codes established by NCES. The results are expressed as vocational degrees compared with the total number of degrees awarded. (CIP describes non–arts and sciences majors as "professional." In Table A.2 and throughout this study, professional majors are referred to as "vocational.")

Table A.3, "Endowments (2007–2008)," shows the market values of the endowment and the endowment per undergraduate full-time equivalent (FTE) at the end of each college's academic year, which in most cases was June 30, 2008. (Interestingly, the 2008 Endowment Study by the National Association of College and University Business Officers showed that the average endowment of all Tier I colleges declined 2.7 percent between 2006–2007 and 2007–2008.)

Table A.4, "Revenues (2007–2008)," gives total revenues (including returns on investments), and the percentage of total revenues accounted for by tuition and required fees payments received. It also shows total revenues per undergraduate FTE.

Table A.5, "Expenses covered by tuition and fees revenues (2007–2008)," shows the percentage of total expenses covered by the tuition and required fees payments received.

Table A.6, "Discounts (2007–2008)," presents the list price published by each college for its tuition and required fees, and the tuition and fees revenues per undergraduate FTE each college actually received, and computes the average discount students received.

Table A.7, "Expenses per full-time equivalent undergraduate (2007–2008)," shows total expenses per undergraduate FTE, and the percentage of those expenses accounted for by salaries, wages, and benefits. Other expenses, such as plant maintenance, depreciation, and interest, vary widely among the colleges. Other than financial aid, salaries, wages, and benefits are the most comparable expenses.

Table A.8, "Total expenses and revenues (2007–2008)," shows total expenses as a percentage of total revenues (including returns on investments).

Table A.1 Colleges and enrollments

College	City	State	Annapolis Group member	1986–1987 fall undergraduate enrollment	2007–2008 fall undergraduate enrollment	Percentage change in enrollment (1986–2007)
Tier I						
Amherst College	Amherst	MA	X	1,570	1,683	7.20%
Bard College	Annandale-on-Hudson	NY		801	2,036	154.18%
Barnard College	New York	NY	X	2,162	2,346	8.51%
Bates College	Lewiston	ME	X	1,543	1,660	7.58%
Bowdoin College	Brunswick	ME	X	1,413	1,716	21.44%
Bryn Mawr College	Bryn Mawr	PA	X	1,254	1,287	2.63%
Bucknell University	Lewisburg	PA	X	3161	3,520	11.36%
Carleton College	Northfield	MN	X	1,867	1,994	6.80%
Centre College	Danville	KY	X	814	1,189	46.07%
Claremont McKenna College	Claremont	CA	X	829	1,135	36.91%
Colby College	Waterville	ME	X	1,802	1,867	3.61%
Colgate University	Hamilton	NY	X	2,685	2,831	5.44%
College of the Holy Cross	Worcester	MA	X	2,658	2,847	7.11%
Colorado College	Colorado Springs	CO	X	1,965	2,053	4.48%
Connecticut College	New London	CT	X	1,860	1,857	−0.16%
Davidson College	Davidson	NC	X	1,397	1,674	19.83%
DePauw University	Greencastle	IN	X	2,307	2,398	3.94%
Dickinson College	Carlisle	PA	X	1,943	2,381	22.54%

Franklin and Marshall College	Lancaster	PA	X	2,684	2,104	−21.61%
Furman University	Greenville	SC	X	2,793	2,774	−0.68%
Gettysburg College	Gettysburg	PA	X	1,923	2,503	30.16%
Grinnell College	Grinnell	IA	X	1,279	1,654	29.32%
Hamilton College	Clinton	NY	X	1,685	1,842	9.32%
Harvey Mudd College	Claremont	CA	X	544	735	35.11%
Haverford College	Haverford	PA	X	1,112	1,169	5.13%
Kenyon College	Gambier	OH	X	1,532	1,662	8.49%
Lafayette College	Easton	PA	X	2,330	2,403	3.13%
Macalester College	St. Paul	MN	X	1,768	1,920	8.60%
Middlebury College	Middlebury	VT	X	2,064	2,500	21.12%
Mount Holyoke College	South Hadley	MA	X	1,926	2,201	14.28%
Oberlin College	Oberlin	OH	X	2,808	2,762	−1.64%
Occidental College	Los Angeles	CA	X	1,652	1,863	12.77%
Pitzer College	Claremont	CA	X	789	999	26.62%
Pomona College	Claremont	CA	X	1,353	1,547	14.34%
Rhodes College	Memphis	TN	X	1,226	1,684	37.36%
St. Olaf College	Northfield	MN	X	3,087	3,040	−1.52%
Sarah Lawrence College	Bronxville	NY	X	946	1,383	46.19%
Scripps College	Claremont	CA	X	600	899	49.83%
Sewanee: The University of the South	Sewanee	TN	X	1084	1,475	36.07%
Skidmore College	Saratoga Springs	NY	X	2,571	2,809	9.26%
Smith College	Northampton	MA	X	2,602	2,596	−0.23%
Swarthmore College	Swarthmore	PA	X	1,334	1,491	11.77%

Table A.1 (continued)

College	City	State	Annapolis Group member	1986–1987 fall undergraduate enrollment	2007–2008 fall undergraduate enrollment	Percentage change in enrollment (1986–2007)
Trinity College	Hartford	CT	X	1,934	2,337	20.84%
Union College	Schenectady	NY	X	2,412	2,177	-9.74%
University of Richmond	Richmond	VA		3,789	3,556	-6.15%
Vassar College	Poughkeepsie	NY	X	2,318	2,450	5.69%
Washington and Lee University	Lexington	VA	X	1,440	1,778	23.47%
Wellesley College	Wellesley	MA	X	2,257	2,380	5.45%
Wesleyan University	Middletown	CT	X	2,828	2,817	-0.39%
Whitman College	Walla Walla	WA	X	1,240	1,489	20.08%
Williams College	Williamstown	MA	X	1,998	2,024	1.30%
Total				93,939	103,497	—
Mean				1,842	2,029	10.17%
Median				1,860	2,024	8.82%
Tier II						
Agnes Scott College	Decatur	GA	X	518	885	70.85%
Albion College	Albion	MI	X	1,587	1,938	22.12%
Allegheny College	Meadville	PA	X	1,875	2,193	16.96%
Augustana College	Rock Island	IL	X	2,081	2,537	21.91%
Austin College	Sherman	TX	X	1,149	1,320	14.88%

College	City	State		Value 1	Value 2	Percent
Beloit College	Beloit	WI	X	1,075	1,366	27.07%
Bennington College	Bennington	VT	X	563	583	3.55%
Berea College	Berea	KY	X	1,585	1,582	−0.19%
Berry College	Mount Berry	GA	X	1,339	1,737	29.72%
Birmingham Southern College	Birmingham	AL	X	1,633	1,339	−18.00%
Calvin College	Grand Rapids	MI		3,988	4,169	4.54%
Central College	Pella	IA		1,528	1,605	5.04%
Coe College	Cedar Rapids	IA	X	1,133	1,298	14.56%
College of St. Benedict	St. Joseph	MN	X	2,045	2,086	2.00%
College of Wooster	Wooster	OH	X	1,851	1,781	−3.78%
Cornell College	Mount Vernon	IA	X	1,161	1,083	−6.72%
Denison University	Granville	OH	X	2,134	2,242	5.06%
Drew University	Madison	NJ	X	1,486	1,666	12.11%
Earlham College	Richmond	IN	X	1,059	1,194	12.75%
Goucher College	Baltimore	MD	X	7,97	1,471	84.57%
Gustavus Adolphus College	St. Peter	MN	X	2,206	2,625	18.99%
Hampden-Sydney College	Hampden-Sydney	VA	X	825	1,122	36.00%
Hampshire College	Amherst	MA	X	1075	1,431	33.12%
Hanover College	Hanover	IN		1084	929	−14.30%
Hendrix College	Conway	AR	X	1,007	1,191	18.27%
Hobart and William Smith Colleges	Geneva	NY	X	1,973	2,001	1.42%
Hollins University	Roanoke	VA	X	766	783	2.22%

(continued)

Table A.1 *(continued)*

College	City	State	Annapolis Group member	1986–1987 fall undergraduate enrollment	2007–2008 fall undergraduate enrollment	Percentage change in enrollment (1986–2007)
Hope College	Holland	MI	X	2,545	3,226	26.76%
Illinois Wesleyan University	Bloomington	IL	X	1,716	2,094	22.03%
Juniata College	Huntingdon	PA	X	1,089	1,506	38.29%
Kalamazoo College	Kalamazoo	MI	X	1,103	1,340	21.49%
Knox College	Galesburg	IL	X	967	1,371	41.78%
Lake Forest College	Lake Forest	IL	X	1,160	1,436	23.79%
Lawrence University	Appleton	WI	X	1,067	1,443	35.24%
Lewis and Clark College	Portland	OR	X	1,651	1,964	18.96%
Linfield College	McMinnville	OR		1,703	1,693	−0.59%
Luther College	Decorah	IA	X	2,041	2,476	21.31%
Lyon College	Batesville	AR		715	497	−30.49%
Millsaps College	Jackson	MS	X	1,277	1,043	−18.32%
Muhlenberg College	Allentown	PA	X	2,087	2,457	17.73%
Ohio Wesleyan University	Delaware	OH	X	1,429	1,986	38.98%
Presbyterian College	Clinton	SC	X	1,041	1,180	13.35%
Randolph College	Lynchburg	VA	X	781	649	−16.90%
Reed College	Portland	OR	X	1,201	1,464	21.90%
St. John's College	Santa Fe	NM	X	391	481	23.02%
St. John's University	Collegeville	MN	X	1,836	1,952	6.32%

St. Lawrence University	Canton	NY	X	2,170	2,198	1.29%
St. Mary's College	Notre Dame	IN	X	1,734	1,604	-7.50%
St. Michael's College	Colchester	VT		1,723	2,008	16.54%
Siena College	Loudonville	NY		3,432	3,217	-6.26%
Southwestern University	Georgetown	TX	X	1,111	1,294	16.47%
Spelman College	Atlanta	GA	X	1,266	2,343	85.07%
Stonehill College	Easton	MA		2,851	2,440	-14.42%
Susquehanna University	Selinsgrove	PA	X	1,751	2,039	16.45%
Sweet Briar College	Sweet Briar	VA	X	66?	800	20.66%
Thomas Aquinas College	Santa Paula	CA		125	360	188.00%
Transylvania University	Lexington	KY	X	970	1,153	18.87%
University of Puget Sound	Tacoma	WA	X	2778	2,537	-8.68%
Ursinus College	Collegeville	PA	X	2,293	1,583	-30.96%
Wabash College	Crawfordsville	IN	X	774	917	18.48%
Washington and Jefferson College	Washington	PA	X	1,354	1,531	13.07%
Washington College	Chestertown	MD	X	841	1,222	45.30%
Westminster College	New Wilmington	PA		1,205	1,349	11.95%
Westmont College	Santa Barbara	CA	X	1,228	1,336	8.79%
Wheaton College	Wheaton	IL		2,236	2,381	6.48%
Wheaton College	Norton	MA	X	1,083	1,657	53.00%
Willamette University	Salem	OR	X	1,435	1,919	33.73%
Wofford College	Spartanburg	SC	X	1,095	1,363	24.47%
Total				99,441	111,666	—
Mean				1,462	1,642	12.29%
Median				1,272	1,519	19.43%

(continued)

177

Table A.1 *(continued)*

College	City	State	Annapolis Group member	1986–1987 fall undergraduate enrollment	2007–2008 fall undergraduate enrollment	Percentage change in enrollment (1986–2007)
Tier III						
Albright College	Reading	PA	X	1,961	2,176	10.96%
Alma College	Alma	MI	X	1,030	1,355	31.55%
American Jewish University	Bel Air	CA		82	96	17.07%
Asbury College	Wilmore	KY		942	1,330	41.19%
Baker University	Baldwin City	KS		776	2,037	162.50%
Bethany College	Bethany	WV		786	815	3.69%
Bridgewater College	Bridgewater	VA		813	1,541	89.54%
Carroll College	Helena	MT		1,412	1,382	−2.12%
Carson-Newman College	Jefferson City	TN		1,681	1,834	9.10%
Cedar Crest College	Allentown	PA		1,145	1,786	55.98%
Centenary College of Louisiana	Shreveport	LA		804	854	6.22%
Clarke College	Dubuque	IA		744	1,022	37.37%
College of Idaho	Caldwell	ID		895	826	−7.71%
College of the Atlantic	Bar Harbor	ME		136	341	150.74%
Concordia College at Moorhead	Moorhead	MN		2,525	2,801	10.93%
Dillard University	New Orleans	LA		1,275	956	−25.02%
Doane College	Crete	NE		739	921	24.63%

Eastern Mennonite University	Harrisonburg	VA		771	970	25.81%
Eckerd College	St. Petersburg	FL	X	1,179	2,544	115.78%
Emory and Henry College	Emory	VA		769	977	27.05%
Fisk University	Nashville	TN		513	761	48.34%
Georgetown College	Georgetown	KY		986	1,368	38.74%
Gordon College	Wenham	MA	X	1,218	1,529	25.53%
Goshen College	Goshen	IN		1,068	955	-10.58%
Grove City College	Grove City	PA		2,140	2,504	17.01%
Guilford College	Greensboro	NC		1,702	2,688	57.93%
Hartwick College	Oneonta	NY		1,464	1,537	4.99%
Hastings College	Hastings	NE		776	1,091	40.59%
Hiram College	Hiram	OH	X	1,186	1,240	4.55%
Houghton College	Houghton	NY		1,126	1,368	21.49%
Illinois College	Jacksonville	IL	X	745	1,014	36.11%
Lycoming College	Williamsport	PA		1,086	1,429	31.58%
Maryville College	Maryville	TN		676	1,176	73.96%
McDaniel College	Westminster	MD	X	1,136	1,731	52.38%
Meredith College	Raleigh	NC		1,735	2,039	17.52%
Merrimack College	North Andover	MA		3,516	2,043	-41.89%
Millikin University	Decatur	IL		1,562	2,335	49.49%
Monmouth College	Monmouth	IL	X	689	1,343	94.92%
Moravian College and Moravian Theological Seminary	Bethlehem	PA	X	1,690	1,784	5.56%

(continued)

179

Table A.1 (continued)

College	City	State	Annapolis Group member	1986–1987 fall undergraduate enrollment	2007–2008 fall undergraduate enrollment	Percentage change in enrollment (1986–2007)
Morehouse College	Atlanta	GA	X	2,121	2,810	32.48%
Mount Union College	Alliance	OH		1,073	2,138	99.25%
Nebraska Wesleyan University	Lincoln	NE	X	1,311	1,888	44.01%
Oglethorpe University	Atlanta	GA	X	869	958	10.24%
Principia College	Elsah	IL		691	not reported	n/a
Randolph-Macon College	Ashland	VA	X	1,013	1,176	16.09%
Ripon College	Ripon	WI	X	833	1,001	20.17%
Roanoke College	Salem	VA		1,527	2,006	31.37%
Russell Sage College	Troy	NY		2,326	682	−70.68%
St. Anselm College	Manchester	NH		1,911	1,968	2.98%
St. John's College	Annapolis	MD	X		435	n/a
St. Norbert College	De Pere	WI		1,708	2,086	22.13%
St. Vincent College	Latrobe	PA		1,249	1,705	36.51%
Salem College	Winston Salem	NC	X	737	768	4.21%
Simpson College	Indianola	IA		1,395	2,017	44.59%
Warren Wilson College	Swannanoa	NC		455	873	91.87%
Wartburg College	Waverly	IA		1,329	1,810	36.19%
Wells College	Aurora	NY		404	552	36.63%
Wesleyan College	Macon	GA	X	424	592	39.62%

Westminster College	Fulton	MO			632	972	53.80%
Whittier College	Whittier	CA	X		982	1,259	28.21%
William Jewell College	Liberty	MO	X		2,061	1,329	−35.52%
Wisconsin Lutheran College	Milwaukee	WI			152	706	364.47%
Wittenberg University	Springfield	OH			2,178	2,066	−5.14%
Total					70,682	86,230	—
Mean					1,159	1,414	22.00%
Median					1,073	1,355	26.28%
Tier IV							
Albertus Magnus College	New Haven	CT			546	1,686	208.79%
Atlantic Union College	South Lancaster	MA			566	551	−2.65%
Bennett College for Women	Greensboro	NC			576	678	17.71%
Bethel College	North Newton	KS			634	541	−14.67%
Bloomfield College	Bloomfield	NJ			1,406	2,056	46.23%
Brevard College	Brevard	NC			593	675	13.83%
Brigham Young University–Hawaii	Laie	HI			1,982	2,397	20.94%
Concordia College	Bronxville	NY			547	708	29.43%
Evangel University	Springfield	MO			1,609	1,534	−4.66%
Ferrum College	Ferrum	VA			1,272	1,233	−3.07%
Franklin Pierce University	Rindge	NH			1,035	2,238	116.23%
Green Mountain College	Poultney	VT			456	770	68.86%

(continued)

Table A.1 (continued)

College	City	State	Annapolis Group member	1986–1987 fall undergraduate enrollment	2007–2008 fall undergraduate enrollment	Percentage change in enrollment (1986–2007)
Greensboro College	Greensboro	NC		553	1,127	103.80%
Huntingdon College	Montgomery	AL		750	954	27.20%
Huston-Tillotson University	Austin	TX		520	727	39.81%
Jarvis Christian College	Hawkins	TX		393	712	81.17%
Johnson C. Smith University	Charlotte	NC		1,130	1,463	29.47%
Judson College	Marion	AL		324	311	−4.01%
Kentucky Wesleyan College	Owensboro	KY		791	956	20.86%
Lambuth University	Jackson	TN		616	751	21.92%
Lane College	Jackson	TN		531	1,766	232.58%
Lindsey Wilson College	Columbia	KY		884	1,621	83.37%
Marlboro College	Marlboro	VT		192	313	63.02%
Marymount Manhattan College	New York	NY		1,484	1,895	27.70%
McPherson College	McPherson	KS		469	544	15.99%
North Greenville University	Tigerville	SC		470	1993	324.04%
Northland College	Ashland	WI		566	682	20.49%
Olivet College	Olivet	MI		731	1,004	37.35%
Paine College	Augusta	GA		789	917	16.22%

Peace College	NC	Raleigh	489	692	41.51%
Pine Manor College	MA	Chestnut Hill	571	450	−21.19%
St. Andrews Presbyterian College	NC	Laurinburg	747	747	0.00%
Sierra Nevada College	NV	Incline Village	94	302	221.28%
Simpson University	CA	Redding	210	892	324.76%
Stephens College	MO	Columbia	1,123	890	−20.75%
Sterling College	KS	Sterling	528	603	14.20%
Talladega College	AL	Talladega	577	350	−39.34%
Texas Lutheran University	TX	Seguin	1,340	1,375	2.61%
Thiel College	PA	Greenville	927	1,219	31.50%
Tougaloo College	MS	Tougaloo	902	856	−5.10%
Virginia Wesleyan College	VA	Norfolk	1,116	1,433	28.41%
West Virginia Wesleyan College	WV	Buckhannon	4,383	3,175	−27.56%
Wingate University	NC	Wingate	1,653	1,471	−11.01%
Total			37,075	47,258	—
Mean			862	1,099	27.47%
Median			683	905	32.53%
All colleges					
Total			301,137	348,651	15.78%
Mean			1,356	1,567	15.60%
Median			1,194	1,490	24.84%

Table A.2 Completions

	1986–1987 completions			2007–2008 completions		
	Vocational degrees awarded	Total degrees awarded	Percent vocational	Vocational degrees awarded	Total degrees awarded	Percent vocational
Tier I						
Amherst College	0	392	0.0%	27	559	4.8%
Bard College	0	160	0.0%	0	358	0.0%
Barnard College	12	534	2.2%	20	618	3.2%
Bates College	2	358	0.6%	12	496	2.4%
Bowdoin College	0	345	0.0%	37	593	6.2%
Bryn Mawr College	0	272	0.0%	4	371	1.1%
Bucknell University	142	642	22.1%	357	1132	31.5%
Carleton College	0	426	0.0%	13	494	2.6%
Centre College	3	179	1.7%	7	351	2.0%
Claremont McKenna College	10	203	4.9%	55	304	18.1%
Colby College	0	441	0.0%	28	665	4.2%
Colgate University	7	605	1.2%	22	824	2.7%
College of the Holy Cross	0	644	0.0%	0	771	0.0%
Colorado College	0	457	0.0%	22	611	3.6%
Connecticut College	18	445	4.0%	44	559	7.9%
Davidson College	0	326	0.0%	0	447	0.0%
DePauw University	25	516	4.8%	153	707	21.6%
Dickinson College	0	452	0.0%	119	626	19.0%

Franklin and Marshall College	0	402	0.0%	110	572	19.2%
Furman University	59	443	13.3%	213	795	26.8%
Gettysburg College	9	308	2.9%	131	741	17.7%
Grinnell College	0	304	0.0%	19	490	3.9%
Hamilton College	0	419	0.0%	37	526	7.0%
Harvey Mudd College	73	124	58.9%	103	189	54.5%
Haverford College	4	288	1.4%	14	320	4.4%
Kenyon College	0	339	0.0%	0	500	0.0%
Lafayette College	140	495	28.3%	105	707	14.9%
Macalester College	0	323	0.0%	23	561	4.1%
Middlebury College	0	558	0.0%	42	746	5.6%
Mount Holyoke College	0	530	0.0%	26	632	4.1%
Oberlin College	11	652	1.7%	63	897	7.0%
Occidental College	6	375	1.6%	32	508	6.3%
Pitzer College	0	146	0.0%	44	287	15.3%
Pomona College	0	333	0.0%	49	411	11.9%
Rhodes College	0	174	0.0%	40	424	9.4%
St. Olaf College	22	646	3.4%	117	942	12.4%
Sarah Lawrence College	0	196	0.0%	0	303	0.0%
Scripps College	0	156	0.0%	4	230	1.7%
Sewanee: The University of the South	11	242	4.5%	16	379	4.2%
Skidmore College	21	404	5.2%	161	727	22.1%
Smith College	13	684	1.9%	55	849	6.5%
Swarthmore College	17	353	4.8%	46	449	10.2%

(continued)

Table A.2 (continued)

	1986–1987 completions			2007–2008 completions		
	Vocational degrees awarded	Total degrees awarded	Percent vocational	Vocational degrees awarded	Total degrees awarded	Percent vocational
Trinity College	21	452	4.6%	66	629	10.5%
Union College	164	591	27.7%	54	530	10.2%
University of Richmond	33	452	7.3%	343	958	35.8%
Vassar College	0	558	0.0%	38	750	5.1%
Washington and Lee University	6	231	2.6%	160	565	28.3%
Wellesley College	17	545	3.1%	28	790	3.5%
Wesleyan University	0	654	0.0%	10	954	1.0%
Whitman College	0	279	0.0%	7	396	1.8%
Williams College	0	522	0.0%	13	707	1.8%
Mean	17	404	4.2%	61	588	10.4%
Median	0	404	0.0%	37	565	6.5%
Tier II						
Agnes Scott College	1	117	0.9%	0	233	0.0%
Albion College	6	215	2.8%	103	543	19.0%
Allegheny College	12	414	2.9%	72	609	11.8%
Augustana College	59	317	18.6%	266	678	39.2%
Austin College	6	167	3.6%	83	428	19.4%
Beloit College	1	185	0.5%	34	389	8.7%

Bennington College	0	95	0.0%	7	180	3.9%
Berea College	65	185	35.1%	152	334	45.5%
Berry College	77	196	39.3%	181	407	44.5%
Birmingham Southern College	18	198	9.1%	85	290	29.3%
Calvin College	192	653	29.4%	443	927	47.8%
Central College	50	217	23.0%	176	389	45.2%
Coe College	8	144	5.6%	162	370	43.8%
College of St. Benedict	118	320	36.9%	162	489	33.1%
College of Wooster	7	311	2.3%	48	427	11.2%
Cornell College	25	263	9.5%	65	321	20.2%
Denison University	8	474	1.7%	109	677	16.1%
Drew University	0	337	0.0%	2	334	0.6%
Earlham College	8	215	3.7%	18	306	5.9%
Goucher College	9	164	5.5%	85	347	24.5%
Gustavus Adolphus College	63	424	14.9%	269	666	40.4%
Hampden-Sydney College	0	140	0.0%	58	264	22.0%
Hampshire College	0	160	0.0%	37	289	12.8%
Hanover College	23	150	15.3%	77	311	24.8%
Hendrix College	9	182	4.9%	17	200	8.5%
Hobart and William Smith Colleges	0	415	0.0%	108	494	21.9%
Hollins University	0	188	0.0%	34	206	16.5%
Hope College	58	323	18.0%	401	844	47.5%
Illinois Wesleyan University	25	216	11.6%	190	549	34.6%

(continued)

Table A.2 (continued)

	1986–1987 completions			2007–2008 completions		
	Vocational degrees awarded	Total degrees awarded	Percent vocational	Vocational degrees awarded	Total degrees awarded	Percent vocational
Juniata College	38	159	23.9%	127	328	38.7%
Kalamazoo College	0	196	0.0%	13	302	4.3%
Knox College	7	176	4.0%	59	370	15.9%
Lake Forest College	0	217	0.0%	106	463	22.9%
Lawrence University	12	252	4.8%	24	377	6.4%
Lewis and Clark College	20	344	5.8%	45	513	8.8%
Linfield College	27	200	13.5%	198	380	52.1%
Luther College	41	332	12.3%	240	649	37.0%
Lyon College	24	57	42.1%	34	98	34.7%
Millsaps College	16	140	11.4%	71	268	26.5%
Muhlenberg College	1	262	0.4%	244	735	33.2%
Ohio Wesleyan University	22	223	9.9%	126	465	27.1%
Presbyterian College	19	135	14.1%	82	270	30.4%
Randolph College	11	186	5.9%	13	168	7.7%
Reed College	0	193	0.0%	0	299	0.0%
St. John's College (NM)	0	65	0.0%	0	89	0.0%
St. John's University	8	236	3.4%	183	483	37.9%
St. Lawrence University	10	559	1.8%	22	613	3.6%
St. Mary's College	32	283	11.3%	157	370	42.4%
St. Michael's College	16	228	7.0%	176	497	35.4%

Siena College	15	4.8%	314	362	781	46.4%
Southwestern University	30	17.0%	176	102	352	29.0%
Spelman College	11	3.7%	298	31	483	6.4%
Stonehill College	56	19.0%	295	254	695	36.5%
Susquehanna University	16	9.2%	173	233	526	44.3%
Sweet Briar College	0	0.0%	159	20	149	13.4%
Thomas Aquinas College	0	0.0%	28	0	80	0.0%
Transylvania University	7	6.7%	104	86	307	28.0%
University of Puget Sound	59	14.9%	396	181	687	26.3%
Ursinus College	7	3.0%	236	98	422	23.2%
Wabash College	0	0.0%	138	0	236	0.0%
Washington and Jefferson College	0	0.0%	152	152	434	35.0%
Washington College	0	0.0%	96	55	243	22.6%
Westminster College (PA)	23	11.8%	195	149	333	44.7%
Westmont College	4	2.0%	197	92	328	28.0%
Wheaton College (IL)	92	20.7%	444	256	737	34.7%
Wheaton College (MA)	0	0.0%	261	3	403	0.7%
Willamette University	14	6.9%	203	40	524	7.6%
Wofford College	2	1.0%	194	106	322	32.9%
Mean	22	9.4%	234	112	416	26.8%
Median	11	5.3%	199	86	379	22.6%
Tier III						
Albright College	26	13.5%	192	183	491	37.3%
Alma College	8	7.0%	115	108	262	41.2%

(continued)

Table A.2 *(continued)*

	1986–1987 completions			2007–2008 completions		
	Vocational degrees awarded	Total degrees awarded	Percent vocational	Vocational degrees awarded	Total degrees awarded	Percent vocational
American Jewish University	0	16	0.0%	6	33	18.2%
Asbury College	86	157	54.8%	137	242	56.6%
Baker University	22	78	28.2%	346	439	78.8%
Bethany College	10	135	7.4%	93	173	53.8%
Bridgewater College	25	92	27.2%	248	411	60.3%
Carroll College	36	139	25.9%	171	315	54.3%
Carson-Newman College	79	215	36.7%	247	380	65.0%
Cedar Crest College	11	79	13.9%	193	353	54.7%
Centenary College of Louisiana	25	93	26.9%	79	229	34.5%
Clarke College	12	99	12.1%	170	264	64.4%
College of Idaho	6	73	8.2%	51	166	30.7%
College of the Atlantic	0	28	0.0%	0	68	0.0%
Concordia College at Moorhead	79	348	22.7%	409	803	50.9%
Dillard University	25	89	28.1%	87	176	49.4%
Doane College	27	99	27.3%	89	213	41.8%
Eastern Mennonite University	79	128	61.7%	187	291	64.3%

Eckerd College	8	145	5.5%	296	650	45.5%
Emory and Henry College	25	95	26.3%	91	256	35.5%
Fisk University	1	69	1.4%	24	117	20.5%
Georgetown College	28	113	24.8%	126	286	44.1%
Gordon College	68	203	33.5%	150	408	36.8%
Goshen College	44	164	26.8%	149	257	58.0%
Grove City College	152	332	45.8%	321	647	49.6%
Guilford College	46	184	25.0%	273	660	41.4%
Hartwick College	4	174	2.3%	93	306	30.4%
Hastings College	43	117	36.8%	149	297	50.2%
Hiram College	14	175	8.0%	108	254	42.5%
Houghton College	51	221	23.1%	213	415	51.3%
Illinois College	18	71	25.4%	61	263	23.2%
Lycoming College	17	121	14.0%	82	411	20.0%
Maryville College	14	67	20.9%	97	222	43.7%
McDaniel College	42	229	18.3%	113	356	31.7%
Meredith College	92	224	41.1%	173	363	47.7%
Merrimack College	71	238	29.8%	228	449	50.8%
Millikin University	47	174	27.0%	325	590	55.1%
Monmouth College	24	121	19.8%	169	339	49.9%
Moravian College and Moravian Theological Seminary	36	200	18.0%	111	408	27.2%
Morehouse College	1	148	0.7%	179	521	34.4%
Mount Union College	25	103	24.3%	289	477	60.6%
Nebraska Wesleyan University	34	146	23.3%	261	464	56.3%

(continued)

Table A.2   (continued)

	1986–1987 completions			2007–2008 completions		
	Vocational degrees awarded	Total degrees awarded	Percent vocational	Vocational degrees awarded	Total degrees awarded	Percent vocational
Oglethorpe University	5	114	4.4%	55	202	27.2%
Principia College	5	133	3.8%	54	128	42.2%
Randolph-Macon College	0	218	0.0%	24	283	8.5%
Ripon College	1	136	0.7%	70	239	29.3%
Roanoke College	38	188	20.2%	176	429	41.0%
Russell Sage College	83	212	39.2%	106	197	53.8%
St. Anselm College	48	310	15.5%	186	426	43.7%
St. John's College (MD)	0	45	0.0%	0	106	0.0%
St. Norbert College	39	201	19.4%	259	514	50.4%
St. Vincent College	5	131	3.8%	121	316	38.3%
Salem College	7	90	7.8%	40	176	22.7%
Simpson College	52	117	44.4%	270	481	56.1%
Warren Wilson College	6	86	7.0%	51	188	27.1%
Wartburg College	43	162	26.5%	211	415	50.8%
Wells College	0	99	0.0%	8	83	9.6%
Wesleyan College	11	67	16.4%	37	87	42.5%
Westminster College (MO)	4	72	5.6%	102	205	49.8%
Whittier College	19	132	14.4%	105	326	32.2%
William Jewell College	36	189	19.0%	192	394	48.7%
Wisconsin Lutheran College	0	6	0.0%	68	148	45.9%

Wittenberg University	46	388	11.9%	138	484	28.5%
Mean	30	145	21.0%	145	326	44.6%
Median	25	132	18.9%	126	306	41.2%
Tier IV						
Albertus Magnus College	0	46	0.0%	285	395	72.2%
Atlantic Union College	21	48	43.8%	49	95	51.6%
Bennett College for Women	18	45	40.0%	50	108	46.3%
Bethel College	41	106	38.7%	83	142	58.5%
Bloomfield College	0	52	0.0%	116	277	41.9%
Brevard College	0	0		70	132	53.0%
Brigham Young University–Hawaii	26	99	26.3%	343	545	62.9%
Concordia College	17	75	22.7%	72	126	57.1%
Evangel University	132	222	59.5%	187	324	57.7%
Ferrum College	22	64	34.4%	92	153	60.1%
Franklin Pierce University	13	89	14.6%	280	448	62.5%
Green Mountain College	12	19	63.2%	51	131	38.9%
Greensboro College	19	58	32.8%	114	195	58.5%
Huntingdon College				136	211	64.5%
Huston-Tillotson University	9	32	28.1%	55	93	59.1%
Jarvis Christian College	8	41	19.5%	40	66	60.6%
Johnson C. Smith University	8	68	11.8%	138	213	64.8%

(continued)

Table A.2 (continued)

	1986–1987 completions			2007–2008 completions		
	Vocational degrees awarded	Total degrees awarded	Percent vocational	Vocational degrees awarded	Total degrees awarded	Percent vocational
Judson College	8	44	18.2%	10	55	18.2%
Kentucky Wesleyan College	29	83	34.9%	81	155	52.3%
Lambuth University	17	81	21.0%	61	124	49.2%
Lane College	8	49	16.3%	99	175	56.6%
Lindsey Wilson College	0	0		84	271	31.0%
Marlboro College	0	26	0.0%	8	105	7.6%
Marymount Manhattan College	1	114	0.9%	127	395	32.2%
McPherson College	31	56	55.4%	100	141	70.9%
North Greenville University	0	0		208	320	65.0%
Northland College	26	100	26.0%	74	142	52.1%
Olivet College	13	70	18.6%	134	188	71.3%
Paine College	12	32	37.5%	42	100	42.0%
Peace College	0	0		59	137	43.1%
Pine Manor College	7	59	11.9%	18	51	35.3%
St. Andrews Presbyterian College	11	74	14.9%	114	179	63.7%
Sierra Nevada College	2	7	28.6%	18	44	40.9%

Simpson University	12	27	44.4%	110	227	48.5%
Stephens College	79	192	41.1%	72	142	50.7%
Sterling College	40	65	61.5%	34	61	55.7%
Talladega College	17	58	29.3%	9	29	31.0%
Texas Lutheran University	44	120	36.7%	142	269	52.8%
Thiel College	1	70	1.4%	124	223	55.6%
Tougaloo College	16	70	22.9%	23	129	17.8%
Virginia Wesleyan College	24	96	25.0%	144	279	51.6%
West Virginia Wesleyan College	68	141	48.2%	139	248	56.0%
Wingate University	67	140	47.9%	160	280	57.1%
Mean	21	68	31.0%	101	189	53.6%
Median	13	62	21.1%	84	153	54.9%
All colleges						
Mean	23	216	10.6%	107	386	27.8%
Median	12	178	6.8%	86	353	24.4%

Table A.3 Endowments (2007–2008)

	Endowment	Endowment/FTE undergraduate
Tier I		
Amherst College	$1,705,916,832	$937,317
Bard College	not reported	n/a
Barnard College	$212,128,959	$93,490
Bates College	$267,220,050	$161,560
Bowdoin College	$831,460,000	$487,374
Bryn Mawr College	$689,334,000	$506,863
Bucknell University	$554,592,000	$158,139
Carleton College	$647,821,803	$330,690
Centre College	$191,326,054	$161,049
Claremont McKenna College	$527,853,000	$466,714
Colby College	$600,248,000	$293,376
Colgate University	$729,249,000	$262,509
College of the Holy Cross	$627,263,848	$208,048
Colorado College	$460,585,743	$211,764
Connecticut College	$215,536,000	$111,909
Davidson College	$513,925,706	$283,623
DePauw University	$544,534,378	$214,299
Dickinson College	$307,759,777	$118,918
Franklin and Marshall College	$271,192,199	$120,745
Furman University	$560,043,828	$211,337
Gettysburg College	$254,729,619	$94,871
Grinnell College	$1,472,448,000	$878,549
Hamilton College	$742,541,000	$411,152
Harvey Mudd College	$249,255,821	$335,924
Haverford College	$521,307,851	$408,229
Kenyon College	$188,695,722	$102,944
Lafayette College	$721,085,562	$290,409
Macalester College	$709,275,000	$354,815
Middlebury College	$885,389,000	$327,437
Mount Holyoke College	$662,094,332	$277,608
Oberlin College	$828,714,935	$305,348
Occidental College	$359,953,560	$194,569
Pitzer College	$100,131,496	$105,847
Pomona College	$1,795,212,000	$1,167,997
Rhodes College	$281,511,695	$167,069
Sarah Lawrence College	$77,939,000	$58,469
Scripps College	$276,010,266	$313,292

	Endowment	Endowment/FTE undergraduate
Sewanee: The University of the South	$313,206,187	$195,266
Skidmore College	$296,330,000	$117,685
Smith College	$1,365,791,923	$518,327
Swarthmore College	$1,412,609,000	$966,878
Trinity College	$434,330,841	$187,941
Union College	$399,538,900	$199,570
University of Richmond	$1,704,350,000	$540,377
Vassar College	$853,643,854	$344,489
Washington and Lee University	not reported	n/a
Wellesley College	$1,629,447,000	$642,273
Wesleyan University	$652,208,000	$220,788
Whitman College	$387,566,000	$268,398
Williams College	$1,755,960,326	$864,579
Total	$31,789,268,067	—
Mean	$662,276,418	$337,517
Median	$549,563,189	$273,003
Tier II		
Agnes Scott College	$307,426,688	$328,799
Albion College	$180,737,242	$97,749
Allegheny College	$157,007,094	$73,816
Augustana College	$113,760,755	$45,215
Austin College	$140,822,803	$112,478
Beloit College	$131,877,612	$104,334
Bennington College	$14,355,439	$25,408
Berea College	$1,023,254,700	$641,941
Berry College	$656,543,056	$381,933
Birmingham Southern College	$101,016,991	$77,112
Calvin College	$112,980,673	$25,973
Central College	$82,231,236	$64,647
Coe College	$81,176,160	$58,191
College of St. Benedict	$41,077,713	$19,806
College of Wooster	$289,021,270	$153,735
Cornell College	$69,253,283	$56,718
Denison University	$690,193,398	$328,977
Drew University	$212,643,000	$119,328
Earlham College	$345,000,467	$328,885

(continued)

	Endowment	Endowment/FTE undergraduate
Goucher College	$203,010,000	$138,573
Gustavus Adolphus College	$114,581,287	$41,590
Hampden-Sydney College	$134,923,952	$120,253
Hampshire College	$43,861,130	$31,397
Hanover College	$150,243,680	$160,517
Hendrix College	$177,273,000	$146,749
Hobart and William Smith Colleges	$185,083,906	$85,608
Hollins University	$120,276,621	$127,682
Hope College	$169,328,092	$52,652
Illinois Wesleyan University	$182,914,462	$87,561
Juniata College	$74,083,985	$50,535
Kalamazoo College	$156,926,548	$191,608
Knox College	$71,423,256	$51,719
Lake Forest College	$76,800,968	$53,186
Lawrence University	$216,494,192	$147,175
Lewis and Clark College	$231,216,656	$109,789
Linfield College	$71,279,513	$41,154
Luther College	$119,928,405	$43,978
Lyon College	$45,952,095	$99,679
Millsaps College	$91,555,007	$81,455
Muhlenberg College	$138,284,000	$50,432
Ohio Wesleyan University	$185,360,761	$93,146
Presbyterian College	$88,254,000	$73,915
Randolph College	$129,048,061	$108,262
Reed College	$427,180,913	$326,092
St. John's College (NM)	$25,653,508	$51,001
St. John's University	$145,232,551	$75,879
St. Lawrence University	$244,832,149	$113,664
St. Mary's College	$140,117,922	$82,277
St. Michael's College	$72,037,946	$34,551
St. Olaf College	$335,689,812	$111,748
Siena College	$139,574,440	$46,003
Southwestern University	$284,272,430	$223,837
Spelman College	$351,705,744	$137,978
Stonehill College	$149,674,677	$64,878
Susquehanna University	$118,609,314	$53,767
Sweet Briar College	$95,439,007	$145,265
Thomas Aquinas College	$12,484,260	$29,237

Table A.3 (continued)

	Endowment	Endowment/FTE undergraduate
Transylvania University	$121,442,000	$104,242
University of Puget Sound	$244,480,000	$100,444
Ursinus College	$124,485,634	$78,988
Wabash College	$366,509,549	$398,380
Washington and Jefferson College	$101,091,273	$66,376
Washington College	$163,204,660	$131,088
Westminster College (PA)	$94,816,893	$62,298
Westmont College	$76,977,698	$59,442
Wheaton College (IL)	$321,929,887	$129,237
Wheaton College (MA)	$186,275,245	$112,012
Willamette University	$283,153,000	$149,896
Wofford College	$162,510,504	$112,386
Total	$12,717,864,173	—
Mean	$184,316,872	$119,342
Median	$140,117,922	$93,146
Tier III		
Albright College	$51,578,260	$24,001
Alma College	$100,994,570	$76,395
American Jewish University	$16,120,031	$161,200
Asbury College	$33,449,230	$25,264
Baker University	$27,634,497	$15,525
Bethany College	$46,807,050	$56,394
Bridgewater College	$64,263,304	$42,362
Carroll College	$28,403,714	$21,518
Carson-Newman College	$42,067,524	$22,496
Cedar Crest College	$18,138,926	$12,256
Centenary College of Louisiana	$118,142,677	$137,856
Clarke College	$24,138,769	$25,707
College of Idaho	$88,849,297	$106,406
College of the Atlantic	$19,480,282	$62,039
Concordia College at Moorhead	$79,641,388	$26,906
Dillard University	$39,835,692	$42,651
Doane College	$86,018,308	$93,498
Eastern Mennonite University	$21,632,206	$21,146
Eckerd College	$30,753,521	$12,228
Emory and Henry College	$84,383,239	$97,779

(continued)

Table A.3   (continued)

	Endowment	Endowment/FTE undergraduate
Fisk University	$13,276,166	$16,679
Georgetown College	$40,742,080	$31,681
Gordon College	$27,787,314	$18,402
Goshen College	$106,263,550	$110,576
Grove City College	not reported	n/a
Guilford College	$73,662,772	$28,277
Hartwick College	$63,672,189	$42,111
Hastings College	$58,225,313	$50,065
Hiram College	$72,618,003	$61,178
Houghton College	$41,727,837	$30,525
Illinois College	$121,011,788	$123,861
Lycoming College	$132,741,908	$89,388
Maryville College	$43,377,903	$33,757
McDaniel College	$82,621,000	$44,206
Meredith College	$82,431,716	$41,971
Merrimack College	$35,373,939	$17,512
Millikin University	$88,738,748	$37,506
Monmouth College	$69,543,797	$53,910
Moravian College and Moravian Theological Seminary	$92,921,470	$50,419
Morehouse College	$128,926,900	$45,477
Mount Union College	$132,812,000	$61,888
Nebraska Wesleyan University	$45,953,864	$23,872
Oglethorpe University	$20,555,912	$22,127
Principia College	$367,252,181	n/a
Randolph College	$155,775,000	$255,788
Ripon College	$55,539,460	$53,301
Roanoke College	$118,611,764	$60,827
Russell Sage College	not reported	n/a
St. Anselm College	$86,906,902	$41,582
St. John's College (MD)	$75,764,845	$156,539
St. Norbert College	$71,100,677	$32,172
St. Vincent College	$66,849,556	$37,201
Salem College	$56,807,530	$70,656
Simpson College	$80,660,171	$42,791
Warren Wilson College	$42,630,075	$48,832
Wartburg College	$50,105,268	$26,680
Wells College	$34,381,456	$61,395

	Endowment	Endowment/FTE undergraduate
Wesleyan College	$54,664,352	$112,943
Westminster College (MO)	$51,079,127	$52,987
Whittier College	$77,108,053	$74,214
William Jewell College	$77,119,000	$64,970
Wisconsin Lutheran College	$24,367,824	$33,704
Wittenberg University	$119,010,536	$55,149
Total	$3,914,367,891	—
Mean	$69,899,427	$56,722
Median	$60,948,751	$42,651
Tier IV		
Albertus Magnus College	$3,314,277	$2,130
Atlantic Union College	$2,203,401	$4,864
Bennett College for Women	$11,381,214	$16,936
Bethel College	$18,680,172	$35,786
Bloomfield College	$8,611,847	$4,640
Brevard College	$22,361,309	$33,325
Brigham Young University–Hawaii	$74,595,000	$28,117
Concordia College	$7,792,199	$10,660
Evangel University	$6,613,116	$4,487
Ferrum College	$42,995,256	$38,769
Franklin Pierce University	$8,188,705	$4,265
Green Mountain College	$2,567,653	$3,503
Greensboro College	$23,728,234	$24,016
Huntingdon College	$47,035,277	$52,730
Huston-Tillotson University	$6,988,586	$11,706
Jarvis Christian College	$11,753,703	$16,079
Johnson C. Smith University	$47,436,278	$31,456
Judson College	$15,247,371	$41,321
Kentucky Wesleyan College	$26,961,003	$30,057
Lambuth University	$10,554,120	$14,379
Lane College	$1,766,517	$937
Lindsey Wilson College	$16,191,436	$11,244
Marlboro College	$35,910,446	$110,494
Marymount Manhattan College	$14,336,485	$8,498
McPherson College	$31,343,253	$53,947
North Greenville University	$15,946,662	$8,165

(continued)

	Endowment	Endowment/FTE undergraduate
Northland College	$18,456,827	$26,905
Olivet College	$12,341,569	$12,697
Paine College	$10,879,798	$12,491
Peace College	$48,628,861	$74,017
Pine Manor College	$10,957,525	$24,350
St. Andrews Presbyterian College	$15,170,952	$21,071
Sierra Nevada College	$3,947,751	$15,301
Simpson University	$3,764,156	$4,653
Stephens College	$26,423,017	$30,267
Sterling College	$11,507,816	$19,276
Talladega College	$4,602,339	$6,565
Texas Lutheran University	$65,670,732	$51,145
Thiel College	$25,741,999	$21,834
Tougaloo College	$8,016,712	$9,670
Virginia Wesleyan College	$52,014,786	$40,384
West Virginia Wesleyan College	$42,097,807	$35,169
Wingate University	$30,195,764	$20,597
Total	$904,921,931	—
Mean	$21,044,696	$23,928
Median	$15,170,952	$19,276

Table A.4 Revenues (2007–2008)

	Total revenues	Tuition and fees revenues	Tuition and fees revenues as percent of total revenues	Total revenues/FTE undergraduate
Tier I				
Amherst College	$270,611,826	$39,234,470	14.5%	$148,688
Bard College	$134,094,968	$45,320,513	33.8%	$62,370
Barnard College	$123,140,991	$54,878,383	44.6%	$54,271
Bates College	$78,186,687	$59,152,608	75.7%	$47,271
Bowdoin College	$130,950,000	$47,772,000	36.5%	$76,758
Bryn Mawr College	$129,956,000	$34,022,000	26.2%	$95,556
Bucknell University	$132,610,000	$92,705,000	69.9%	$37,813
Carleton College	$89,648,816	$48,213,980	53.8%	$45,763
Centre College	$32,180,719	$27,125,461	84.3%	$27,088
Claremont McKenna College	$254,326,000	$25,796,000	10.1%	$224,868
Colby College	$101,845,000	$52,311,000	51.4%	$49,778
Colgate University	$159,479,000	$71,564,000	44.9%	$57,408
College of the Holy Cross	$103,482,571	$68,408,629	66.1%	$34,323
Colorado College	$91,410,977	$50,121,944	54.8%	$42,028
Connecticut College	$87,449,000	$53,844,000	61.6%	$45,404
Davidson College	$107,507,688	$31,680,218	29.5%	$59,331
DePauw University	$72,720,980	$31,670,358	43.6%	$28,619
Dickinson College	$123,480,396	$59,367,552	48.1%	$47,713
Franklin and Marshall College	$88,785,779	$58,918,961	66.4%	$39,531
Furman University	$151,742,047	$53,762,765	35.4%	$57,261

(continued)

203

	Total revenues	Tuition and fees revenues	Tuition and fees revenues as percent of total revenues	Total revenues/FTE undergraduate
Gettysburg College	$102,104,782	$62,787,389	61.5%	$38,028
Grinnell College	−$141,314,000	$24,152,000	−17.1%	−$84,316
Hamilton College	$66,881,000	$49,318,000	73.7%	$37,033
Harvey Mudd College	$50,169,980	$15,165,742	30.2%	$67,615
Haverford College	$51,241,868	$30,902,349	60.3%	$40,127
Kenyon College	$86,248,232	$41,184,770	47.8%	$47,053
Lafayette College	$68,178,655	$52,204,142	76.6%	$27,458
Macalester College	$104,529,000	$35,110,000	33.6%	$52,291
Middlebury College	$144,099,000	$115,489,000	80.1%	$53,291
Mount Holyoke College	$172,932,541	$43,612,060	25.2%	$72,508
Oberlin College	$101,105,116	$59,621,446	59.0%	$37,253
Occidental College	$69,278,757	$41,356,027	59.7%	$37,448
Pitzer College	$39,374,913	$36,581,305	92.9%	$41,623
Pomona College	$152,244,000	$30,714,000	20.2%	$99,053
Rhodes College	$53,345,142	$31,349,030	58.8%	$31,659
Sarah Lawrence College	$68,680,867	$39,687,766	57.8%	$51,524
Scripps College	$41,694,293	$23,454,064	56.3%	$47,326
Sewanee: The University of the South	$89,383,988	$36,271,720	40.6%	$55,726
Skidmore College	$143,224,000	$74,274,000	51.9%	$56,880
Smith College	$203,169,951	$61,076,661	30.1%	$77,104
Swarthmore College	$88,352,000	$34,322,000	38.8%	$60,474

Trinity College	$105,234,493	$58,315,046	55.4%	$45,536
Union College	$116,912,690	$49,187,930	42.1%	$58,398
University of Richmond	$267,278,989	$81,070,224	30.3%	$84,743
Vassar College	$133,671,070	$66,574,321	49.8%	$53,943
Washington and Lee University	$127,626,000	$54,661,000	42.8%	$71,299
Wellesley College	$144,767,000	$48,438,000	33.5%	$57,062
Wesleyan University	$107,832,000	$73,760,000	68.4%	$36,504
Whitman College	$49,953,265	$30,746,355	61.6%	$34,594
Williams College	$97,580,898	$49,024,011	50.2%	$48,046
Mean				$54,382
Median				$48,912
Tier II				
Agnes Scott College	$19,402,177	$9,141,973	47.1%	$20,751
Albion College	$38,129,355	$24,591,761	64.5%	$20,622
Allegheny College	$68,296,520	$36,596,348	53.6%	$32,109
Augustana College	$60,826,452	$41,205,602	67.7%	$24,176
Austin College	$46,168,460	$21,427,640	46.4%	$36,876
Beloit College	$42,067,629	$20,598,448	49.0%	$33,281
Bennington College	$44,645,130	$19,150,973	42.9%	$79,018
Berea College	−$9,439,811	$2,035,067	−21.6%	−$5,922
Berry College	$32,698,874	$19,776,399	60.5%	$19,022
Birmingham Southern College	$37,368,059	$16,907,048	45.2%	$28,525
Calvin College	$136,651,984	$62,052,190	45.4%	$31,414

(continued)

205

	Total revenues	Tuition and fees revenues	Tuition and fees revenues as percent of total revenues	Total revenues/FTE undergraduate
Central College	$41,026,833	$20,075,943	48.9%	$32,254
Coe College	$34,007,704	$14,717,454	43.3%	$24,378
College of St. Benedict	$57,358,770	$32,787,501	57.2%	$27,656
College of Wooster	$75,619,341	$33,606,594	44.4%	$40,223
Cornell College	$35,837,015	$12,336,095	34.4%	$29,351
Denison University	$140,609,098	$42,075,274	29.9%	$67,021
Drew University	$49,455,000	$38,967,000	78.8%	$27,753
Earlham College	$23,008,579	$21,349,872	92.8%	$21,934
Goucher College	$64,305,000	$31,676,000	49.3%	$43,894
Gustavus Adolphus College	$76,644,562	$43,599,289	56.9%	$27,820
Hampden-Sydney College	$39,780,531	$17,035,802	42.8%	$35,455
Hampshire College	$50,619,665	$38,957,693	77.0%	$36,235
Hanover College	$12,486,776	$9,703,953	77.7%	$13,341
Hendrix College	$29,648,402	$10,949,686	36.9%	$24,543
Hobart and William Smith Colleges	$95,980,629	$44,890,566	46.8%	$44,394
Hollins University	$29,143,680	$12,982,175	44.5%	$30,938
Hope College	$112,052,059	$46,765,362	41.7%	$34,842
Illinois Wesleyan University	$49,116,102	$36,687,377	74.7%	$23,512
Juniata College	$49,409,308	$22,048,382	44.6%	$33,703
Kalamazoo College	$32,809,742	$21,889,306	66.7%	$40,061
Knox College	$35,309,393	$22,708,276	64.3%	$25,568

Lake Forest College	$48,246,281	$22,651,470	46.9%	$33,412
Lawrence University	$43,105,035	$33,696,352	78.2%	$29,303
Lewis and Clark College	$106,983,455	$70,751,673	66.1%	$50,799
Linfield College	$51,673,930	$35,217,957	68.2%	$29,835
Luther College	$73,877,074	$40,614,268	55.0%	$27,091
Lyon College	$8,416,346	$3,010,676	35.8%	$18,257
Millsaps College	$25,447,348	$12,140,876	47.7%	$22,640
Muhlenberg College	$78,119,959	$52,339,394	67.0%	$28,490
Ohio Wesleyan University	$68,928,021	$30,303,959	44.0%	$34,637
Presbyterian College	$21,582,111	$12,198,585	56.5%	$18,075
Randolph College	$35,390,570	$17,758,490	50.2%	$29,690
Reed College	$51,774,135	$32,895,783	63.5%	$39,522
St. John's College (NM)	$20,879,093	$12,268,997	58.8%	$41,509
St. John's University	$64,694,516	$31,544,702	48.8%	$33,801
St. Lawrence University	$79,363,808	$46,657,120	58.8%	$36,845
St. Mary's College	$54,181,854	$27,185,054	50.2%	$31,816
St. Michael's College	$69,292,188	$49,265,379	71.1%	$33,234
St. Olaf College	$123,731,917	$57,651,302	46.6%	$41,189
Siena College	$80,251,781	$43,409,247	54.1%	$26,451
Southwestern University	$18,823,855	$20,247,454	107.6%	$14,822
Spelman College	$105,923,249	$28,593,348	27.0%	$41,555
Stonehill College	$63,851,379	$45,146,694	70.7%	$27,677
Susquehanna University	$54,004,559	$35,837,233	66.4%	$24,481
Sweet Briar College	$30,271,172	$13,304,581	44.0%	$46,075
Thomas Aquinas College	$15,809,406	$7,093,367	44.9%	$37,024
Transylvania University	$9,490,963	$13,465,288	141.9%	$8,147

(continued)

	Total revenues	Tuition and fees revenues	Tuition and fees revenues as percent of total revenues	Total revenues/FTE undergraduate
University of Puget Sound	$102,247,000	$58,255,000	57.0%	$42,008
Ursinus College	$41,444,302	$29,835,245	72.0%	$26,297
Wabash College	–$7,368,869	$11,164,266	–151.5%	–$8,010
Washington and Jefferson College	$45,973,450	$26,829,172	58.4%	$30,186
Washington College	$50,957,361	$27,102,241	53.2%	$40,930
Westminster College (PA)	$29,259,789	$17,360,559	59.3%	$19,225
Westmont College	$57,274,553	$28,882,672	50.4%	$44,227
Wheaton College (IL)	$70,143,562	$47,961,205	68.4%	$28,159
Wheaton College (MA)	$74,964,144	$40,627,169	54.2%	$45,078
Willamette University	$78,183,000	$44,304,000	56.7%	$41,389
Wofford College	$44,766,714	$20,508,166	45.8%	$30,959
Mean				$31,182
Median				$30,938
Tier III				
Albright College	$48,401,601	$30,645,182	63.3%	$22,523
Alma College	$22,499,340	$13,938,813	62.0%	$17,019
American Jewish University	$27,315,503	$3,598,374	13.2%	$273,155
Asbury College	$28,507,517	$17,154,008	60.2%	$21,531
Baker University	$35,163,846	$29,152,305	82.9%	$19,755

Bethany College	$26,851,949	$6,820,288	25.4%	$32,352
Bridgewater College	$32,123,614	$17,016,571	53.0%	$21,176
Carroll College	$38,035,730	$24,733,755	65.0%	$28,815
Carson-Newman College	$37,487,412	$19,504,270	52.0%	$20,047
Cedar Crest College	$28,409,497	$20,865,818	73.4%	$19,196
Centenary College of Louisiana	$32,018,951	$8,064,573	25.2%	$37,362
Clarke College	$31,545,583	$13,874,208	44.0%	$33,595
College of Idaho	$48,077,262	$6,536,841	13.6%	$57,578
College of the Atlantic	$17,345,940	$9,057,263	52.2%	$55,242
Concordia College at Moorhead	$83,139,178	$40,300,952	48.5%	$28,088
Dillard University	$60,222,734	$12,940,317	21.5%	$64,478
Doane College	$14,664,816	$7,536,535	51.4%	$15,940
Eastern Mennonite University	$26,154,815	$17,287,021	66.1%	$25,567
Eckerd College	$69,096,158	$45,567,152	65.9%	$27,474
Emory and Henry College	$27,361,673	$10,065,434	36.8%	$31,705
Fisk University	$29,137,942	$7,682,517	26.4%	$36,605
Georgetown College	$31,754,830	$17,348,775	54.6%	$24,693
Gordon College	$50,047,915	$28,074,846	56.1%	$33,144
Goshen College	$8,663,791	$12,413,383	143.3%	$9,015
Grove City College	not reported	not reported	n/a	n/a
Guilford College	$47,632,714	$27,729,489	58.2%	$18,285
Hartwick College	$52,907,680	$27,903,789	52.7%	$34,992
Hastings College	$15,165,584	$10,005,931	66.0%	$13,040

(continued)

Table A.4 (continued)

	Total revenues	Tuition and fees revenues	Tuition and fees revenues as percent of total revenues	Total revenues/FTE undergraduate
Hiram College	$25,385,314	$16,054,309	63.2%	$21,386
Houghton College	$35,879,548	$19,337,513	53.9%	$26,247
Illinois College	$18,726,849	$10,050,237	53.7%	$19,168
Lycoming College	$31,805,915	$21,277,492	66.9%	$21,418
Maryville College	$42,588,634	$14,007,352	32.9%	$33,143
McDaniel College	$52,123,000	$33,942,000	65.1%	$27,888
Meredith College	$46,878,203	$34,002,415	72.5%	$23,869
Merrimack College	$52,346,406	$33,406,556	63.8%	$25,914
Millikin University	$44,360,309	$30,279,605	68.3%	$18,749
Monmouth College	$32,404,537	$14,753,263	45.5%	$25,120
Moravian College and Moravian Theological Seminary	$51,798,383	$31,078,499	60.0%	$28,105
Morehouse College	$79,682,400	$33,658,900	42.2%	$28,107
Mount Union College	$38,754,000	$25,883,913	66.8%	$18,059
Nebraska Wesleyan University	$31,113,000	$22,385,000	71.9%	$16,163
Oglethorpe University	$19,521,088	$10,032,879	51.4%	$21,013
Principia College	$4,055,141	$3,556,317	87.7%	n/a
Randolph College	$29,322,476	$6,736,883	23.0%	$48,149
Ripon College	$19,228,267	$10,726,796	55.8%	$18,453
Roanoke College	$53,512,120	$28,986,363	54.2%	$27,442

Russell Sage College	not reported	not reported	n/a	n/a
St. Anselm College	$55,469,885	$38,418,662	69.3%	$26,541
St. John's College (MD)	$32,704,041	$12,786,342	39.1%	$67,570
St. Norbert College	$54,957,223	$31,568,704	57.4%	$24,868
St. Vincent College	$58,065,025	$23,891,485	41.1%	$32,312
Salem College	$14,568,035	$6,308,205	43.3%	$18,119
Simpson College	$35,782,493	$20,508,725	57.3%	$18,983
Warren Wilson College	$32,413,170	$13,706,917	42.3%	$37,128
Wartburg College	$49,065,356	$22,747,126	46.4%	$26,126
Wells College	$19,685,808	$4,819,738	24.5%	$35,153
Wesleyan College	$20,452,000	$4,049,756	19.8%	$42,256
Westminster College (MO)	$19,507,492	$5,864,743	30.1%	$20,236
Whittier College	$57,855,626	$38,879,469	67.2%	$55,684
William Jewell College	$28,402,955	$13,623,144	48.0%	$23,928
Wisconsin Lutheran College	$22,226,450	$7,024,203	31.6%	$30,742
Wittenberg University	$53,743,839	$30,731,169	57.2%	$24,904
Mean				$32,724
Median				$26,126
Tier IV				
Albertus Magnus College	$25,735,916	$20,180,805	78.4%	$16,540
Atlantic Union College	$12,807,964	$5,246,118	41.0%	$28,274
Bennett College for Women	$16,343,083	$5,964,198	36.5%	$24,320
Bethel College	$10,751,558	$5,701,100	53.0%	$20,597
Bloomfield College	$33,633,014	$25,651,826	76.3%	$18,121
Brevard College	$19,053,927	$8,109,750	42.6%	$28,396

(continued)

Table A.4 (continued)

	Total revenues	Tuition and fees revenues	Tuition and fees revenues as percent of total revenues	Total revenues/FTE undergraduate
Brigham Young University–Hawaii	$100,958,000	$6,069,000	6.0%	$38,054
Concordia College	$18,396,127	$10,211,194	55.5%	$25,166
Evangel University	$27,644,256	$17,447,078	63.1%	$18,755
Ferrum College	$23,443,184	$14,702,630	62.7%	$21,139
Franklin Pierce University	$50,094,936	$35,503,237	70.9%	$26,091
Green Mountain College	$18,860,106	$11,798,032	62.6%	$25,730
Greensboro College	$21,679,461	$11,313,374	52.2%	$21,943
Huntingdon College	$14,504,054	$6,996,622	48.2%	$16,260
Huston-Tillotson University	$14,363,495	$5,521,988	38.4%	$24,059
Jarvis Christian College	$11,478,419	$4,121,944	35.9%	$15,702
Johnson C. Smith University	$34,862,333	$20,035,154	57.5%	$23,118
Judson College	$6,122,479	$1,598,417	26.1%	$16,592
Kentucky Wesleyan College	$9,261,188	$3,805,057	41.1%	$10,325
Lambuth University	$12,938,758	$4,023,633	31.1%	$17,628
Lane College	$25,996,346	$7,969,738	30.7%	$13,784
Lindsey Wilson College	$22,697,869	$13,618,095	60.0%	$15,762
Marlboro College	$12,308,849	$6,665,817	54.2%	$37,873
Marymount Manhattan College	$42,474,004	$29,977,326	70.6%	$25,177
McPherson College	$11,778,992	$4,177,808	35.5%	$20,274
North Greenville University	$28,585,562	$11,714,688	41.0%	$14,637

Northland College	$14,910,562	$7,644,356	51.3%	$21,736
Olivet College	$17,712,945	$10,164,438	57.4%	$18,223
Paine College	$17,654,009	$7,898,607	44.7%	$20,269
Peace College	$15,073,392	$8,906,686	59.1%	$22,943
Pine Manor College	$14,698,412	$3,860,925	26.3%	$32,663
St. Andrews Presbyterian College	$17,729,548	$5,993,092	33.8%	$24,624
Sierra Nevada College	$10,690,005	$6,220,659	58.2%	$41,434
Simpson University	$17,008,426	$10,522,510	61.9%	$21,024
Stephens College	$16,878,939	$9,159,827	54.3%	$19,334
Sterling College	$14,141,952	$8,388,208	59.3%	$23,688
Talladega College	$11,698,030	$2,145,370	18.3%	$16,688
Texas Lutheran University	$31,775,408	$14,727,515	46.3%	$24,747
Thiel College	$25,586,369	$13,367,893	52.2%	$21,702
Tougaloo College	$22,473,942	$5,088,165	22.6%	$27,110
Virginia Wesleyan College	$30,326,806	$19,382,760	63.9%	$23,546
West Virginia Wesleyan College	$23,361,835	$10,801,389	46.2%	$19,517
Wingate University	$37,578,582	$19,684,574	52.4%	$25,633
Mean				$22,539
Median				$21,736

Table A.5 Expenses covered by tuition and fees revenues (2007–2008)

	Total expenses	Tuition and fees revenues	Tuition and fees revenues as percent of total expenses
Tier I			
Amherst College	$130,918,257	$39,234,470	30.0%
Bard College	$115,288,609	$45,320,513	39.3%
Barnard College	$109,008,798	$54,878,383	50.3%
Bates College	$83,394,783	$59,152,608	70.9%
Bowdoin College	$117,198,000	$47,772,000	40.8%
Bryn Mawr College	$96,507,000	$34,022,000	35.3%
Bucknell University	$166,761,000	$92,705,000	55.6%
Carleton College	$102,857,333	$48,213,980	46.9%
Centre College	$46,595,614	$27,125,461	58.2%
Claremont McKenna College	$72,383,000	$25,796,000	35.6%
Colby College	$98,369,000	$52,311,000	53.2%
Colgate University	$146,206,000	$71,564,000	48.9%
College of the Holy Cross	$133,464,239	$68,408,629	51.3%
Colorado College	$104,666,896	$50,121,944	47.9%
Connecticut College	$90,098,000	$53,844,000	59.8%
Davidson College	$91,721,726	$31,680,218	34.5%
DePauw University	$93,333,653	$31,670,358	33.9%
Dickinson College	$102,150,206	$59,367,552	58.1%
Franklin and Marshall College	$96,086,995	$58,918,961	61.3%
Furman University	$117,095,989	$53,762,765	45.9%
Gettysburg College	$104,602,432	$62,787,389	60.0%

Grinnell College	$90,111,000	$24,152,000	26.8%
Hamilton College	$107,606,000	$49,318,000	45.8%
Harvey Mudd College	$45,965,656	$15,165,742	33.0%
Haverford College	$77,997,901	$30,902,349	39.6%
Kenyon College	$82,499,636	$41,184,770	49.9%
Lafayette College	$123,434,285	$52,204,142	42.3%
Macalester College	$83,124,000	$35,110,000	42.2%
Middlebury College	$212,686,000	$115,489,000	54.3%
Mount Holyoke College	$116,126,195	$43,612,060	37.6%
Oberlin College	$142,442,614	$59,621,446	41.9%
Occidental College	$86,472,812	$41,356,027	47.8%
Pitzer College	$41,407,737	$36,581,305	88.3%
Pomona College	$117,795,000	$30,714,000	26.1%
Rhodes College	$59,573,707	$31,349,030	52.6%
Sarah Lawrence College	$68,143,873	$39,687,766	58.2%
Scripps College	$45,747,031	$23,454,064	51.3%
Sewanee: The University of the South	$75,749,062	$36,271,720	47.9%
Skidmore College	$127,472,000	$74,274,000	58.3%
Smith College	$189,267,093	$61,076,661	32.3%
Swarthmore College	$118,204,000	$34,322,000	29.0%
Trinity College	$129,384,562	$58,315,046	45.1%
Union College	$101,738,002	$49,187,930	48.3%
University of Richmond	$186,128,173	$81,070,224	43.6%
Vassar College	$155,662,273	$66,574,321	42.8%
Washington and Lee University	$117,201,000	$54,661,000	46.6%

(continued)

	Total expenses	Tuition and fees revenues	Tuition and fees revenues as percent of total expenses
Wellesley College	$188,332,000	$48,438,000	25.7%
Wesleyan University	$177,849,000	$73,760,000	41.5%
Whitman College	$57,566,463	$30,746,355	53.4%
Williams College	$181,192,585	$49,024,011	27.1%
Mean	$110,511,744	$49,125,604	44.5%
Median	$104,666,896	$49,024,011	46.8%
Tier II			
Agnes Scott College	$46,001,335	$9,141,973	19.9%
Albion College	$51,869,186	$24,591,761	47.4%
Allegheny College	$63,532,193	$36,596,348	57.6%
Augustana College	$66,426,258	$41,205,602	62.0%
Austin College	$42,417,260	$21,427,640	50.5%
Beloit College	$45,267,227	$20,598,448	45.5%
Bennington College	$28,527,005	$19,150,973	67.1%
Berea College	$67,964,732	$2,035,067	3.0%
Berry College	$61,085,372	$19,776,399	32.4%
Birmingham Southern College	$56,909,025	$16,907,048	29.7%
Calvin College	$115,707,673	$62,052,190	53.6%
Central College	$42,565,655	$20,075,943	47.2%

Coe College	$32,784,536	44.9%
College of St. Benedict	$55,737,568	58.8%
College of Wooster	$76,070,428	44.2%
Cornell College	$31,332,314	39.4%
Denison University	$98,145,736	42.9%
Drew University	$81,378,000	47.9%
Earlham College	$47,620,179	44.8%
Goucher College	$58,515,000	54.1%
Gustavus Adolphus College	$72,279,421	60.3%
Hampden-Sydney College	$44,412,498	38.4%
Hampshire College	$48,926,858	79.6%
Hanover College	$31,379,013	30.9%
Hendrix College	$40,989,538	26.7%
Hobart and William Smith Colleges	$78,032,865	57.5%
Hollins University	$32,481,584	40.0%
Hope College	$94,648,917	49.4%
Illinois Wesleyan University	$75,546,665	48.6%
Juniata College	$45,271,242	48.7%
Kalamazoo College	$43,069,996	50.8%
Knox College	$41,747,786	54.4%
Lake Forest College	$43,748,720	51.8%
Lawrence University	$54,794,035	61.5%
Lewis and Clark College	$103,026,393	68.7%
Linfield College	$54,114,903	65.1%
Luther College	$63,247,936	64.2%

(continued)

217

	Total expenses	Tuition and fees revenues	Tuition and fees revenues as percent of total expenses
Lyon College	$17,219,269	$3,010,676	17.5%
Millsaps College	$35,689,686	$12,140,876	34.0%
Muhlenberg College	$75,626,593	$52,339,394	69.2%
Ohio Wesleyan University	$60,031,180	$30,303,959	50.5%
Presbyterian College	$32,409,981	$12,198,585	37.6%
Randolph College	$39,189,980	$17,758,490	45.3%
Reed College	$69,553,401	$32,895,783	47.3%
St. John's College (NM)	$20,981,802	$12,268,997	58.5%
St. John's University	$64,421,742	$31,544,702	49.0%
St. Lawrence University	$106,976,435	$46,657,120	43.6%
St. Mary's College	$55,310,656	$27,185,054	49.1%
St. Michael's College	$69,627,188	$49,265,379	70.8%
St. Olaf College	$100,821,310	$57,651,302	57.2%
Siena College	$76,778,319	$43,409,247	56.5%
Southwestern University	$53,644,745	$20,247,454	37.7%
Spelman College	$77,190,850	$28,593,348	37.0%
Stonehill College	$72,209,311	$45,146,694	62.5%
Susquehanna University	$59,148,843	$35,837,233	60.6%
Sweet Briar College	$40,292,492	$13,304,581	33.0%
Thomas Aquinas College	$14,806,733	$7,093,367	47.9%
Transylvania University	$31,527,757	$13,465,288	42.7%
University of Puget Sound	$94,397,000	$58,255,000	61.7%

Ursinus College	$52,654,440	56.7%
Wabash College	$48,641,478	23.0%
Washington and Jefferson College	$43,953,110	61.0%
Washington College	$49,954,332	54.3%
Westminster College (PA)	$35,840,087	48.4%
Westmont College	$49,798,311	58.0%
Wheaton College (IL)	$101,280,139	47.4%
Wheaton College (MA)	$71,252,250	57.0%
Willamette University	$81,675,000	54.2%
Wofford College	$44,870,683	45.7%
Mean	$57,758,698	50.1%
Median	$54,114,903	50.2%

Tier III

Albright College	$46,491,275	65.9%
Alma College	$33,931,443	41.1%
American Jewish University	$27,896,334	12.9%
Asbury College	$24,918,434	68.8%
Baker University	$39,854,588	73.1%
Bethany College	$29,249,914	23.3%
Bridgewater College	$31,940,753	53.3%
Carroll College	$39,090,519	63.3%
Carson-Newman College	$37,347,849	52.2%
Cedar Crest College	$31,636,314	66.0%
Centenary College of Louisiana	$30,924,609	26.1%

(continued)

Table A.5   (continued)

	Total expenses	Tuition and fees revenues	Tuition and fees revenues as percent of total expenses
Clarke College	$20,404,194	$13,874,208	68.0%
College of Idaho	$21,371,775	$6,536,841	30.6%
College of the Atlantic	$17,421,738	$9,057,263	52.0%
Concordia College at Moorhead	$83,336,363	$40,300,952	48.4%
Dillard University	$49,911,574	$12,940,317	25.9%
Doane College	$23,739,208	$7,536,535	31.7%
Eastern Mennonite University	$28,708,548	$17,287,021	60.2%
Eckerd College	$64,533,369	$45,567,152	70.6%
Emory and Henry College	$24,450,639	$10,065,434	41.2%
Fisk University	$26,856,838	$7,682,517	28.6%
Georgetown College	$37,674,084	$17,348,775	46.0%
Gordon College	$51,950,741	$28,074,846	54.0%
Goshen College	$30,029,708	$12,413,383	41.3%
Grove City College	not reported	not reported	n/a
Guilford College	$50,024,779	$27,729,489	55.4%
Hartwick College	$46,149,136	$27,903,789	60.5%
Hastings College	$22,965,026	$10,005,931	43.6%
Hiram College	$32,977,497	$16,054,309	48.7%
Houghton College	$35,536,672	$19,337,513	54.4%
Illinois College	$24,819,013	$10,050,237	40.5%
Lycoming College	$32,560,381	$21,277,492	65.3%

Maryville College	$28,385,028	$14,007,352	49.3%
McDaniel College	$57,990,000	$33,942,000	58.5%
Meredith College	$54,122,497	$34,002,415	62.8%
Merrimack College	$54,057,156	$33,406,556	61.8%
Millikin University	$48,126,975	$30,279,605	62.9%
Monmouth College	$27,595,858	$14,753,263	53.5%
Moravian College and Moravian Theological Seminary	$48,294,867	$31,078,499	64.4%
Morehouse College	$85,678,300	$33,658,900	39.3%
Mount Union College	$44,263,843	$25,883,913	58.5%
Nebraska Wesleyan University	$32,964,000	$22,385,000	67.9%
Oglethorpe University	$21,461,339	$10,032,879	46.7%
Principia College	$36,129,886	$3,556,317	9.8%
Randolph College	$27,274,674	$6,736,883	24.7%
Ripon College	$24,697,671	$10,726,796	43.4%
Roanoke College	$52,431,322	$28,986,363	55.3%
Russell Sage College	not reported	not reported	n/a
St. Anselm College	$62,849,204	$38,418,662	61.1%
St. John's College (MD)	$27,048,048	$12,786,342	47.3%
St. Norbert College	$50,282,509	$31,568,704	62.8%
St. Vincent College	$45,967,819	$23,891,485	52.0%
Salem College	$22,537,974	$6,308,205	28.0%
Simpson College	$34,746,478	$20,508,725	59.0%
Warren Wilson College	$27,625,679	$13,706,917	49.6%
Wartburg College	$46,845,523	$22,747,126	48.6%

(continued)

Table A.5 (continued)

	Total expenses	Tuition and fees revenues	Tuition and fees revenues as percent of total expenses
Wells College	$27,238,265	$4,819,738	17.7%
Wesleyan College	$15,813,979	$4,049,756	25.6%
Westminster College (MO)	$20,618,641	$5,864,743	28.4%
Whittier College	$57,727,958	$38,879,469	67.3%
William Jewell College	$36,185,483	$13,623,144	37.6%
Wisconsin Lutheran College	$26,070,924	$7,024,203	26.9%
Wittenberg University	$58,190,972	$30,731,169	52.8%
Mean	$37,555,932	$19,013,935	50.6%
Median	$32,970,749	$17,220,515	52.2%
Tier IV			
Albertus Magnus College	$24,228,622	$20,180,805	83.3%
Atlantic Union College	$12,999,410	$5,246,118	40.4%
Bennett College for Women	$18,331,710	$5,964,198	32.5%
Bethel College	$12,621,864	$5,701,100	45.2%
Bloomfield College	$33,329,673	$25,651,826	77.0%
Brevard College	$20,651,103	$8,109,750	39.3%
Brigham Young University– Hawaii	$76,255,000	$6,069,000	8.0%
Concordia College	$16,818,875	$10,211,194	60.7%
Evangel University	$29,440,121	$17,447,078	59.3%

Ferrum College	$25,415,545	$14,702,630	57.8%
Franklin Pierce University	$49,845,665	$35,503,237	71.2%
Green Mountain College	$17,997,700	$11,798,032	65.6%
Greensboro College	$20,967,104	$11,313,374	54.0%
Huntingdon College	$17,149,742	$6,996,622	40.8%
Huston-Tillotson University	$14,376,516	$5,521,988	38.4%
Jarvis Christian College	$12,971,342	$4,121,944	31.8%
Johnson C. Smith University	$38,395,086	$20,035,154	52.2%
Judson College	$8,253,047	$1,598,417	19.4%
Kentucky Wesleyan College	$14,538,574	$3,805,057	26.2%
Lambuth University	$15,111,476	$4,023,633	26.6%
Lane College	$25,023,032	$7,969,738	31.8%
Lindsey Wilson College	$23,045,579	$13,618,095	59.1%
Marlboro College	$12,919,700	$6,665,817	51.6%
Marymount Manhattan College	$41,276,955	$29,977,326	72.6%
McPherson College	$12,552,160	$4,177,808	33.3%
North Greenville University	$23,741,112	$11,714,688	49.3%
Northland College	$18,024,074	$7,644,356	42.4%
Olivet College	$17,050,287	$10,164,438	59.6%
Paine College	$19,340,958	$7,898,607	40.8%
Peace College	$18,594,725	$8,906,686	47.9%
Pine Manor College	$16,590,534	$3,860,925	23.3%
St. Andrews Presbyterian College	$17,727,389	$5,993,092	33.8%
Sierra Nevada College	$15,039,147	$6,220,659	41.4%

(continued)

Table A.5 *(continued)*

	Total expenses	Tuition and fees revenues	Tuition and fees revenues as percent of total expenses
Simpson University	$17,187,637	$10,522,510	61.2%
Stephens College	$19,646,983	$9,159,827	46.6%
Sterling College	$11,283,635	$8,388,208	74.3%
Talladega College	$10,859,736	$2,145,370	19.8%
Texas Lutheran University	$28,574,998	$14,727,515	51.5%
Thiel College	$27,190,965	$13,367,893	49.2%
Tougaloo College	$22,039,203	$5,088,165	23.1%
Virginia Wesleyan College	$33,091,912	$19,382,760	58.6%
West Virginia Wesleyan College	$24,622,571	$10,801,389	43.9%
Wingate University	$34,755,853	$19,684,574	56.6%
Mean	$22,555,287	$10,746,084	47.6%
Median	$18,594,725	$8,388,208	45.1%

Table A.6 Discounts (2007–2008)

	List price (tuition and required fees)	Tuition and fees revenues/FTE undergraduate	Average discount
Tier I			
Amherst College	$36,232	$21,557	40.5%
Bard College	$36,534	$21,079	42.3%
Barnard College	$35,190	$24,186	31.3%
Bates College	not reported	$35,763	n/a
Bowdoin College	$36,370	$28,002	23.0%
Bryn Mawr College	$34,650	$25,016	27.8%
Bucknell University	$38,134	$26,434	30.7%
Carleton College	$36,156	$24,612	31.9%
Centre College	$28,000	$22,833	18.5%
Claremont McKenna College	$35,190	$22,808	35.2%
Colby College	not reported	$25,567	n/a
Colgate University	$37,660	$25,761	31.6%
College of the Holy Cross	$35,142	$22,689	35.4%
Colorado College	$33,972	$23,045	32.2%
Connecticut College	not reported	$27,956	n/a
Davidson College	$31,794	$17,484	45.0%
DePauw University	$29,700	$12,464	58.0%
Dickinson College	$35,784	$22,940	35.9%
Franklin and Marshall College	$36,480	$26,233	28.1%
Furman University	$31,560	$20,288	35.7%
Gettysburg College	$35,770	$23,385	34.6%

(continued)

Table A.6 (continued)

	List price (tuition and required fees)	Tuition and fees revenues/FTE undergraduate	Average discount
Grinnell College	$33,910	$14,411	57.5%
Hamilton College	$36,860	$27,308	25.9%
Harvey Mudd College	$34,891	$20,439	41.4%
Haverford College	$35,390	$24,199	31.6%
Kenyon College	$38,140	$22,469	41.1%
Lafayette College	$33,811	$21,025	37.8%
Macalester College	$33,694	$17,564	47.9%
Middlebury College	not reported	$42,710	n/a
Mount Holyoke College	$35,940	$18,286	49.1%
Oberlin College	$36,282	$21,968	39.5%
Occidental College	$35,373	$22,355	36.8%
Pitzer College	$35,912	$38,669	−7.7%
Pomona College	$33,932	$19,983	41.1%
Rhodes College	$30,652	$18,605	39.3%
Sarah Lawrence College	$38,090	$29,773	21.8%
Scripps College	$35,850	$26,622	25.7%
Sewanee: The University of the South	$30,660	$22,613	26.2%
Skidmore College	$36,860	$29,497	20.0%
Smith College	$34,186	$23,179	32.2%
Swarthmore College	$34,884	$23,492	32.7%
Trinity College	$36,870	$25,234	31.6%
Union College	not reported	$24,569	n/a

University of Richmond	$37,610	$25,704	31.7%
Vassar College	$38,115	$26,866	29.5%
Washington and Lee University	$35,445	$30,537	13.8%
Wellesley College	$34,994	$19,093	45.4%
Wesleyan University	$36,806	$24,970	32.2%
Whitman College	$32,980	$21,292	35.4%
Williams College	$35,670	$24,138	32.3%
Mean	$35,069	$24,153	33.5%
Median	$35,418	$23,492	32.5%
Tier II			
Agnes Scott College	$27,387	$9,778	64.3%
Albion College	$27,530	$13,300	51.7%
Allegheny College	$30,000	$17,206	42.6%
Augustana College	$26,484	$16,377	38.2%
Austin College	$24,920	$17,115	31.3%
Beloit College	$29,908	$16,296	45.5%
Bennington College	$36,800	$33,896	7.9%
Berea College	$790	$1,277	−61.6%
Berry College	$20,570	$11,505	44.1%
Birmingham Southern College	$24,300	$12,906	46.9%
Calvin College	$21,685	$14,265	34.2%
Central College	$22,510	$15,783	29.9%
Coe College	$26,390	$10,550	60.0%
College of St. Benedict	$26,570	$15,809	40.5%
College of Wooster	$31,870	$17,876	43.9%

(continued)

227

Table A.6 (continued)

	List price (tuition and required fees)	Tuition and fees revenues/FTE undergraduate	Average discount
Cornell College	$26,280	$10,103	61.6%
Denison University	$33,010	$20,055	39.2%
Drew University	$34,790	$21,867	37.1%
Earlham College	$31,514	$20,353	35.4%
Goucher College	$31,082	$21,622	30.4%
Gustavus Adolphus College	$28,515	$15,826	44.5%
Hampden-Sydney College	$27,732	$15,183	45.2%
Hampshire College	$36,545	$27,887	23.7%
Hanover College	$24,220	$10,367	57.2%
Hendrix College	$24,498	$9,064	63.0%
Hobart and William Smith Colleges	$36,718	$20,763	43.5%
Hollins University	$25,645	$13,782	46.3%
Hope College	$23,800	$14,541	38.9%
Illinois Wesleyan University	$30,750	$17,562	42.9%
Juniata College	$28,920	$15,040	48.0%
Kalamazoo College	$28,716	$26,727	6.9%
Knox College	$29,178	$16,443	43.6%
Lake Forest College	$30,964	$15,687	49.3%
Lawrence University	$31,080	$22,907	26.3%
Lewis and Clark College	$31,840	$33,595	−5.5%
Linfield College	$25,644	$20,334	20.7%
Luther College	$28,840	$14,893	48.4%

Lyon College	$15,960	$6,531	59.1%
Millsaps College	$23,352	$10,801	53.7%
Muhlenberg College	$33,090	$19,088	42.3%
Ohio Wesleyan University	$31,930	$15,228	52.3%
Presbyterian College	$26,320	$10,217	61.2%
Randolph College	$26,830	$14,898	n/a
Reed College	$36,420	$25,111	31.1%
St. John's College (NM)	$36,596	$24,392	33.3%
St. John's University	$26,570	$16,481	38.0%
St. Lawrence University	$35,600	$21,661	39.2%
St. Mary's College	$26,875	$15,963	40.6%
St. Michael's College	$29,945	$23,628	21.1%
St. Olaf College	$30,600	$19,192	37.3%
Siena College	$22,685	$14,308	36.9%
Southwestern University	$25,740	$15,943	38.1%
Spelman College	$18,615	$11,217	39.7%
Stonehill College	$28,440	$19,569	31.2%
Susquehanna University	$28,320	$16,245	42.6%
Sweet Briar College	$25,015	$20,251	19.0%
Thomas Aquinas College	$20,400	$16,612	18.6%
Transylvania University	$22,300	$11,558	48.2%
University of Puget Sound	$31,895	$23,934	25.0%
Ursinus College	$35,160	$18,931	46.2%
Wabash College	$26,350	$12,135	53.9%
Washington and Jefferson College	$29,532	$17,616	40.3%
Washington College	$32,160	$21,769	32.3%

(continued)

Table A.6 (continued)

	List price (tuition and required fees)	Tuition and fees revenues/FTE undergraduate	Average discount
Westminster College (PA)	$25,530	$11,406	55.3%
Westmont College	$31,212	$22,303	28.5%
Wheaton College (IL)	$23,730	$19,254	18.9%
Wheaton College (MA)	$36,690	$24,430	33.4%
Willamette University	$31,968	$23,454	26.6%
Wofford College	$27,830	$14,183	49.0%
Mean	$27,995	$17,201	37.6%
Median	$28,320	$16,377	40.0%
Tier III			
Albright College	$28,884	$14,260	50.6%
Alma College	$23,688	$10,544	55.5%
American Jewish University	$21,300	$35,984	−68.9%
Asbury College	$21,286	$12,956	39.1%
Baker University	$18,830	$16,378	13.0%
Bethany College	$18,203	$8,217	54.9%
Bridgewater College	$21,490	$11,217	47.8%
Carroll College	$19,620	$18,738	4.5%
Carson-Newman College	$16,980	$10,430	38.6%
Cedar Crest College	$25,340	$14,099	44.4%
Centenary College of Louisiana	$20,950	$9,410	55.1%

Clarke College	$21,312	$14,776	30.7%
College of Idaho	$17,680	$7,829	55.7%
College of the Atlantic	$29,970	$28,845	3.8%
Concordia College at Moorhead	$22,350	$13,615	39.1%
Dillard University	$12,240	$13,855	−13.2%
Doane College	$19,150	$8,192	57.2%
Eastern Mennonite University	$21,960	$16,898	23.0%
Eckerd College	$29,160	$18,118	37.9%
Emory and Henry College	$22,320	$11,663	47.7%
Fisk University	$15,620	$9,651	38.2%
Georgetown College	$22,360	$13,490	n/a
Gordon College	$25,748	$18,593	27.8%
Goshen College	$21,300	$12,917	39.4%
Grove City College	$11,500	not reported	n/a
Guilford College	$24,470	$10,645	56.5%
Hartwick College	$31,035	$18,455	40.5%
Hastings College	$19,604	$8,604	56.1%
Hiram College	$24,885	$13,525	45.6%
Houghton College	$21,620	$14,146	34.6%
Illinois College	$18,800	$10,287	45.3%
Lycoming College	$26,749	$14,328	46.4%
Maryville College	$25,350	$10,901	57.0%
McDaniel College	$28,940	$18,161	37.2%
Meredith College	$22,400	$17,313	22.7%
Merrimack College	$27,040	$16,538	38.8%
Millikin University	$23,945	$12,798	46.6%

(continued)

	List price (tuition and required fees)	Tuition and fees revenues/FTE undergraduate	Average discount
Monmouth College	$22,000	$11,437	48.0%
Moravian College and Moravian Theological Seminary	$28,388	$16,863	40.6%
Morehouse College	$18,678	$11,873	36.4%
Mount Union College	$22,050	$12,061	45.3%
Nebraska Wesleyan University	$20,252	$11,629	42.6%
Oglethorpe University	$24,442	$10,800	55.8%
Principia College	$22,080	not reported	n/a
Randolph College	$25,860	$11,062	57.2%
Ripon College	$23,323	$10,294	55.9%
Roanoke College	$26,250	$14,865	43.4%
Russell Sage College	$25,790	$0	100.0%
St. Anselm College	$27,690	$18,382	33.6%
St. John's College (MD)	$36,596	$26,418	27.8%
St. Norbert College	$24,653	$14,284	42.1%
St. Vincent College	$24,106	$13,295	44.8%
Salem College	$19,190	$7,846	59.1%
Simpson College	$23,596	$10,880	53.9%
Warren Wilson College	$21,384	$15,701	26.6%
Wartburg College	$24,300	$12,112	50.2%
Wells College	$17,810	$8,607	51.7%
Wesleyan College	$16,500	$8,367	49.3%

Westminster College (MO)	$15,946	$6,084	61.8%
Whittier College	$30,160	$37,420	−24.1%
William Jewell College	$21,400	$11,477	46.4%
Wisconsin Lutheran College	$19,564	$9,715	50.3%
Wittenberg University	$31,400	$14,241	54.6%
Mean	$22,742	$13,628	40.2%
Median	$22,335	$12,937	44.4%
Tier IV			
Albertus Magnus College	$21,114	$12,970	38.6%
Atlantic Union College	$16,080	$11,581	28.0%
Bennett College for Women	$14,648	$8,875	39.4%
Bethel College	$17,800	$10,922	38.6%
Bloomfield College	$18,000	$13,821	23.2%
Brevard College	$18,750	$12,086	35.5%
Brigham Young University–Hawaii	$3,250	$2,288	29.6%
Concordia College	$22,450	$13,969	37.8%
Evangel University	$13,915	$11,837	14.9%
Ferrum College	$20,840	$13,258	36.4%
Franklin Pierce University	$26,516	$18,491	30.3%
Green Mountain College	$24,565	$16,096	34.5%
Greensboro College	$20,810	$11,451	45.0%
Huntingdon College	$18,270	$7,844	57.1%
Huston-Tillotson University	$10,040	$9,250	7.9%
Jarvis Christian College	$8,208	$5,639	31.3%
Johnson C. Smith University	$15,754	$13,286	15.7%

(continued)

Table A.6 (continued)

	List price (tuition and required fees)	Tuition and fees revenues/FTE undergraduate	Average discount
Judson College	$11,120	$4,332	61.0%
Kentucky Wesleyan College	$14,550	$4,242	70.8%
Lambuth University	$17,400	$5,482	68.5%
Lane College	$7,620	$4,226	44.5%
Lindsey Wilson College	$15,806	$9,457	40.2%
Marlboro College	$30,680	$20,510	33.1%
Marymount Manhattan College	$20,600	$17,770	13.7%
McPherson College	$16,400	$7,191	56.2%
North Greenville University	$11,180	$5,998	46.3%
Northland College	$21,901	$11,143	49.1%
Olivet College	$18,684	$10,457	44.0%
Paine College	$10,694	$9,068	15.2%
Peace College	$21,628	$13,557	37.3%
Pine Manor College	$17,750	$8,580	51.7%
St. Andrews Presbyterian College	$18,192	$8,324	54.2%
Sierra Nevada College	$22,005	$24,111	−9.6%
Simpson University	$18,600	$13,007	30.1%
Stephens College	$21,730	$10,492	51.7%
Sterling College	$15,500	$14,051	9.4%
Talladega College	$7,128	$3,060	57.1%
Texas Lutheran University	$20,060	$11,470	42.8%
Thiel College	$20,024	$11,338	43.4%

Tougaloo College	$9,710	$6,138	36.8%
Virginia Wesleyan College	$24,515	$15,049	38.6%
West Virginia Wesleyan College	$21,830	$9,024	58.7%
Wingate University	$18,480	$13,427	27.3%
Mean	$17,321	$10,818	37.6%
Median	$18,192	$11,143	38.6%

Table A.7 Expenses per full-time equivalent undergraduate (2007–2008)

	Total expenses per FTE	Salaries, wages, and benefits per FTE	Salaries, wages, and benefits per FTE/total expenses per FTE
Tier I			
Amherst College	$71,933	$31,024	43.1%
Bard College	$53,623	$17,825	33.2%
Barnard College	$48,043	$24,130	50.2%
Bates College	$50,420	$24,032	47.7%
Bowdoin College	$68,698	$30,443	44.3%
Bryn Mawr College	$70,961	$30,236	42.6%
Bucknell University	$47,551	$20,367	42.8%
Carleton College	$52,505	$23,062	43.9%
Centre College	$39,222	$14,093	35.9%
Claremont McKenna College	$63,999	n/a	n/a
Colby College	$48,079	$20,132	41.9%
Colgate University	$52,630	$21,855	41.5%
College of the Holy Cross	$44,267	$18,559	41.9%
Colorado College	$48,123	$20,690	43.0%
Connecticut College	$46,780	$21,933	46.9%
Davidson College	$50,619	$24,028	47.5%
DePauw University	$36,731	$15,253	41.5%
Dickinson College	$39,471	$17,025	43.1%
Franklin and Marshall College	$42,781	$17,224	40.3%
Furman University	$44,187	$18,345	41.5%
Gettysburg College	$38,958	$15,004	38.5%

Grinnell College	$53,766	41.6%
Hamilton College	$59,583	39.0%
Harvey Mudd College	$61,948	45.4%
Haverford College	$61,079	41.7%
Kenyon College	$45,008	40.5%
Lafayette College	$49,712	38.1%
Macalester College	$41,583	46.3%
Middlebury College	$78,656	46.2%
Mount Holyoke College	$48,690	47.1%
Oberlin College	$52,484	45.8%
Occidental College	$46,742	45.7%
Pitzer College	$43,771	41.0%
Pomona College	$76,640	40.5%
Rhodes College	$35,355	41.8%
Sarah Lawrence College	$51,121	44.7%
Scripps College	$51,926	36.9%
Sewanee: The University of the South	$47,225	40.7%
Skidmore College	$50,624	42.0%
Smith College	$71,828	44.7%
Swarthmore College	$80,906	42.6%
Trinity College	$55,986	34.4%
Union College	$50,818	42.0%
University of Richmond	$59,013	43.5%
Vassar College	$62,818	46.1%
Washington and Lee University	$65,475	44.8%
Wellesley College	$74,234	47.1%

(continued)

Table A.7 *(continued)*

	Total expenses per FTE	Salaries, wages, and benefits per FTE	Salaries, wages, and benefits per FTE/total expenses per FTE
Wesleyan University	$60,206	$25,611	42.5%
Whitman College	$39,866	$18,032	45.2%
Williams College	$89,213	$35,669	40.0%
Mean	$54,517	$23,206	42.6%
Median	$51,121	$22,161	42.6%
Tier II			
Agnes Scott College	$49,199	$17,553	35.7%
Albion College	$28,053	$11,512	41.0%
Allegheny College	$29,869	$11,666	39.1%
Augustana College	$26,402	$12,313	46.6%
Austin College	$33,880	$13,271	39.2%
Beloit College	$35,813	$16,335	45.6%
Bennington College	$50,490	$24,337	48.2%
Berea College	$42,638	$18,057	42.3%
Berry College	$35,535	$12,606	35.5%
Birmingham Southern College	$43,442	$13,205	30.4%
Calvin College	$26,599	$10,716	40.3%
Central College	$33,464	$12,564	37.5%
Coe College	$23,501	$10,153	43.2%
College of St. Benedict	$26,874	$12,568	46.8%
College of Wooster	$40,463	$16,727	41.3%

238

Cornell College	$25,661	43.7%
Denison University	$46,781	37.6%
Drew University	$45,667	43.2%
Earlham College	$45,396	38.4%
Goucher College	$39,942	42.6%
Gustavus Adolphus College	$26,236	44.0%
Hampden-Sydney College	$39,583	40.2%
Hampshire College	$35,023	44.0%
Hanover College	$33,525	41.7%
Hendrix College	$33,932	38.4%
Hobart and William Smith Colleges	$36,093	39.7%
Hollins University	$34,482	40.2%
Hope College	$29,431	41.0%
Illinois Wesleyan University	$36,164	42.4%
Juniata College	$30,881	40.2%
Kalamazoo College	$52,589	41.0%
Knox College	$30,230	41.5%
Lake Forest College	$30,297	46.0%
Lawrence University	$37,250	44.6%
Lewis and Clark College	$48,920	43.6%
Linfield College	$31,244	42.7%
Luther College	$23,193	43.6%
Lyon College	$37,352	39.5%
Millsaps College	$31,752	42.3%
Muhlenberg College	$27,581	37.7%
Ohio Wesleyan University	$30,166	39.8%
Presbyterian College	$27,144	44.3%

(continued)

Table A.7 (continued)

	Total expenses per FTE	Salaries, wages, and benefits per FTE	Salaries, wages, and benefits per FTE/total expenses per FTE
Randolph College	$32,878	$14,536	n/a
Reed College	$53,094	$21,693	40.9%
St. John's College (NM)	$41,713	$21,491	51.5%
St. John's University	$33,658	$14,669	43.6%
St. Lawrence University	$49,664	$19,518	39.3%
St. Mary's College	$32,478	$13,631	42.0%
St. Michael's College	$33,394	$13,896	41.6%
St. Olaf College	$33,562	$14,200	42.3%
Siena College	$25,306	$11,126	44.0%
Southwestern University	$42,240	$19,404	45.9%
Spelman College	$30,283	$13,301	43.9%
Stonehill College	$31,300	$13,218	42.2%
Susquehanna University	$26,813	$9,730	36.3%
Sweet Briar College	$61,328	$24,326	39.7%
Thomas Aquinas College	$34,676	$12,555	36.2%
Transylvania University	$27,062	$12,611	46.6%
University of Puget Sound	$38,783	$17,996	46.4%
Ursinus College	$33,410	$13,122	39.3%
Wabash College	$52,871	$17,671	33.4%
Washington and Jefferson College	$28,860	$10,404	36.1%
Washington College	$40,124	$13,865	34.6%
Westminster College (PA)	$23,548	$9,887	42.0%
Westmont College	$38,454	$15,997	41.6%

Wheaton College (IL)	$40,658	$17,690	43.5%
Wheaton College (MA)	$42,846	$19,482	45.5%
Willamette University	$43,237	$18,168	42.0%
Wofford College	$31,031	$13,238	42.7%
Mean	$35,884	$14,840	41.5%
Median	$33,880	$13,865	41.8%
Tier III			
Albright College	$21,634	$9,296	43.0%
Alma College	$25,667	$9,505	37.0%
American Jewish University	$278,963	$95,758	34.3%
Asbury College	$18,821	$9,073	48.2%
Baker University	$22,390	$10,021	44.8%
Bethany College	$35,241	$10,178	28.9%
Bridgewater College	$21,055	$9,285	44.1%
Carroll College	$29,614	$8,635	29.2%
Carson-Newman College	$19,972	$8,378	41.9%
Cedar Crest College	$21,376	$11,365	53.2%
Centenary College of Louisiana	$36,085	$14,199	39.3%
Clarke College	$21,730	$9,663	44.5%
College of Idaho	$25,595	$10,268	40.1%
College of the Atlantic	$55,483	$15,061	27.1%
Concordia College at Moorhead	$28,154	$12,625	44.8%
Dillard University	$53,439	$12,179	22.8%
Doane College	$25,803	$11,880	46.0%
Eastern Mennonite University	$28,063	$13,995	49.9%

(continued)

Table A.7 *(continued)*

	Total expenses per FTE	Salaries, wages, and benefits per FTE	Salaries, wages, and benefits per FTE/total expenses per FTE
Eckerd College	$25,659	$8,878	34.6%
Emory and Henry College	$28,332	$11,046	39.0%
Fisk University	$33,740	$13,509	40.0%
Georgetown College	$29,296	$11,393	38.9%
Gordon College	$34,404	$13,394	38.9%
Goshen College	$31,248	$12,093	38.7%
Grove City College	not reported	not reported	n/a
Guilford College	$19,203	$6,482	33.8%
Hartwick College	$30,522	$11,528	37.8%
Hastings College	$19,746	$8,436	42.7%
Hiram College	$27,782	$10,618	38.2%
Houghton College	$25,996	$10,742	41.3%
Illinois College	$25,403	$10,171	40.0%
Lycoming College	$21,926	$9,024	41.2%
Maryville College	$22,090	$10,409	47.1%
McDaniel College	$31,027	$12,757	41.1%
Meredith College	$27,557	$11,581	42.0%
Merrimack College	$26,761	$10,625	39.7%
Millikin University	$20,341	$8,162	40.1%
Monmouth College	$21,392	$8,782	41.1%
Moravian College and Moravian Theological Seminary	$26,204	$11,637	44.4%

Morehouse College	$30,222	$10,796	35.7%
Mount Union College	$20,626	$8,437	40.9%
Nebraska Wesleyan University	$17,124	$8,173	47.7%
Oglethorpe University	$23,102	$10,214	44.2%
Principia College	not reported	not reported	n/a
Randolph College	$44,786	$18,544	41.4%
Ripon College	$23,702	$7,995	33.7%
Roanoke College	$26,888	$11,825	44.0%
Russell Sage College	not reported	not reported	n/a
St. Anselm College	$30,071	$12,807	42.6%
St. John's College (MD)	$55,884	$22,621	40.5%
St. Norbert College	$22,752	$11,175	49.1%
St. Vincent College	$25,580	$9,330	36.5%
Salem College	$28,032	$12,207	43.5%
Simpson College	$18,433	$7,831	42.5%
Warren Wilson College	$31,645	$10,332	32.6%
Wartburg College	$24,944	$9,814	39.3%
Wells College	$48,640	$15,447	31.8%
Wesleyan College	$32,674	$14,275	43.7%
Westminster College (MO)	$21,389	$8,310	38.9%
Whittier College	$55,561	$24,435	44.0%
William Jewell College	$30,485	$11,827	38.8%
Wisconsin Lutheran College	$36,059	$11,644	32.3%
Wittenberg University	$26,965	$11,032	40.9%
Mean	$32,888	$12,695	40.1%
Median	$26,824	$10,769	40.7%

(continued)

Table A.7 *(continued)*

	Total expenses per FTE	Salaries, wages, and benefits per FTE	Salaries, wages, and benefits per FTE/total expenses per FTE
Tier IV			
Albertus Magnus College	$15,571	$6,406	41.1%
Atlantic Union College	$28,696	$11,315	39.4%
Bennett College for Women	$27,279	$10,517	38.6%
Bethel College	$24,180	$10,338	42.8%
Bloomfield College	$17,958	$8,521	47.4%
Brevard College	$30,777	$11,185	36.3%
Brigham Young University–Hawaii	$28,743	$12,221	42.5%
Concordia College	$23,008	$8,662	37.6%
Evangel University	$19,973	$6,577	32.9%
Ferrum College	$22,918	$10,645	46.4%
Franklin Pierce University	$25,961	$10,142	39.1%
Green Mountain College	$24,553	$8,546	34.8%
Greensboro College	$21,222	$9,617	45.3%
Huntingdon College	$19,226	$7,323	38.1%
Huston-Tillotson University	$24,081	$8,657	35.9%
Jarvis Christian College	$17,745	$6,585	37.1%
Johnson C. Smith University	$25,461	$10,007	39.3%
Judson College	$22,366	$9,403	42.0%
Kentucky Wesleyan College	$16,208	$5,221	32.2%
Lambuth University	$20,588	$7,862	38.2%
Lane College	$13,268	$4,965	37.4%

Lindsey Wilson College	$16,004	44.0%
Marlboro College	$39,753	46.5%
Marymount Manhattan College	$24,468	41.0%
McPherson College	$21,604	39.1%
North Greenville University	$12,156	49.4%
Northland College	$26,274	40.1%
Olivet College	$17,541	39.8%
Paine College	$22,205	36.6%
Peace College	$28,302	42.5%
Pine Manor College	$36,868	44.4%
St. Andrews Presbyterian College	$24,621	37.0%
Sierra Nevada College	$58,291	47.8%
Simpson University	$21,246	42.8%
Stephens College	$22,505	40.3%
Sterling College	$18,901	38.6%
Talladega College	$15,492	46.2%
Texas Lutheran University	$22,255	37.6%
Thiel College	$23,063	35.9%
Tougaloo College	$26,585	41.2%
Virginia Wesleyan College	$25,692	43.4%
West Virginia Wesleyan College	$20,570	42.0%
Wingate University	$23,708	43.1%
Mean	$23,672	40.6%
Median	$22,918	40.1%

Table A.8 Total expenses and revenues (2007–2008)

	Total expenses	Total revenues	Total expenses as percent of total revenues
Tier I			
Amherst College	$130,918,257	$270,611,826	48.4%
Bard College	$115,288,609	$134,094,968	86.0%
Barnard College	$109,008,798	$123,140,991	88.5%
Bates College	$83,394,783	$78,186,687	106.7%
Bowdoin College	$117,198,000	$130,950,000	89.5%
Bryn Mawr College	$96,507,000	$129,956,000	74.3%
Bucknell University	$166,761,000	$132,610,000	125.8%
Carleton College	$102,857,333	$89,648,816	114.7%
Centre College	$46,595,614	$32,180,719	144.8%
Claremont McKenna College	$72,383,000	$254,326,000	28.5%
Colby College	$98,369,000	$101,845,000	96.6%
Colgate University	$146,206,000	$159,479,000	91.7%
College of the Holy Cross	$133,464,239	$103,482,571	129.0%
Colorado College	$104,666,896	$91,410,977	114.5%
Connecticut College	$90,098,000	$87,449,000	103.0%
Davidson College	$91,721,726	$107,507,688	85.3%
DePauw University	$93,333,653	$72,720,980	128.3%
Dickinson College	$102,150,206	$123,480,396	82.7%
Franklin and Marshall College	$96,086,995	$88,785,779	108.2%
Furman University	$117,095,989	$151,742,047	77.2%
Gettysburg College	$104,602,432	$102,104,782	102.4%

Grinnell College	$90,111,000	−$141,314,000	−63.8%
Hamilton College	$107,606,000	$66,881,000	160.9%
Harvey Mudd College	$45,965,656	$50,169,980	91.6%
Haverford College	$77,997,901	$51,241,868	152.2%
Kenyon College	$82,499,636	$86,248,232	95.7%
Lafayette College	$123,434,285	$68,178,655	181.0%
Macalester College	$83,124,000	$104,529,000	79.5%
Middlebury College	$212,686,000	$144,099,000	147.6%
Mount Holyoke College	$116,126,195	$172,932,541	67.2%
Oberlin College	$142,442,614	$101,105,116	140.9%
Occidental College	$86,472,812	$69,278,757	124.8%
Pitzer College	$41,407,737	$39,374,913	105.2%
Pomona College	$117,795,000	$152,244,000	77.4%
Rhodes College	$59,573,707	$53,345,142	111.7%
Sarah Lawrence College	$68,143,873	$68,680,867	99.2%
Scripps College	$45,747,031	$41,694,293	109.7%
Sewanee: The University of the South	$75,749,062	$89,383,988	84.7%
Skidmore College	$127,472,000	$143,224,000	89.0%
Smith College	$189,267,093	$203,169,951	93.2%
Swarthmore College	$118,204,000	$88,352,000	133.8%
Trinity College	$129,384,562	$105,234,493	122.9%
Union College	$101,738,002	$116,912,690	87.0%
University of Richmond	$186,128,173	$267,278,989	69.6%
Vassar College	$155,662,273	$133,671,070	116.5%
Washington and Lee University	$117,201,000	$127,626,000	91.8%
Wellesley College	$188,332,000	$144,767,000	130.1%

(continued)

Table A.8 (continued)

	Total expenses	Total r venues	Total expenses as percent of total revenues
Wesleyan University	$177,849,000	$107,832,000	164.9%
Whitman College	$57,566,463	$49,953,265	115.2%
Williams College	$181,192,585	$97,580,898	185.7%
Mean	$110,511,744	$107,387,799	102.9%
Median	$104,666,896	$103,482,571	101.1%
Tier II			
Agnes Scott College	$46,001,335	$19,402,177	237.1%
Albion College	$51,869,186	$38,129,355	136.0%
Allegheny College	$63,532,193	$68,296,520	93.0%
Augustana College	$66,426,258	$60,826,452	109.2%
Austin College	$42,417,260	$46,168,460	91.9%
Beloit College	$45,267,227	$42,067,629	107.6%
Bennington College	$28,527,005	$44,645,130	63.9%
Berea College	$67,964,732	−$9,439,811	−720.0%
Berry College	$61,085,372	$32,698,874	186.8%
Birmingham Southern College	$56,909,025	$37,368,059	152.3%
Calvin College	$115,707,673	$136,651,984	84.7%
Central College	$42,565,655	$41,026,833	103.8%
Coe College	$32,784,536	$34,007,704	96.4%
College of St. Benedict	$55,737,568	$57,358,770	97.2%

College of Wooster	$76,070,428	$75,619,341	100.6%
Cornell College	$31,332,314	$35,837,015	87.4%
Denison University	$98,145,736	$140,609,098	69.8%
Drew University	$81,378,000	$49,455,000	164.5%
Earlham College	$47,620,179	$23,008,579	207.0%
Goucher College	$58,515,000	$64,305,000	91.0%
Gustavus Adolphus College	$72,279,421	$76,644,562	94.3%
Hampden-Sydney College	$44,412,498	$39,780,531	111.6%
Hampshire College	$48,926,858	$50,619,665	96.7%
Hanover College	$31,379,013	$12,486,776	251.3%
Hendrix College	$40,989,538	$29,648,402	138.3%
Hobart and William Smith Colleges	$78,032,865	$95,980,629	81.3%
Hollins University	$32,481,584	$29,143,680	111.5%
Hope College	$94,648,917	$112,052,059	84.5%
Illinois Wesleyan University	$75,546,665	$49,116,102	153.8%
Juniata College	$45,271,242	$49,409,308	91.6%
Kalamazoo College	$43,069,996	$32,809,742	131.3%
Knox College	$41,747,786	$35,309,393	118.2%
Lake Forest College	$43,748,720	$48,246,281	90.7%
Lawrence University	$54,794,035	$43,105,035	127.1%
Lewis and Clark College	$103,026,393	$106,983,455	96.3%
Linfield College	$54,114,903	$51,673,930	104.7%
Luther College	$63,247,936	$73,877,074	85.6%
Lyon College	$17,219,269	$8,416,346	204.6%
Millsaps College	$35,689,686	$25,447,348	140.2%
Muhlenberg College	$75,626,593	$78,119,959	96.8%

(continued)

Table A.8 (continued)

	Total expenses	Total revenues	Total expenses as percent of total revenues
Ohio Wesleyan University	$60,031,180	$68,928,021	87.1%
Presbyterian College	$32,409,981	$21,582,111	150.2%
Randolph College	$39,189,980	$35,390,570	110.7%
Reed College	$69,553,401	$51,774,135	134.3%
St. John's College (NM)	$20,981,802	$20,879,093	100.5%
St. John's University	$64,421,742	$64,694,516	99.6%
St. Lawrence University	$106,976,435	$79,363,808	134.8%
St. Mary's College	$55,310,656	$54,181,854	102.1%
St. Michael's College	$69,627,188	$69,292,188	100.5%
St. Olaf College	$100,821,310	$123,731,917	81.5%
Siena College	$76,778,319	$80,251,781	95.7%
Southwestern University	$53,644,745	$18,823,855	285.0%
Spelman College	$77,190,850	$105,923,249	72.9%
Stonehill College	$72,209,311	$63,851,379	113.1%
Susquehanna University	$59,148,843	$54,004,559	109.5%
Sweet Briar College	$40,292,492	$30,271,172	133.1%
Thomas Aquinas College	$14,806,733	$15,809,406	93.7%
Transylvania University	$31,527,757	$9,490,963	332.2%
University of Puget Sound	$94,397,000	$102,247,000	92.3%
Ursinus College	$52,654,440	$41,444,302	127.0%
Wabash College	$48,641,478	−$7,368,869	−660.1%

Washington and Jefferson College	$43,953,110	$45,973,450	95.6%
Washington College	$49,954,332	$50,957,361	98.0%
Westminster College (PA)	$35,840,087	$29,259,789	122.5%
Westmont College	$49,798,311	$57,274,553	86.9%
Wheaton College (IL)	$101,280,139	$70,143,562	144.4%
Wheaton College (MA)	$71,252,250	$74,964,144	95.0%
Willamette University	$81,675,000	$78,183,000	104.5%
Wofford College	$44,870,683	$44,766,714	100.2%
Mean	$57,758,698	$52,797,131	109.4%
Median	$54,114,903	$49,116,102	110.2%

Tier III

Albright College	$46,491,275	$48,401,601	96.1%
Alma College	$33,931,443	$22,499,340	150.8%
American Jewish University	$27,896,334	$27,315,503	102.1%
Asbury College	$24,918,434	$28,507,517	87.4%
Baker University	$39,854,588	$35,163,846	113.3%
Bethany College	$29,249,914	$26,851,949	108.9%
Bridgewater College	$31,940,753	$32,123,614	99.4%
Carroll College	$39,090,519	$38,035,730	102.8%
Carson-Newman College	$37,347,849	$37,487,412	99.6%
Cedar Crest College	$31,636,314	$28,409,497	111.4%
Centenary College of Louisiana	$30,924,609	$32,018,951	96.6%
Clarke College	$20,404,194	$31,545,583	64.7%
College of Idaho	$21,371,775	$48,077,262	44.5%

(continued)

Table A.8 *(continued)*

	Total expenses	Total revenues	Total expenses as percent of total revenues
College of the Atlantic	$17,421,738	$17,345,940	100.4%
Concordia College at Moorhead	$83,336,363	$83,139,178	100.2%
Dillard University	$49,911,574	$60,222,734	82.9%
Doane College	$23,739,208	$14,664,816	161.9%
Eastern Mennonite University	$28,708,548	$26,154,815	109.8%
Eckerd College	$64,533,369	$69,096,158	93.4%
Emory and Henry College	$24,450,639	$27,361,673	89.4%
Fisk University	$26,856,838	$29,137,942	92.2%
Georgetown College	$37,674,084	$31,754,830	n/a
Gordon College	$51,950,741	$50,047,915	103.8%
Goshen College	$30,029,708	$8,663,791	346.6%
Grove City College	not reported	not reported	n/a
Guilford College	$50,024,779	$47,632,714	105.0%
Hartwick College	$46,149,136	$52,907,680	87.2%
Hastings College	$22,965,026	$15,165,584	151.4%
Hiram College	$32,977,497	$25,385,314	129.9%
Houghton College	$35,536,672	$35,879,548	99.0%
Illinois College	$24,819,013	$18,726,849	132.5%
Lycoming College	$32,560,381	$31,805,915	102.4%
Maryville College	$28,385,028	$42,588,634	66.6%
McDaniel College	$57,990,000	$52,123,000	111.3%
Meredith College	$54,122,497	$46,878,203	115.5%

Merrimack College	$54,057,156	103.3%
Millikin University	$48,126,975	108.5%
Monmouth College	$27,595,858	85.2%
Moravian College and Moravian Theological Seminary	$48,294,867	93.2%
Morehouse College	$85,678,300	107.5%
Mount Union College	$44,263,843	114.2%
Nebraska Wesleyan University	$32,964,000	105.9%
Oglethorpe University	$21,461,339	n/a
Principia College	$36,129,886	891.0%
Randolph College	$27,274,674	93.0%
Ripon College	$24,697,671	128.4%
Roanoke College	$52,431,322	98.0%
Russell Sage College	not reported	n/a
St. Anselm College	$62,849,204	113.3%
St. John's College (MD)	$27,048,048	82.7%
St. Norbert College	$50,282,509	91.5%
St. Vincent College	$45,967,819	79.2%
Salem College	$22,537,974	154.7%
Simpson College	$34,746,478	97.1%
Warren Wilson College	$27,625,679	85.2%
Wartburg College	$46,845,523	95.5%
Wells College	$27,238,265	138.4%
Wesleyan College	$15,813,979	77.3%
Westminster College (MO)	$20,618,641	105.7%
Whittier College	$57,727,958	99.8%
William Jewell College	$36,185,483	127.4%

(continued)

	Total expenses	Total revenues	Total expenses as percent of total revenues
Wisconsin Lutheran College	$26,070,924	$22,226,450	117.3%
Wittenberg University	$58,190,972	$53,743,839	108.3%
Mean	$37,736,495	$36,624,894	103.0%
Median	$32,977,497	$32,404,537	101.8%
Tier IV			
Albertus Magnus College	$24,228,622	$25,735,916	94.1%
Atlantic Union College	$12,999,410	$12,807,964	101.5%
Bennett College for Women	$18,331,710	$16,343,083	112.2%
Bethel College	$12,621,864	$10,751,558	117.4%
Bloomfield College	$33,329,673	$33,633,014	99.1%
Brevard College	$20,651,103	$19,053,927	108.4%
Brigham Young University–Hawaii	$76,255,000	$100,958,000	75.5%
Concordia College	$16,818,875	$18,396,127	91.4%
Evangel University	$29,440,121	$27,644,256	106.5%
Ferrum College	$25,415,545	$23,443,184	108.4%
Franklin Pierce University	$49,845,665	$50,094,936	99.5%
Green Mountain College	$17,997,700	$18,860,106	95.4%
Greensboro College	$20,967,104	$21,679,461	96.7%
Huntingdon College	$17,149,742	$14,504,054	118.2%
Huston-Tillotson University	$14,376,516	$14,363,495	100.1%

Jarvis Christian College	$12,971,342	$11,478,419	113.0%
Johnson C. Smith University	$38,395,086	$34,862,333	110.1%
Judson College	$8,253,047	$6,122,479	134.8%
Kentucky Wesleyan College	$14,538,574	$9,261,188	157.0%
Lambuth University	$15,111,476	$12,938,758	116.8%
Lane College	$25,023,032	$25,996,346	96.3%
Lindsey Wilson College	$23,045,579	$22,697,869	101.5%
Marlboro College	$12,919,700	$12,308,849	105.0%
Marymount Manhattan College	$41,276,955	$42,474,004	97.2%
McPherson College	$12,552,160	$11,778,992	106.6%
North Greenville University	$23,741,112	$28,585,562	83.1%
Northland College	$18,024,074	$14,910,562	120.9%
Olivet College	$17,050,287	$17,712,945	96.3%
Paine College	$19,340,958	$17,654,009	109.6%
Peace College	$18,594,725	$15,073,392	123.4%
Pine Manor College	$16,590,534	$14,698,412	112.9%
St. Andrews Presbyterian College	$17,727,389	$17,729,548	100.0%
Sierra Nevada College	$15,039,147	$10,690,005	140.7%
Simpson University	$17,187,637	$17,008,426	101.1%
Stephens College	$19,646,983	$16,878,939	116.4%
Sterling College	$11,283,635	$14,141,952	79.8%
Talladega College	$10,859,736	$11,698,030	92.8%
Texas Lutheran University	$28,574,998	$31,775,408	89.9%
Thiel College	$27,190,965	$25,586,369	106.3%
Tougaloo College	$22,039,203	$22,473,942	98.1%

(continued)

255

Table A.8 *(continued)*

	Total expenses	Total revenues	Total expenses as percent of total revenues
Virginia Wesleyan College	$33,091,912	$30,326,806	109.1%
West Virginia Wesleyan College	$24,622,571	$23,361,835	105.4%
Wingate University	$34,755,853	$37,578,582	92.5%
Mean	$22,555,287	$22,466,815	100.4%
Median	$18,594,725	$17,729,548	104.9%

Notes

Introduction

1. National Center for Education Statistics (NCES), *Digest of Education Statistics 2008,* www.nces.ed.gov.

2. Ibid.

1. Liberal Arts Colleges and Why We Should Care about Them

1. *Webster's Third New International Dictionary of the English Language* (Springfield, Mass.: G. & C. Merriam Company, 1963).

2. John Henry Newman, *The Idea of a University* (New Haven: Yale University Press, 1996), 89.

3. The *Oxford English Dictionary* is on the same page as *Webster's,* distinguishing liberal education from "servile" education, and calling liberal education "a pastime practiced for pleasure not for profit."

4. On "definition by negation" see, e.g., Jane E. Aaron, *The Compact Reader* (Boston: Bedford/St. Martin's, 1999), 254.

5. The trivium comprises the study of grammar, rhetoric, and logic; the quadrivium, arithmetic, geometry, astronomy, and music.

6. If there are any lingering doubts about the unacceptably obscure nature of the adjective *liberal,* Shakespeare's reference to "liberal shepherds" in *Hamlet,* and to a "liberal villain" in *Much Ado about Nothing,* should resolve them.

7. Even though "general education" acquired a somewhat technical meaning in the 1920s and 1930s, when it was debated in the academy as a pedagogical alternative to "specialized education."

8. Carnegie Foundation, *A Classification of Institutions of Higher Education* (Princeton: Carnegie Foundation for the Advancement of Teaching, 1994), vii.

9. Ibid., xx. Finer subclassifications are provided by the National Center

for Education Statistics using Classification of Instructional Programs (CIP) codes. More than ninety academic majors are classified by CIP codes as arts and sciences.

10. Ibid., xx–xxi. The word *professional* is used by the Carnegie Foundation to describe these fields of study, even though most of them have nothing to do with what is ordinarily understood to be the professions, i.e., medicine, law, and the ministry. More descriptive terms are *vocational* and *career-oriented*. Vocational is used here.

11. Actually, the Liberal Arts Colleges I definition stated that more than half of the degrees offered were in "liberal arts and sciences" fields, whereas the group II definition referred only to "liberal arts" fields. This was apparently an error. The footnote listing the included fields used the same descriptor for both groups of colleges. Generally, and in this book, the term *liberal arts* includes both arts and sciences.

12. The error described above, in note 11, was caught and eliminated.

13. In its original 1970 definitions, Carnegie had called the occupational and technical disciplines "occupational/pre-professional."

14. "The Carnegie Classification of Institutions of Higher Education," http://classifications.carnegiefoundation.org/ (accessed 6/21/10).

15. Absalom Peters, *Colleges Religious Institutions: A Discourse Delivered in the Park Presbyterian Church, Newark, N.J., Oct. 29, 1851 before the Society for the Promotion of Collegiate and Theological Education at the West* (New York: John F. Trow, 1851), 13, Cornell University Library Digital Collections, www.library.cornell.edu (accessed 10/23/09).

16. Frederick Rudolph, *The American College and University* (Athens: University of Georgia Press, 1990), 48, 49.

17. Associated Press, "Universities Seek Better Ways to Teach Large Classes," *Wisconsin State Journal,* November 26, 2007, A8.

18. *Wisconsin State Journal,* "Course Cuts Hurt Quality, UW Fears," August 19, 2007, A1. Course offerings at the University of Wisconsin–Madison in 2007 represented a substantial decline from 1975 (239 majors and 16,467 courses). Ibid.

19. Hugh Hawkins, "The Making of the Liberal Arts College Identity," in Steven Koblik and Stephen R. Graubard, eds., *Distinctively American* (New Brunswick, N.J.: Transactions Publishers, 2000), 23.

20. Pew Charitable Trusts, *Policy Perspectives* 5, no. 4 (January 1995): 2A.

21. David L. Kirp, "This Little Student Went to Market," in Richard H. Hersh and John Merrow, eds., *Declining by Degrees: Higher Education at Risk* (New York: Palgrave Macmillan, 2005), 123.

22. *New York Times,* "State Colleges Also Face Cuts in Ambitions," March 17,

2009, 18. (Citations to the *New York Times* in this book are to the National Edition.) Wellman is executive director of the Delta Project on Postsecondary Costs, Productivity, and Accountability.

23. David W. Breneman, *Liberal Arts Colleges: Thriving, Surviving, or Endangered?* (Washington, D.C.: Brookings Institution, 1994).

24. Michael S. McPherson and Morton Owen Schapiro, "The Future Economic Challenges for the Liberal Arts Colleges," in Steven Koblik and Stephen R. Graubard, eds., *Distinctively American* (New Brunswick, N.J.: Transactions Publishers, 2000), 49–50.

25. "The Carnegie Classification of Institutions of Higher Education."

26. See Appendix, Table A.1. Four of the 130 Annapolis Group members are classified by *U.S. News and World Report* as "Masters Universities" rather than liberal arts colleges.

27. There is, for example, no good reason to believe the college ranked thirty-fifth is any better than the college ranked thirty-sixth. Indeed, the very notion of a "better" college is suspect. Had *U.S. News* called its list the "economically strongest" or "most popular" colleges, it would have obviated a lot of carping from the academy.

28. See Appendix, Table A.1. Thirteen additional private colleges are listed by *U.S. News and World Report* but not ranked, for a variety of reasons, including the fact that they do not use SAT or ACT scores in making admissions decisions. One of them, Sarah Lawrence College—ranked in Tier I for many years and then excluded from the rankings after a dispute with *U.S. News*—is included in Tier I in the analysis here. The remaining twelve are not included.

29. John Henry Newman, *The Idea of a University* (New Haven: Yale University Press, 1996), 77.

30. Lord Henry Peter Brougham, address to the House of Commons, 1828, quoted in Angela Partington, ed., *Oxford Dictionary of Quotations,* 4th ed. (Oxford: Oxford University Press, 1992), 144.

31. Martha C. Nussbaum, *Cultivating Humanity* (Cambridge, Mass.: Harvard University Press, 1997), ch. 3.

32. Elia Kazan, unpublished speech, delivered at Williams College on the occasion of the fiftieth reunion of the class of 1930, June 14, 1980, 1. See also Elia Kazan, "Pursuit of the 'Usey-Less,'" *Williams Alumni Review,* November 1964, 4.

33. Marilynne Robinson, "A Great Amnesia," *Harper's Magazine,* May 2008, 20–21.

34. Warren Goldstein, "What Would Plato Do? A (Semi-)Careerist Defense of the Liberal Arts," *Yale Alumni Magazine,* July/August 2005, www.yalealumnimagazine.com (accessed 2/15/10).

35. Franklin was provost from 1749 to 1754. At that time the university was known as the Academy of Philadelphia.

36. H. W. Brands, *The First American* (New York: Doubleday, 2000), 194–195.

37. Edward H. Levi, *Points of View* (Chicago: University of Chicago Press, 1970), 169.

38. Jaraslav Pelikan, *The Idea of the University* (New Haven: Yale University Press, 1992), 92.

39. *Presidents:* William Harrison (Hampden-Sydney College), Pierce (Bowdoin College), Buchanan (Dickinson College), Hayes (Kenyon College), Garfield (Hiram College, Williams College), Arthur (Union College), McKinley (Allegheny College), Harding (Ohio Central College), Coolidge (Amherst College), Nixon (Whittier College), Reagan (Eureka College), and Obama (Occidental College). *Chief Justices:* Roger Brooke Taney (Dickinson College), Melville Weston Fuller (Bowdoin College), Edward Douglas White (Mount St. Mary's College), Charles Evans Hughes (Colgate University), Harlan Fiske Stone (Amherst College), and Fred M. Vinson (Centre College).

40. See www.sefora.org (accessed 2/15/10).

41. Including former United Nations secretary-general Kofi A. Annan, a graduate of Macalester College; see www.nobelprize.org (accessed 10/23/09).

42. See www.macfound.org (accessed 2/15/10).

43. See www.law.harvard.edu (accessed 2/15/10).

44. See www.president.harvard.edu (accessed 2/15/10); www.umich.edu (accessed 2/15/10); www.wfu.edu (accessed 2/15/10).

45. National Science Foundation, Division of Science Resources Statistics, *Survey of Earned Doctorates, 1997–2006*, and special tabulations from U.S. Department of Education, National Center for Education Statistics, Integrated Postsecondary Data System, *Completions Survey, 1988–1997.*

46. Examples of many other current leaders in a variety of fields who are liberal arts college graduates are included in Chapter 11.

47. Pew Charitable Trusts, *Policy Perspectives* 5, no. 4 (January 1995): 2A.

48. Ibid.

2. The Economic Health of Liberal Arts Colleges

1. Frederick Rudolph, *The American College and University* (Athens: University of Georgia Press, 1990), 181.

2. Ibid., 186–187.

3. See Lee Smith, "A Small College Scores Big in the Investment Game," *Fortune*, December 18, 1978, 68–72; Barry Stavro, "Grinnell College's Quantum Jumps,"

Forbes, December 31, 1984, 80–81; and Jason Zweig, "The Best Investor You've Never Heard Of," *Money,* June 2000, 140–144.

4. National Association of College and University Business Officers (NACUBO), *2008 NACUBO Endowment Study* (Washington, D.C.: NACUBO, 2009), xvi.

5. Ibid., xxiii.

6. These were Williams, Pomona, Amherst, Wellesley, Grinnell, Swarthmore, Smith, and Berea Colleges, and the University of Richmond. The endowments of 21 additional Tier I and Tier II colleges exceeded $500 million.

7. NACUBO, *2008 NACUBO Endowment Study.* Significantly, given the recession surge in the second half of 2008, most endowments in the report are stated as of June 30, 2008, the end of the 2007–2008 fiscal year for most colleges.

8. Ibid., xxi.

9. Ibid.

10. Ibid., xx.

11. Although 25 percent reported lowering them. See www.nacubo.org (accessed 2/16/10).

12. Data from www.campusgrotto.com, October 21, 2009.

13. Integrated Postsecondary Education Data System, Peer Analysis System (PAS).

14. See Appendix, Table A.5.

15. See http://nces.ed.gov/ipeds/datacenter.

16. Gordon C. Winston and Stephen R. Lewis, Jr., "Costs, Prices, and Subsidies in Higher Education," unpublished paper, April 13, 1996, 2. And see Roger T. Kaufman and Geoffrey Woglom, "Financial Changes and Measures of Success among the Second Tier of Top Liberal Arts Colleges," unpublished paper, March 2005, www.amherst.edu~grwoglom/LibArts.12doc.

17. National Center for Education Statistics (NCES), *2003–2004 Postsecondary Student Aid Study* (NPSAS: 04) (Washington, D.C.: NCES, 2005), nces.ed.gov.

18. Williams College, *Handbook for Parents* (2008).

19. Dickinson College, *Financial Aid News* (2008).

20. *New York Times,* "College Presidents Defend Rising Tuition, but Lawmakers Sound Skeptical," September 9, 2008, A19.

21. The facts on increasing financial aid in this and the following three paragraphs were culled from various newspaper reports.

22. *New York Times,* "Feeling Pressure from Harvard on College Cost," December 29, 2007, 1.

23. See, e.g., *New York Times,* "Senate Looking at Endowments as Tuition Rises," January 25, 2008, 1.

24. Tamar Lewin, "Investment Losses Cause Steep Dip in University Endowments, Study Finds," *New York Times,* January 28, 2010, A13.

25. Robert J. Massa, "The Cost of Competition," *Dickinson Magazine* 86, no. 1 (2008): 4 (emphasis in the original).

26. NACUBO, *2008 NACUBO Endowment Study.* Dickinson's 2006–2007 endowment ($288 million) placed it forty-fifth among the 224 colleges included in this volume. For 2007–2008 endowments, see Appendix A, Table A.3.

27. *New York Times,* "Feeling Pressure from Harvard on College Cost," 1.

28. See, e.g. *Washington Post,* "Private Colleges Looking to Rein in Financial Aid," February 2, 2010, www.washingtonpost.com; *New York Times,* "Williams College Will Bring Loans Back to Aid Packages," February 2, 2010, www.nytimes.com.

29. Clark Kerr, "Foreword," in Earl F. Cheit, *The New Depression in Higher Education: A Study of Financial Conditions at 41 Colleges and Universities* (Hightstown, N.J.: McGraw-Hill Book Company, 1971), x.

30. Howard R. Bowen and W. John Minter, *First Annual Report on Financial and Educational Trends in the Private Sector of American Higher Education* (Washington, D.C.: Association of American Colleges, 1975).

31. Virginia Ann Fadil and Nancy A. Carter, *Openings, Closings, Mergers, and Accreditation Status of Independent Colleges, Winter 1970 through Summer 1979* (Washington, D.C.: National Association of Independent Colleges and Universities, 1980).

32. Carnegie Foundation, *A Classification of Institutions of Higher Learning,* foreword by Ernest L. Boyer (Princeton: Carnegie Foundation for the Advancement of Teaching, 1994), vii.

33. Hugh Hawkins, "The Making of the Liberal Arts College Identity," in Steven Koblik and Stephen R. Graubard, eds., *Distinctively American* (New Brunswick, N.J.: Transactions Publishers, 2000), 21. No support was provided for this statement.

34. Jeff Long, "The College That Went Away to School," *Chicago Tribune,* October 9, 2006, www.iit.edu.

35. See AAUP Investigating Committee, *College and University Government: Antioch University and the Closing of Antioch College,* September 1, 2009, www.aaup.org.

36. Ibid., 52.

37. Gregory L. Smith, "Milton College: An Evaluative Case Study in Decline," Ph.D. diss., University of Wisconsin–Madison, 1985.

3. The Declining Demand for Liberal Arts Education

1. Henry Adams, *The Education of Henry Adams* (Boston: Houghton Mifflin, 1961), 54, 64.

2. Richard H. Hersh, "Intentions and Perceptions: A National Survey of Public Attitudes towards Liberal Arts Education," *Change,* March/April 1997, 1.

3. William M. Chace, "The Decline of the English Department," *American Scholar,* Autumn 2009, www.theamericanscholar.org.

4. U.S. Census Bureau, *Current Population Survey, 1955–2007.*

5. Hersh, "Intentions and Perceptions," 1.

6. Such institutions include many of the Tier III and IV colleges—and a number of the Tier II colleges—in this study.

7. For a nice, concise statement of changing student experience and expectations in the twentieth century, see Roger L. Geiger, "The Ten Generations of American Higher Education," in Philip G. Altbach et al., eds., *American Higher Education in the Twenty-First Century* (Baltimore: Johns Hopkins University Press, 2005), 54–66.

8. John Williams, *Stoner* (New York: New York Review Books, 2003), 6.

9. Derek Bok, *Our Underachieving Colleges* (Princeton: Princeton University Press, 2006), 26–27.

10. *New York Times,* letter to the editor, June 29, 2008, WK9.

11. Alexandra Robbins, *The Overachievers* (New York: Hyperion, 2006), 389.

12. Stamats, Inc., *2008 Teens TALK,* July 20, 2008, 10.

13. Steven Kappler, former executive director of consulting, Stamats, Inc., personal communication, April 14, 2009.

14. GDA Integrated Services, *Three Cues* newsletter 2007, www.dehne.com.

15. Telephone interview with Metro Editorial Services official Jennifer Flack, May 26, 2009. Metro Editorial Services is a division of Metro Creative Graphics, Inc.

16. Metro Editorial Services, "Tips for Finding the Right College," published in *Congratulations Class of 2009,* special supplement to the Brodhead, Wisconsin, *Independent-Register,* May 20, 2009, 24.

17. U.S. Department of Education, *A Test of Leadership: Charting the Future of U.S. Higher Education* (Washington, D.C.: U.S. Department of Education, 2006).

18. See www.whitehouse.gov/issues/education/higher-education, accessed August 8, 2010.

19. See www.college.georgetown.edu, accessed August 8, 2010.

20. Anthony P. Carnevale, Nicole Smith, and Jeff Strohl, *Help Wanted: Projections of Jobs and Education Requirements through 2018: Executive Summary* (Washington, D.C.: Georgetown University Center on Education and the Workforce, June 2010), 1–5, www9.georgetown.edu/grad/gppi/hpi/cew/pdfs/ExecutiveSummary-web.pdf.

21. David Jason Fischer, interview with Anthony Carnevale, Center for

an Urban Future, May 2009, www.nycfuture.org/content/articles/article_view. cfm?article_id=1239.

22. *Inside Higher Ed,* "A Jobs Mismatch," June 15, 2010, www.insidehighered. com.

23. Anthony P. Carnevale, "All One System," in Nancy Hoffman et al., eds., *Minding the Gap: Why Integrating High School with College Makes Sense and How to Do It* (Cambridge, Mass: Harvard Education Press, 2007), 88, 286n2.

24. Fischer, interview with Carnevale, May 2009. National Center for Education Statistics, Integrated Postsecondary Education Data System, Classification of Instructional Programs (CIP), http://nces.ed.gov/ipeds/cipcode/cipdetail. Beloit College is typical in that it does not have any programs that fall into this category.

25. See http://nces.ed.gov/ipeds/cipcode/cipdetail.

26. Hersh, "Intentions and Perceptions," 2, 4, 6.

27. Reported in *Chronicle of Higher Education,* August 18, 2005, 18. In addition, 72 percent answered "to be able to get a better job" and 70 percent answered "to be able to make more money."

28. 2009 UCLA Higher Education Research Institute Freshman Survey, www. heri.ucla.edu.

29. Richard H. Hersh, "The Liberal Arts College," *Liberal Education,* Summer 1997, 26–33.

30. Interviews with students at Parkview High School, Orfordville, Wisconsin, October 6, 2008.

31. The word Jacques Barzun uses to define the curriculum of U.S. public high schools is *liberal.* See Jacques Barzun, *From Dawn to Decadence* (New York: Harper Collins, 2000), 745.

32. Interview with student at Parkview High School, Orfordville, Wisconsin, October 6, 2008.

33. Motoko Rich, "Literary Debate: R U Really Reading?" *New York Times,* July 27, 2008, www.nytimes.com.

34. Quoted in ibid., 3.

35. See, e.g., National Endowment for the Arts, *To Read or Not to Read,* Research Report 47 (Washington, D.C.: National Endowment for the Arts, 2007), 7–8, www.nea.gov/research/toread.pdf. The National Assessment of Educational Progress (NAEP) reported very small gains in national average reading skills for fourth- and eighth-graders between 1992 and 2005, but only 31 percent of both groups were rated proficient. Between 1992 and 2002, average scores of twelfth-graders fell. National Center for Education Statistics, *The Condition of Education 2006 in Brief* (NCES 2006-072), 7, http://nces.ed.gov.

36. James Harvey, "Goodwill and Growing Worry: Public Perceptions of Higher

Education in America," unpublished remarks presented at the annual meeting of the Council for Advancement and Support of Education, Chicago, July 11, 1994, 15.

37. Art and Science Group, LLC, Fall 1996 Survey, www.artsci.com.

38. Fields of study are determined by the appropriate Classification of Instructional Programs (CIP) code.

39. Appendix, Table A.2.

40. David W. Breneman, *Liberal Arts Colleges: Thriving, Surviving, or Endangered?* (Washington, D.C.: Brookings Institution, 1994), 3.

41. David F. Swensen, "Endowment Management," unpublished paper presented at the Association for Investment Management and Research [AIMR, now the CFA Institute] Seminar on Investment Policy, Tokyo, Japan, April 18–20, 1994, 1. See also David F. Swensen, *Pioneering Portfolio Management: An Unconventional Approach to Institutional Investment* (New York: Free Press, 2000), 10.

42. Paul Neely, "The Threats to Liberal Arts Colleges," in Steven Koblik and Stephen R. Graubard, eds., *Distinctively American* (New Brunswick, N.J.: Transactions Publishers, 2000), 29.

43. Michael S. McPherson and Morton Owen Schapiro, "The Future Economic Challenges for the Liberal Arts Colleges," in Steven Koblik and Stephen R. Graubard, eds., *Distinctively American* (New Brunswick, N.J.: Transactions Publishers, 2000), 51.

4. Competing

1. As opposed to "negative externalities," unwanted side effects such as air pollution. Competitive markets do not handle either positive or negative externalities efficiently because their benefits and costs are not fully reflected in the prices that enter the profit and loss calculus of private individuals and firms.

2. Stephen Happel, "Tenure Has Outlived Its Usefulness," letter to the editor, *Wall Street Journal* (Eastern Edition), November 13, 1996, A23.

3. See "Epilogue: A Fable" (pp. 163–167), which carries the automobile-dealership analogy a good bit further, exploring the similarities and differences between the pricing policies of private and public educational institutions.

4. At least this is the case now. We may be approaching a time when some undergraduates will pay negative tuition. This in fact happens today at top graduate schools.

5. See www.moreheadcain.org (accessed 10/23/09).

6. What is the best is, of course, highly subjective. The high-pressure atmo-

sphere of Swarthmore may not be the best for some students, and the party-school atmosphere of a sunbelt university may not suit others.

7. See, e.g., Marquis W. Childs, *Sweden: The Middle Way* (New Haven: Yale University Press, 1936).

8. The University of Minnesota's Honors Program now serves 10 percent of the university's undergraduate population. Like a liberal arts college, it features individual advising, faculty-directed undergraduate research, study- and work-abroad opportunities, and a close-knit community. Admission is competitive. See www.umn.edu (accessed 10/23/09).

9. Tibor Scitovsky, "Ignorance as a Source of Oligopoly Power," *American Economic Review* 40 (1950): 48–53.

10. Roger Rosenblatt, *Beet* (New York: Harper Collins, 2008), 6.

11. National Center for Public Policy and Higher Education, *Measuring Up 2008* (San Jose, Calif.: National Center for Public Policy and Higher Education, 2008), 8; www.highereducation.org (accessed 2/18/10).

12. National Center for Education Statistics, *Digest of Education Statistics* (annual reports), www.nces.ed.gov.

13. Thorstein Veblen, *The Theory of the Leisure Class* (New York: New American Library, 1953), ch. 4. Veblen, of course, ascribed "conspicuous consumption" to the leisure class, but one can reasonably conclude that, by virtue of attending a liberal arts college, students belong to that class.

14. Tibor Scitovsky, *Welfare and Competition* (London: Routledge, 2003), 403–406.

15. It is interesting to note that while tuition increases at top-rated colleges for 2010–2011, the academic year following the 2008 recession, tended to be somewhat smaller than in prior years, they were not eliminated and exceeded the cost-of-living index. Changes will be felt in the form of reduced financial aid packages, fewer outright grants, and more loans.

16. Gordon C. Winston and David J. Zimmerman, "Where Is Aggressive Price Competition Taking Higher Education?" Williams Project on the Economics of Higher Education Discussion Paper No. 56 (June 2000), 20.

17. Private baccalaureate colleges as classified by the Carnegie Foundation. College Board, *Trends in College Pricing 2009,* October 20, 2009, www.trends-collegeboard.com.

18. Confusingly, they are not discriminating if they are viewed as buying students rather than selling educational services. In that case, their discounts represent paying different prices for presumably different-quality students.

19. James C. Garland, *Saving Alma Mater* (Chicago: University of Chicago Press, 2009), 5, 208.

20. Ibid., 207.

21. Ibid., 38.

22. In Wisconsin, the state university system has more than 100 registered lobbyists working assiduously to see that the low-tuition advantage for middle- and upper-income families is maintained. All of the Wisconsin private colleges and universities combined have only 2 lobbyists.

23. See www.osu.edu/costs.

24. See www.wisconsin.edu/news (April 8, 2010).

25. Garland, *Saving Alma Mater*, xvi–xvii.

26. Ibid., 225–226. Also, Miami University competes with high-tuition/high-aid private colleges and universities, so the change was not as shocking to its potential customers as it would be for most public schools. Indeed, Miami University is perceived as "privatelike" and "fundamentally different from other state schools." Ibid., 227.

27. Ibid., 199.

28. Garland, *Saving Alma Mater*, 211–212.

29. Daniel F. Sullivan, unpublished speech at the Hardwick-Day/Lawlor Group Summer Seminar, Minneapolis, June 13, 2008. States in which the average family income of public flagship university students exceeds that of private-college students include California, Florida, Oregon, and Minnesota. Jenny B. Wahl, *A Bigger Bang for the Public Buck: Achieving Efficiency and Equity in Higher Education* (St. Paul: Minnesota Private College Research Foundation, 2002), 32.

30. Garland, *Saving Alma Mater*, 212.

31. Ibid., 203.

32. Charles M. Vest, *Industry, Philanthropy, and Universities: The Roles and Influences of the Private Sector in Higher Education* (Berkeley: University of California Press, 2006), 15. The distinction President Vest draws seems to assume that poor students are less excellent than well-to-do students.

33. Quoted by Lewis H. Lapham in "Playing with Fire," *Lapham's Quarterly* (Fall 2008): 15.

5. Cooperating

1. Paul Neely, "The Threats to Liberal Arts Colleges," in Steven Koblik and Stephen R. Graubard, eds., *Distinctively American* (New Brunswick, N.J.: Transactions Publishers, 2000), 32.

2. See www.cuc.claremont.edu (accessed 7/13/09).

3. See www.waicu.org (accessed 8/8/09).

4. See www.mainegrads.org (accessed 8/8/09).

5. See www.glca.org (accessed 8/9/09); www.acm.edu (accessed 8/8/09).

6. See www.colleges.org (accessed 8/8/09).

7. See www.womenscollege.org (accessed 8/8/09).

8. See www.boston-consortium.org (accessed 8/8/09).

9. See www.occc.edu (accessed 8/8/09).

10. See www.fivecolleges.edu (accessed 8/8/09).

11. Julia Colatrella, "Five College Courses Give Students a Chance to 'Get Out of the Smith Bubble,'" *NewSmith*, Summer 2010, 3.

12. Quoted in "Consortiums, Collaboration, Centralization . . . Conflict?" *Inside Higher Ed*, July 1, 2009, www.insidehighered.com.

13. Ibid.

14. See www.brynmawr.edu (accessed 2/26/10).

15. See www.cuc.claremont.edu (accessed 7/13/09).

16. See www.sunoikisis.org (accessed 2/16/10).

17. See www.colleges.org (accessed 2/25/10).

18. See www.colorado.edu (accessed 2/20/10).

19. See www.liberalarts.org (accessed 2/20/10).

20. See www.nitle.org (accessed 2/25/10).

21. *Chronicle of Higher Education*, "Liberal-Arts Colleges Create Joint Effort for Online Courses," February 24, 2006, http://chronicle.com/article/Liberal-Arts-Colleges-Create/1864.

22. www.ocicu.org (accessed 10/21/10).

23. Quoted in Jennifer Epstein, "Mergers and Survival," *Inside Higher Ed*, July 13, 2010, www.insidehighered.com.

24. See, e.g., John Brooks, "The Marts of Trade: The Law School and the Noodle Factory," *New Yorker*, December 26, 1977, 48–53.

25. A Baccalaureate College, in *U.S. News and World Report*'s terms, is an institution focusing on undergraduate education and offering a range of degree programs in the liberal arts, which account for fewer than half of its bachelor's degrees, and in professional fields, such as business, nursing, and education. U.S. News and World Report, *America's Best Colleges*, 2008 ed. (Washington, D.C.: U.S. News and World Report, Inc., 2007), 167. Before 2008, *U.S. News* called Baccalaureate Colleges "Comprehensive Colleges—Bachelor's," but the definition was the same.

26. See www.citytowninfo.com (accessed 8/9/09).

27. *Montpelier Times Argus*, "CCV to Make Former Woodbury College Building Its Headquarters," November 11, 2008, www.timesargus.com.

28. Enrollment and majors data for Mount St. Clare College and its succes-

sors, Franciscan University and Ashford University, are from various editions of *U.S. News's America's Best Colleges,* unless otherwise indicated.

29. North Central Association of Colleges and Schools, Higher Learning Commission, www.ncahlc.org (accessed 8/9/09).

30. *Inside Higher Ed,* March 2, 2005, www.insidehighered.com.

31. See www.bridgepointeducation.com (accessed 8/9/09).

32. See www.ashfordathletics.com (accessed 8/9/09).

33. See www.bridgepointeducation.com (accessed 8/9/09).

34. *Inside Higher Ed,* May 9, 2009, www.insidehighered.com.

35. Ibid.

36. The information in this and the following two paragraphs is taken from contemporaneous news reports in the local newspaper, the *Forest City Summit,* www.forestcitysummit.com.

37. *Inside Higher Ed,* May 9, 2009, www.insidehighered.com.

38. *Business Week,* April 9, 2009, 56.

39. All of the facts in this and the following two paragraphs are taken from news reports in the *Santa Fe New Mexican,* www.santafenewmexican.com. And see Robin Romm, "School for Brides," Week in Review, *New York Times,* July 4, 2010, 9.

40. All of the facts in this and the following paragraph are taken from reports published by the *Omaha World-Herald,* www.omaha.com.

41. *Nashua Telegraph,* www.nashuatelegraph.com.

42. Tamar Lewin, "Inquiry Is Sought into Practices of For-Profit College," *New York Times,* June 22, 2010, A14.

43. Peter S. Goodman, "In Hard Times, Lured into Trade School," *New York Times,* March 13, 2010, www.nytimes.com.

44. See, generally, Richard S. Ruch, *Higher Ed., Inc.* (Baltimore: Johns Hopkins University Press, 2001); David W. Breneman, Brian Pusser, and Sarah T. Turner, eds., *Earnings from Learning* (Albany: SUNY Press, 2006); David L. Kirp, *Shakespeare, Einstein, and the Bottom Line* (Cambridge, Mass.: Harvard University Press, 2003), ch. 13 ("They're All Business: DeVry University").

45. See www.collegenews.org (accessed 5/9/10).

46. Steven Koblik and Stephen R. Graubard, eds., *Distinctively American* (New Brunswick, N.J.: Transactions Publishers, 2000).

47. Russell Edgerton, "Forward," *National Survey of Student Engagement (NSSE) Annual Results 2009,* 5.

48. Nicholas Thompson, "Playing with Numbers," *Washington Monthly,* September 2000, www.washingtonmonthly.com.

49. See www.washingtonpost.com, March 9, 2007; U.S. News, *America's Best Colleges,* 2008 ed., 91.

50. *Inside Higher Ed,* June 20, 2007, www.insidehighered.com.

51. See www.educationconservancy.org (accessed 8/9/09).

52. *Inside Higher Ed,* September 10, 2007, www.insidehighered.com.

53. *Washington Post,* "Some Colleges Are Opting Out of Magazine's Annual Survey," May 3, 2010, www.washingtonpost.com.

54. The same *Washington Post* article also reported that some university officials gave competing universities low scores on the so-called reputational survey to make their own institution look better, including one official who rated the quality of all but two of his university's peers—including Harvard and Yale—as merely "adequate." No efforts by university administrators to end this deceptive practice were reported.

55. 15 U.S.C. 1 et seq.

56. See, e.g., *Northern Pacific Ry. Co. v. United States,* 356 U.S. 1 (1958).

57. According to Newberry Library president David Spadafora, then associate dean of Yale's Graduate School of Arts and Sciences.

58. Charles M. Vest, *Industry, Philanthropy, and Universities: The Roles and Influences of the Private Sector in Higher Education* (Berkeley: University of California, 2006), 17, www.escholarship.org/uc/item/3r51g7nw.

59. Ibid., 17.

60. *New York Times,* "Ivy Universities Deny Price-Fixing But Agree to Avoid It in the Future," May 23, 1991, A1.

61. MIT, *Tech,* May 28, 1993, www.tech.mit.edu.

62. Gordon C. Winston and David J. Zimmerman, "Where Is Aggressive Price Competition Taking Higher Education?" Williams Project on the Economics of Higher Education, Discussion Paper 56 (June 2000), 3, www.williams.edu/wpehe/DPs/DP.56.pdf.

63. Vest, *Industry, Philanthropy, and Universities,* 16.

64. *New York Times,* "Ivy Universities Deny Price-Fixing," A1.

65. Dennis W. Carlton, Gustavo E. Bamberger, and Roy J. Epstein, "Antitrust and Higher Education," University of Chicago, Center for the Study of the Economy and the State, Working Paper No. 107 (January 1994), 12, http://research.chicagobooth.edu/economy/research/articles/107.pdf.

66. Ibid., 20.

67. Ibid., 28–29.

68. Ibid.

69. *New York Times,* "Paying in Full as the Ticket into Colleges," March 31, 2009, A16.

70. *Federal Club v. National League,* 259 U.S. 200, 208 (1922).

71. Vest, *Industry, Philanthropy, and Universities,* 16.

6. Recruiting Students

1. And by others. To take one example, New York University professor Ken Bain's excellent book, *What the Best College Teachers Do* (Cambridge, Mass.: Harvard University Press, 2004), references only universities in its index and mentions the name of only one college in its text (a passing reference to Wellesley College on page 42; Wellesley is not included in the index).

2. Eva T. H. Brann, "Four Appreciative Queries," in Robert Orrill, executive ed., *The Condition of American Liberal Education: Pragmatism and a Changing Tradition* (New York: College Board, 1995), 175.

3. Mark Schneider, "How Much Is That Bachelor's Degree Really Worth? The Million Dollar Misunderstanding," American Enterprise Institute, *Education Outlook* 5 (May 4, 2009), www.aei.org/outlook/1000034.

4. Jane Smiley, *Moo* (New York: Knopf, 1995), 24.

5. *News at Princeton,* September 21, 2009, www.princeton.edu.

6. Lisa W. Foderaro, "Princeton's Type-A-Plus Students Chafe at Grade Deflation," *New York Times,* January 31, 2010, 30.

7. Richard H. Hersh, "Intentions and Perceptions: A National Survey of Public Attitudes towards Liberal Arts Education," *Change,* March/April 1997, 3.

7. Liberal Arts Teachers

1. Arthur M. Schlesinger, Jr., *Journals, 1952–2000* (New York: Penguin Press, 2007), 516.

2. Quoted in Bruce J. Schulman, *The Seventies* (New York: Free Press, 2002), 41.

3. James M. Redfield, "The Aims of Education," in *The Aims of Education* (Chicago: University of Chicago, 1997), 183.

4. David L. Kirp, "This Little Student Went to Market," in Richard H. Hersh and John Merrow, eds., *Declining by Degrees: Higher Education at Risk* (New York: Palgrave Macmillan, 2005), 123.

5. Andrew Delbanco, "The College Idea," in *Lapham's Quarterly,* Fall 2008, 184.

6. Richard Pells, "For Academics, Too, It's All in the Telling," *International Herald Tribune,* March 24, 1999, 9.

7. Ibid.

8. Employing and Deploying Faculty for Teaching Excellence

1. It is not uncommon for candidates for administrative positions to request that their candidacy be kept confidential so as not to jeopardize their current employment. Such requests are frequently honored, making obtaining reliable information about the candidates difficult.

2. Area, ethnic, cultural, and gender studies; computer and information sciences; English language and literature/letters; foreign languages, literatures, and linguistics; liberal arts and sciences, general studies, and humanities; mathematics and statistics; multi/interdisciplinary studies; philosophy and religious studies; physical sciences and science technologies; psychology; social sciences and history; and visual and performing arts. See http://nces.ed.gov/programs/digest/d09.

3. William James, "The Ph.D. Octopus," in Bruce W. Wilshire, ed., *William James: The Essential Writings* (Albany, N.Y.: SUNY Press, 1984), 343–345.

4. David W. Breneman, "The University of Phoenix," in David W. Breneman, Brian Pusser, and Sarah T. Turner, eds., *Earnings from Learning* (Albany, N.Y.: SUNY Press, 2006), 76.

5. Ibid., 85.

6. Brian C. Rosenberg, president, Macalester College, "Can Liberal-Arts Colleges Survive?" *Chronicle of Higher Education Media Daily Report,* audio interview, May 8, 2009, www.insight24.com.

7. See, e.g., George D. Kuh, *High-Impact Educational Practices: What They Are, Who Has Access to Them, and Why They Matter* (Washington, D.C.: AAC&U Publications, 2008); Teagle Working Group on the Teacher-Scholar, *Student Learning and Faculty Research: Connecting Teaching and Scholarship,* Teagle Foundation White Paper (New York: American Council of Learned Societies, May 2007).

8. See American Association of University Professors, *AAUP Policy Documents and Reports,* 10th ed. (Baltimore: Johns Hopkins University Press, 2006), 24–25. AAUP addresses permissible justifications for termination. At issue here is not terminating faculty but effectively deploying faculty and planning for future needs so that termination will not be an issue.

9. Emma L. Carew and Paul Fain, "Paychecks Top More Than $1-Million for 23 Private-College Presidents," *Chronicle of Higher Education,* November 1, 2009, www.chronicle.com.

10. Ibid.

11. Ibid.

12. Russell Edgerton, president emeritus, American Association for Higher Education, "Foreword," in National Survey of Student Engagement, *Assessment for*

Improvement: Tracking Student Engagement over Time: Annual Results 2009 (Bloomington: Indiana University Center for Postsecondary Research, 2009), 5 (emphasis in the original).

9. Tenure

1. Richard A. Posner, "Tenure: Posner's Reply to Comments," Becker-Posner Blog, January 21, 2006, www.becker-posner-blog.com.

2. Richard P. Chait, "Why Academe Needs More Employment Options," *Chronicle of Higher Education,* February 7, 1997, B4. See also Richard P. Chait, ed., *The Questions of Tenure* (Cambridge, Mass.: Harvard University Press, 2002).

3. American Association of University Professors, *AAUP Policy Documents and Reports,* 10th ed. (Baltimore: Johns Hopkins University Press, 2006), 294 (emphasis added). *AAUP Policy Documents and Reports* is often referred to as the Redbook.

4. Ibid., 300.

5. Ibid., 295.

6. Ibid., 298.

7. Ibid., 300 (emphasis added).

8. Ibid., 295.

9. Ibid., 297. The last point, about the "tyranny of public opinion," is an odd one given the committee's view that "the responsibility of the university teacher is primarily to the public itself" (295).

10. Ibid., 295.

11. Ibid., 296.

12. Ibid., 298, 299.

13. AAUP, "American Freedom and Tenure," *AAUP Bulletin* 42, no. 1 (Spring 1956): 42.

14. American Association of University Professors, *AAUP Policy Documents and Reports,* 4.

15. Carolyn J. Mooney, "Dismissals 'for Cause,'" *Chronicle of Higher Education,* December 7, 1994, A17.

16. *Wall Street Journal,* January 10, 2005.

17. John Kenneth Galbraith, *The Tenured Professor* (Boston: Houghton Mifflin, 1990), 38–39, 71 (emphasis in original).

18. See Richard A. Posner, "Tenured Employment," Becker-Posner Blog, January 15, 2006, www.becker-posner-blog.com.

19. See, e.g., Robert M. O'Neil, "Academic Freedom," in Philip G. Altbach et

al., eds., *American Higher Education in the Twenty-First Century* (Baltimore: Johns Hopkins University Press, 2005), 103–105.

20. National Center for Education Statistics, IPEDS DAS, National Study of Postsecondary Faculty (NSOPF), nces.ed.gov/surveys/nsopf. Over the same period the percentage of untenured faculty on a tenure track also fell, from 14.7 percent to 12.2 percent.

21. Armen A. Alchian, *Economic Forces at Work* (Indianapolis: Liberty Fund, 1977), 186.

10. Curriculums

1. See www.stjohnscollege.edu (accessed 2/24/10).

2. See www.middlebury.edu (accessed 2/24/10).

3. See www.williams.edu (accessed 2/24/10); www.carleton.edu (accessed 2/24/10).

4. See www.pomona.edu (accessed 2/24/10).

5. Lewis H. Lapham, "Playing with Fire," *Lapham's Quarterly,* Fall 2008, 19.

6. Francis Oakley, *Community of Learning* (New York: Oxford University Press, 1992), 157–158 (emphasis in the original).

7. Michael N. Bastedo, "Curriculum in Higher Education: The Historical Roots of Contemporary Issues," in Philip G. Altbach, Robert O. Berdahl, and Patricia J. Gumport, eds., *American Higher Education in the Twenty-First Century* (Baltimore: Johns Hopkins University Press, 2005), 463.

8. For a delightful exploration of virtually every aspect of the Great Books concept, including curriculums, see Alex Beam, *A Great Idea at the Time* (New York: Public Affairs, 2008).

9. Ibid., 169.

10. David B. Ellis, "What Is the Role of a Mathematician at a Liberal Arts College?" unpublished paper, 1996.

11. David McCullough, remarks made on accepting the National Book Foundation Medal for Distinguished Contribution to American Letters, November 15, 1995, quoted in McCullough, *Why History?* (New York: Simon and Schuster, 1996), 13.

11. At the Brink

1. David Brooks, "History for Dollars," *New York Times,* June 8, 2010, A23.

2. Michael Roth, "Coming to the Defense of Liberal Education," *Huffington*

Post, June 9, 2010, www.huffingtonpost.com. And see Leigh A. Bortins, *The Core: Teaching Your Child the Foundations of Classical Education* (New York: Macmillan, 2010); Martha C. Nussbaum, *Not for Profit: Why Democracy Needs the Humanities* (Princeton: Princeton University Press, 2010); Diane Ravitch, *The Death and Life of the Great American School System: How Testing and Choice Are Undermining Education* (New York: Basic Books, 2010); Stanley Fish, "A Classical Education: Back to the Future," Opinionator, *New York Times,* http://opinionator.blogs.nytimes.com, June 7, 2010.

3. David W. Breneman, *Liberal Arts Colleges: Thriving, Surviving, or Endangered?* (Washington, D.C.: Brookings Institution, 1994), 3.

4. Vitruvius, *The Ten Books on Architecture,* trans. Morris Hicky Morgan (Cambridge, Mass.: Harvard University Press, 1914; New York: Dover Publications, 1960), 5–12 (1960 ed.).

5. I cannot resist sharing a favorite quatrain: "The law locks up the man or woman / Who steals the goose from off the common / But leaves the greater villain loose / Who steals the common from off the goose." One can speculate (although probably not profitably) about who or what is the "greater villain" in the case of liberal arts colleges.

6. Roger G. Baldwin and Vicki L. Baker, "The Case of the Disappearing Liberal Arts College," *Inside Higher Ed,* July 9, 2009, www.insidehighered.com.

7. Mark Slouka, "Dehumanized: When Math and Science Rule the School," *Harper's Magazine,* September 2009, www.harpers.org.

8. Carol G. Schneider, "Liberal Education: Slip-Sliding Away?" in Richard H. Hersh and John Merrow, eds., *Declining by Degrees* (New York: Palgrave Macmillan, 2005), 74.

9. Council of Independent Colleges, *Strategic Planning Initiative: Report to the Membership,* January 2002, 4, www.cic.edu.

10. Francis Oakley, *Community of Learning* (New York: Oxford University Press, 1992), 151–152.

11. Breneman, *Liberal Arts Colleges,* 135–137.

12. Paul Neely, "The Threats to Liberal Arts Colleges," in Steven Koblik and Stephen R. Graubard, eds., *Distinctively American: The Residential Liberal Arts Colleges* (New Brunswick, N.J.: Transaction Publishers, 2000), 32.

13. Personal communication, December 10, 2009.

14. Warren Goldstein, "What Would Plato Do? A (Semi-)Careerist Defense of the Liberal Arts," *Yale Alumni Magazine,* July/August 2005, www.yalealumnimagazine.com (accessed 2/15/10).

Acknowledgments

I am indebted not only to people who helped me in writing *Liberal Arts at the Brink,* but also to those who inspired me to write it. In the latter group are the faculty of my alma maters, Oberlin College and Yale Law School (which, when I attended, provided—and probably still provides—what is tantamount to a postgraduate liberal education). Prominent in the former group are my Beloit College family—faculty, staff, students, alumni, and trustees—and the many friends who read and constructively criticized portions of the drafts.

Liberal Arts at the Brink would never have been published without the skillful guidance of Elizabeth Knoll, my editor at Harvard University Press, and the support of Cynthia Gray, the most talented and imaginative researcher and data analyst I know. Finally, the book has been immeasurably strengthened by my beloved life editor-in-chief and wife, Linda K. Smith.

Index

Academia, culture of, 121
Academic freedom, 62, 139, 140, 142, 143, 144
Accreditation, 39, 91, 93, 94
Adams, Henry, 40, 43, 112
Administrators, 53–54, 68; compensation for, 135–136; and curriculum, 153; and faculty training, 131; recruiting of, 128; of state universities, 75, 76; and student aid, 76, 98; and tenure, 140, 141
Admission, need-blind, 78–80
Admissions officers, 111–112
Albee, Edward, 162
Albright, Madeleine, 162
Alchian, Armen, 145
Alexander, Jane, 162
Alumni, 68, 69, 160
American Association of Colleges and Universities, 157
American Association of Collegiate Registrars and Admissions Officers (AACRAO), 95
American Association of University Professors (AAUP), 95; history of *Statement of Principles on Academic Freedom and Tenure*, 139–143
Amherst College, 14, 34–35, 37, 84, 98, 100
Andresen, Martha, 127
Annan, Kofi, 162
Annapolis Group, 4, 15–16, 58, 95–97, 105, 159

Antioch College, 38
Antioch University, 38
Antitrust laws, 97, 101, 102, 103
Apollo Group, 92
Apple, 24
Arizona State University, 14
Armstrong, Richard, 127
Ashford University, 88–89
Associated Colleges of the Midwest (ACM), 83
Associated Colleges of the South (ACS), 83, 86
Association of Governing Boards (AGB), 95
Associations, national, 95–104

Barat College, 38
Bard College, 12, 58
Barnard College, 98, 100
Barry, Dave, 161
Bastedo, Michael, 148
Bates College, 35
Belichick, Bill, 162
Beloit College, x, xi, 12, 13, 152
Berklee College of Music, 83
Berkshire Hathaway, 24
Berra, Yogi, 162
Beschloss, Michael, 161
Bloom, Allan, 148
Boards of trustees, 69–70, 135, 140, 141
Bok, Derek, 44
Boston Consortium for Higher Education (BCHE), 83–84

Bowdoin College, 36, 98, 100
Bowen, Howard, 37
Boyer, Ernest, 37
Bradford College, 38
Brann, Eva, 106
Breneman, David W., 14–15, 16, 58, 87,
    132, 154; *Liberal Arts Colleges,* 158
Bridgepoint Education, 88–89, 93
Brooks, David, 154
Brougham, Lord, 17
Brown University, 35, 98, 99–100, 150
Bryn Mawr College, 12, 84–85, 98, 100
Bucknell University, 35
Buffett, Warren, 24
Burns, Ken, 161
Business: colleges and universities as,
    62–70, 74, 75, 102; partnership with,
    157, 158; postsecondary education
    as, 1; programs in, 19, 44, 45, 47, 107,
    109; testimonials from leaders in, 19,
    112, 160–161

Career(s): after liberal arts education,
    41, 42, 108–109, 116; and demand
    for liberal arts education, 45–51; and
    liberal arts orientation, 18; progams
    oriented toward, 3, 30, 59, 67, 107,
    151–152; and recruiting, 107. *See
    also* Vocational education
Carleton, William, 23
Carleton College, x, 22, 41, 42, 147
Carlton, Dennis, 100, 101
Carlyle, Thomas, 60
Carnegie Foundation for the Advance-
    ment of Teaching, 8–12, 15–16, 155
Carnevale, Anthony P., 48–50
Carter, Nancy, 37
Chace, William M., 42–43
Chait, Richard, 139
Champlain College, 87
Charity, 79, 102–103
Chase, Chevy, 162

Choate School, 40
Church, affiliation with, 23
Citizens, 16–17
Claremont Graduate University, 85
Claremont McKenna College, 85
Claremont University Consortium
    (CUC), 82, 85–86
Coe College, 57
Colby College, 36, 98, 100
Coleman, Mary Sue, 22
College, for-profit, 72, 88–94, 95. *See
    also* Liberal arts college(s); Univer-
    sity/universities
Colorado College, 30
Colorado School of Professional Psy-
    chology, 89
Columbia Southern University (CSU),
    91, 92, 93
Columbia University, 23, 35, 98, 99–
    100
Community College of Vermont
    (CCV), 88
Community colleges, 30, 35, 49
Competition: for admission, 44;
    among liberal arts institutions, 4, 44,
    57, 62, 71–80; among private and
    public colleges, 65–66; economic,
    60–80; and financial aid, 35; free-
    market, 4, 71–80; and marketing, 64;
    and Overlap Group, 102; and public
    universities, 78, 157; with richest
    colleges and universities, 3; for stu-
    dents, 71, 72, 98–100, 104; with tax-
    supported public institutions, 3; and
    tuition, 34, 36–37, 52, 72–74, 81; and
    unique programs, 53
Completions, 55–58, 184–195
Computers, 51
Congress, 21
Consortia, 82–87, 159
Consortium of Liberal Arts Colleges
    (CLAC), 86

Cooperation, 4, 81–104
Cornell University, 35, 98, 99–100
Cotton, Raymond D., 135
Council for Advancement and Support of Education (CASE), 95
Council of Independent Colleges (CIC), 95, 158, 159
Crown, Susan, 19
Curriculum, 147–153; and attitude toward learning and knowing, 150–151; autonomy in, 4; and career paths, 151–152; debates over, 148–150; interdisciplinary, 152; required courses in, 67, 68, 109; review of, 5; unique, 53

Dana College, 93
Daniel Webster College, 93
Dartmouth College, 12
Dartmouth University, 35, 98, 99–100
Davenport, Iowa, 35
Davidson College, 58
Dayton, Ohio, 35
Debt, 29, 39, 54, 91, 92, 93
Degree(s), sale of, 71–72
Delbanco, Andrew, 117
Denison, William, 23
Denver, 35
DePaul University, 38
DePauw University, 135
Dickinson College, 33, 36–37
Doctorow, E. L., 162
Donations, 23, 25, 79
Dubinsky, Donna, 19
Duke, Paul, 161
Duke University, 35
Durden, William, 37

Economy, 48, 60–62, 63. See also Recession
Education, 8; as big business, 1; and

citizenship, 16–17; democratization of, 43; elementary and secondary, 159–160; good-enough, 65; sale of, 61, 63, 64, 71, 77. See also Liberal arts education
Ellis, David, 152
Employer(s), 44, 71–72. See also Career(s); Vocational education; Work
Endowment, 23–30, 62, 196–202, 261n6; disparities between institutions, 24, 26, 27–29, 30; investment of, 81; and recession, 29–30; and spending, 26–28, 54; and tuition, 34, 59
Enrollment, 1–3, 172–183; declining, 43–44; at for-profit colleges, 72; increases in, 43, 54–55, 81; of liberal arts colleges, 15; and Mount St. Clare College, 88; and public universities, 76; and Waldorf College, 90, 91
Entrepreneurship, 161
Evangelical Lutheran Churches of America, 93
Expenses, 23, 26, 28, 30–32, 52, 214–224, 236–245, 246–256

Facilities, 30, 53–54, 81, 84, 85, 94
Faculty: academic contributions of, 120; adjunct, 68, 144; assessment of, 132–133; character of, 113–114; and choice of academic life, 115–116; circumstances of, 5; and committees, 123–124; compensation for, 30, 52, 134–136, 139–140, 144; and curriculum debates, 148–150; deployment of, 133–134; disciplining or dismissal of, 140–141, 143; formation of, 114–115; graduate education of, 115, 116–118; guidance of, 41; hiring of, 127–130; hours worked by, 120; in liberal arts, 113–125; as

Faculty *(continued)*
mentors for new faculty, 118, 131, 132; as mentors for students, 115, 118, 123, 124–125, 148; minority, 130; with Ph.D.s, 68, 69, 129; publication by, 119, 122; ratio to students, 68, 69; and research, 117–118; and sabbaticals, 121; self-regulation of, 140–141; specialization by, 122; and tenure, 119–120, 121, 138–146; training of, 118–119, 131–132; and undergraduate education, 13–14; workload reductions for, 81; writing by, 122–123. *See also* Teaching; Tenure
Fadil, Virginia, 37
Faust, Drew Gilpin, 22
Finances, 3, 23–39, 52, 158. *See also* Fund accounting; Fund-raising; Investment; Revenues; Spending; Tax subsidization; Tuition
Financial aid: and accounting, 70; and choice of college, 53; competition through, 63; expense of, 69; as grants, 33, 34, 35; as loans, 33, 34–35, 37; merit-based, 78–80; need-based, 78–80; and Overlap Group, 98–99; percentages of, 33; reductions in, 52; and tuition, 72; and tuition discounting, 35. *See also* Scholarships; Student(s); Tuition
Five Colleges, Inc., 84
Fordham University, 38
Franciscan University, 88–89
Franklin, Benjamin, 20
Franklin and Marshall College, 136
Franzen, Jonathan, 162
Free enterprise, 142
Fund accounting, 69–70. *See also* Finances
Fund-raising, 23, 25, 39, 53, 79, 106. *See also* Finances

Galbraith, John Kenneth, 143
Garland, James C., 21, 76–77, 78; *Saving Alma Mater*, 74, 75
Gates, Bill, 20
Georgetown University, 48–49
George Washington University, 38
Gettysburg College, 136
GI Bill, 43
Goldstein, Warren, 19, 112, 160
Goodwin, Doris Kearns, 161
Government: assistance with tuition by, 35–36; city, 35–36; and education, 61; federal, 33, 34, 93–94; and free market, 60–61; and grants and loans, 33, 93–94; and public universities, 75, 76–77; state, 33, 34, 75, 76–77; support from, 23, 34; and vocational education, 47–48. *See also* State legislatures; Tax subsidization
Grade inflation, 67, 110
Graduate school, 99, 110, 115, 116–118
Graduate student assistants, 118
Grassley, Charles, 34, 36
Graubard, Stephen, *Distinctively American*, 96, 159
Great Lakes College Association (GLCA), 83
Grinnell College, 22, 24, 34
Griswold, Erwin, x, 138
Groton School, 40
Gumbel, Bryant, 161

Hamilton, Lee, 162
Hampshire College, 84, 144
Hanson, Dick, 90–92
Happel, Stephen, 62
Hartwick College, 136
Harvard Law School, 22
Harvard University, 22, 40, 83; Center for Hellenic Studies, 86; early state support of, 23; financial aid at, 35; and Overlap Group, 98, 99–100; and

Radcliffe College, 38; and tuition assistance, 36; wealth of, 26
Harvey Mudd College, 22, 85
Hatch, Nathan O., 22
Haverford College, 84–85
Hawkins, Hugh, 13, 37
Higher Education Roundtable, 22
Higher Learning Commission, 93, 94
High school, 40, 79; class rank in, 68; counselors in, 46, 66, 159–160; diploma from, 43; students in, 46–47, 49; teachers in, 46
History, 18, 41, 153
Holmes, Oliver Wendell, 103
Holy Cross College, 58
Hope College, 57
Hutchins, Robert, 38, 148

Illinois Institute of Technology, 38
Information technology, 51
Intel, 24
Internet, 51, 86, 159
Investment, 24, 25, 28–29. *See also* Finances
ITT Educational Services, 93
Ivins, Molly, 161
Ivy League, 40–41, 42, 98, 99–100

James, William, 129
Jobs, Steve, 20
Judson, Pieter, 127
Justice Department, 4, 98, 101, 102

Kalamazoo, Michigan, 35
Kazan, Elia, 18, 155
Keck Graduate Institute of Applied Life Sciences, 85
Kenyon College, 58
Kerr, Clark, 8, 37
Kirp, David, 14, 117
Koblik, Steven, *Distinctively American*, 96, 159

La Crosse, Wisconsin, 35
Lapham, Lewis, 148
Laureate Education, 92, 93
Lawrenceville School, 40
Levi, Edward, 20
Lewis, Sinclair, 161
Lewis, Stephen, 32
Liberal arts college(s): Carnegie Foundation definition of, 9–12; changing reasons for attending, 40–51; characteristics of, 13–14; collective interests of, 156; consumer ignorance about, 66; economic uniqueness of, 62–70; familiarity of public high school teachers with, 46; goal of, 132; intimacy of, 13, 14; judgment of quality of, 68, 72–73; marketing by, 64, 66–67; measures of excellence of, 68–69; media attention to, 105–106; mergers and acquisitions of, 4, 38, 87–95; in nineteenth century, 12–13; percentage of students attending, 43–44; poorer, 25–26, 27, 28–29, 31, 36, 37, 53–54, 63, 72, 73, 81, 103; prestigious, 41, 42, 71, 72–73, 79, 102, 106; promotion of, 106–107; and public universities, 74–78; rescue of, 157–162; survival of, 37–39; testimonials for, 160–162; value of, 20–21, 22; wealthy, 16, 25–26, 31, 34, 35, 37, 57, 71, 72, 73, 78–79, 81, 156–157. *See also* Competition; Ivy League; Tier I colleges; Tier II colleges; Tier III colleges; Tier IV colleges
Liberal arts education: and attitude toward knowledge, 17, 18, 20, 150; collective action for, 159; and communication skills, 17, 108, 110; and creativity, 17, 18; and credential-seeking, 110; and critical thinking, 17, 19, 107–108, 110, 152; and cul-

Liberal arts education *(continued)*
ture, x, 19, 20, 41, 111; decline in demand for, 3, 4, 40, 43–59, 154–162,
158; definition of, 7–12; fields of
study in, 9–12; and future income,
107; general understanding of, 50–
51, 66, 111–112; history of, 40–45;
and leaders, 21–22; negative public-
ity about, 48–49; and Olivet College,
39; as preparation for multiple careers, 108–109; as privilege versus
earned, 80; and public universities,
78; and self-examination, 17, 18, 20;
skills nurtured by, x, 17–19, 20, 111–
112; suitability of, 18; value of, 105,
106–107
Lincoln, Abraham, 20
Lobbyists, 75, 95, 267n22
Lugar, Richard, 162
Luther College, 57

MacArthur Fellowships, 21–22
Maine College Career Consortium, 83
Major League Baseball, 103, 130
Marquette University, 82
Marymount College, 28, 38
Massa, Robert J., 36
Massachusetts Institute of Technology,
35, 98, 99, 100
Matthews, Chris, 161
Maydew, Mary Jo, 84
Mayes, Robert, Jr., 92
McCown, Clint, 150
McCullough, David, 52, 153
McPherson, Michael, 15, 59
Meacham, Jon, 161
Mellon Foundation, 86
Menand, Louis, 161
Metro Editorial Services, 47
Miami University of Ohio, 76, 77,
267n26
Middlebury College, 98, 100, 147

Midland Lutheran College, 93
Midwest, colleges in, 41–42
Milton College, 39
Minter, W. John, 37
Mitchell, John, 113
Montessori, Maria, 109
Morehead-Cain Scholarships, 65
Morrill Act of 1862, 12
Morris, Donald, 39
Mount Holyoke College, 84, 85, 98, 100
Mount St. Clare College, 88–89, 92
Mount Vernon College, 38
Mudd, Roger, 161
Muhlenberg College, 57
Myers, Michele T., 159–160

National Association of College and
University Business Officers (NA-
CUBO), 95
National Association of Independent
Colleges and Universities (NAICU),
95, 159
National Institute for Technology in
Liberal Education, 86
National Survey of Student Engage-
ment (NSSE), 95, 136–137
Navasky, Victor, 161
Neely, Paul, 59, 81, 159
Newman, John Henry, 7
New Mexico Highlands University, 92
1960s culture, 42–43
Nobel laureates, 21
Northland College, 82
Noyce, Robert, 24
Nussbaum, Martha, 17, 148

Oakley, Francis, 148, 158
Obama, Barack, 21, 105, 162
Obama administration, 47–48
Oberlin College, ix–x, 41, 42
Ohio State University (Columbus), 75
OKC Downtown College, 84

Olivet College, 39
Online Consortium of Independent
   Colleges and Universities (OCICU),
   86–87
Online programs, 4, 30, 68, 72, 86–87,
   88, 89, 91, 92
Overlap Group, 4, 97–104, 159

Partnership, 35, 91, 92
Pelikan, Jaroslav, 21
Pell Grants, 94
Pells, Richard, 122
Peters, Absalom, 13
Pew Foundation Roundtable, 105
Philadelphia, 35
Pinkwater, Daniel, 161
Pitzer College, 85–86
Pomona College, 28, 85, 147
Posner, Richard A., 138
Pound, Roscoe, 139, 141
Presidents, 21, 260n39
Princeton University, 26, 28, 35, 40, 98,
   99–100, 110
Professional school, 59, 110, 132, 150,
   151
Proulx, Annie, 162

Radcliffe College, 38
Reading, 51–52, 264n35
Reagan, Ron, 162
Reagan, Ronald, 162
Recession, 3, 29–30, 37, 103; and career
   decisions, 50; and Grassley, 36; and
   tuition, 52, 73, 266n15; and vocational programs, 59; vulnerability to,
   81. See also Economy
Redfield, James, 114–115
Reed College, 22, 96
Regnery, Alfred, 161
Research and scholarship, 21, 94, 133
Research grants, 106
Revenues, 203–213, 246–256; and en-
dowment, 28; and fund accounting,
   70; and fund-raising, 79; and gov-
   ernment aid, 89, 93; as inadequate,
   23; from increased enrollment, 54–
   55; and Overlap Group, 99, 101, 103,
   104; of prestigious colleges, 59; and
   public universities, 76; from tuition,
   30–33, 52–53, 72; from vocational
   programs, 54, 55. See also Finances
Richardson, Bill, 92
Rickey, Branch, 130
Robbins, Tom, 162
Roberts, Cokie, 161
Robinson, Jackie, 130
Robinson, Marilynne, 18–19
Rooney, Andy, 161
Rosenblatt, Roger, Beet, 67
Rosenfield, James, 24
Roth, Michael, 154
Roth, Philip, 162
Rubin, Robert M., 19
Rudolph, Frederick, 13

San Francisco, 35
Santa Fe, 92–93
Santa Fe University of Art and Design
   (College of Santa Fe), 92–93
Santayana, George, 153
Sarah Lawrence College, 30, 58, 96
SAT/ACT test scores, 68, 69, 96
Sawyer, Diane, 161
Schapiro, Morton, 15, 59, 103
Schlesinger, Arthur, 113
Schmidt, Benno, 98
Scholarships: and economic unique-
   ness of colleges, 64–65; and Miami
   University (Ohio), 76, 77; and Over-
   lap Group, 98–99; undertaken or
   planned by cities, 37. See also Finan-
   cial aid; Tuition
Schulze, Franz, 127
Scitovsky, Tibor, 66

Scripps College, 85
Selectivity, 55, 68, 69
Sequoia Fund, 24
Seven Sisters colleges, 42
Sherman Antitrust Act, 97
Shimer College, 38
Sinclair, Upton, *The Goose-Step,* xi
Smiley, Jane, *Moo,* 107
Smith, Adam, 60
Smith College, 9, 84, 98, 100
Spellings, Margaret, 47
Spending, 26–28, 52. *See also* Finances
Sports, 94
Stanford University, 26, 35
Starr, Frederick, 86
State legislatures, 53, 75, 76. *See also* Government
St. John's College, 147, 149
St. Lawrence University, 136
Student athletes, 64–65, 69, 78, 98
Student(s): and academic freedom, 142; competition for, 71, 72, 98–100, 104; and competition for admission, 45–46; as customers, 63; diversity of, 130; faculty relationships with, 115, 118, 123, 124–125, 148; and family income, 71, 77–78, 267n29; in-state vs. out-of-state, 74, 75; as integral ingredient of education service, 63; international, 69; less-qualified, 55; minority, 43, 69, 98; poor/needy, 4, 34, 35, 70, 75, 78, 98–99, 101, 102, 103, 104; privileged, 79, 81; purchase of, 63, 64, 71, 77, 78–79, 103; quality of, 63, 71–72, 78–80; ratio to faculty, 68, 69; recruitment of, 67, 105–112; and social-service work abroad, 35; total subsidies received, 32–33. *See also* Financial aid
Sullivan, Daniel, 77–78
Sunoikisis, 86
Supreme Court chief justices, 21

Swarthmore College, ix, xii, 9, 14, 22, 36, 84–85
Sweden, 65
Swensen, David F., 59

Tax-exempt status, 34
Tax subsidization, 3, 61, 65, 74, 106, 157. *See also* Finances; Government
Teaching, 41; excellence in, 4, 5, 113, 126–137, 138, 143, 144–145, 146, 147, 151, 157, 158–159; at liberal arts and for-profit colleges, 94; at liberal arts colleges vs. universities, 21; and tenure, 5; training for, 47; of undergraduates, 21. *See also* Faculty
Technical colleges, 30
Tenure, 121, 138–146; history of, 139–143; improvements in, 145–146; process of, 119–120; and teaching quality, 5, 143. *See also* Faculty
Thomas, Clarence, 162
Thornburgh, Richard, 99
Tier I colleges, 155; and Consortium of Liberal Arts Colleges, 86; as credential generators, 156–157; endowments of, 27, 28; expenses of, 31–32; and financial aid grants, 33; and Great Lakes College Association, 83; tuition discounting by, 34; and *U.S. News* rankings, 16; and vocational programs, 57, 58, 59, 95
Tier II colleges, 157; and Consortium of Liberal Arts Colleges, 86; endowments of, 27, 28, 29; expenses of, 31–32; and financial aid grants, 33; and Great Lakes College Association, 83; and recession, 30; tuition discounting by, 33–34; and *U.S. News* rankings, 16; and vocational programs, 57, 95
Tier III colleges: endowments of, 27, 28; expenses of, 31–32; and falling

demand, 156; and *U.S. News* rankings, 16; and vocational programs, 55, 57, 95
Tier IV colleges, 31, 88; endowments of, 27, 28; expenses of, 31–32; and falling demand, 156; and *U.S. News* rankings, 16; and vocational programs, 55, 57, 58, 95
Tri-College library system, 85
Trinity College, 38, 98, 100
Tufts University, 98, 100
Tuition: and 2008 recession, 266n15; and accounting, 70; city government assistance with, 35–36; and competition, 72–74, 81; discounting of, 3, 32, 33–37, 72–74, 78, 97, 98, 225–235; and economic uniqueness of colleges, 64–65; and endowment, 23, 59; and free market competition, 71; and Garland, 76–77; and increased enrollments, 55; increases in, 52–53; and liberal arts colleges vs. public universities, 75; and Milton College, 39; negative, 34, 64, 65, 99; and Overlap Group, 97–104; and price discrimination, 76–77; and public universities, 75–76; revenue from, 30–33, 52–53, 72; and Waldorf College, 90. *See also* Finances; Financial aid; Scholarships

Unions, 135
University/universities, 74–78; and family income, 77–78, 267n29; and financial aid, 35; for-profit, 4, 62, 64, 87–95, 131–132, 156; fund-raising by, 106; Ivy League, 40–41, 42, 98, 99–100; land-grant, 12, 44; and liberal arts education, 20; media attention to, 105–106; not-for-profit, 86; online, 4, 88, 91; president of, 22; private, 62; public, 20, 23, 35, 53, 65, 74–78, 267n29; state, 12, 62, 106; and state support for private institutions, 23; tax subsidization of, 65; and teacher training, 131–132; teaching vs. research at, 14; and tenure, 139, 144; tuition increases at, 53; undergraduate experience at, 20–21; virtual, 62
University of Chicago, ix
University of Colorado, 13, 86
University of Florida, 35
University of Indiana, 35
University of Massachusetts–Amherst, 84
University of Michigan, 35
University of Minnesota, 266n8
University of North Carolina, 35
University of Pennsylvania, 35, 98, 99–100
University of Phoenix, 92, 132
University of Texas, 26
University of the Rockies, 89
University of Virginia, 35
University of Wisconsin, ix, 76
University of Wisconsin–Madison, 13
Upshaw, Dawn, 162
U.S. News and World Report, 15–16, 68, 69, 96–97, 156, 159, 270n54
Utley, Garrick, 161

Vassar College, 98, 100
Veblen, Thorstein, *The Theory of the Leisure Class*, 72
Vest, Charles M., 78, 98–99, 103, 104
Virtual Geography Department Project, 86
Vocational education, 68, 86, 92, 158; Carnegie Foundation definition of, 9; change to, 4; and competition, 81; demand for, 3, 44–45, 154, 155; and for-profit colleges, 94; and Georgetown University, 48–49; increased

Vocational education *(continued)*
programs in, 4, 47, 54, 55–59, 154–
155; and intrinsic value of knowledge, 18; and liberal arts colleges, 13,
94–95; and liberal arts education, 8,
107, 108; and Milton College, 39;
and Mount St. Clare College, 88;
Myers on, 160; and Obama administration, 47–48; and Olivet College,
39; and public universities, 78; quality of, 71; and recession, 30; social
emphasis on, 112; suitability of, 18;
and Waldorf College, 90, 91. *See also*
Career(s)

Waldorf College, 89–92
Waldorf Lutheran College Association,
91
Walters, Barbara, 161
Warch, Rik, 7
Wellesley College, 98, 100
Wellman, Jane, 14
Wesleyan University, 98, 100
Western canon, 41
Westminster College (Pa.), 136
Will, George, 161
Williams, John, *Stoner,* 44

Williams College, xii, 33, 98, 100, 103,
147
Wilson, Woodrow, 79–80
Winston, Gordon, 32, 73, 99
Wisconsin, x, 267n22
Wisconsin Association of Independent
Colleges and Universities (WAICU),
82–83, 84
Wolfe, Tom, 162
Women's College Coalition (WCC), 83
Woodbury College, 87–88
Woodruff, Bob, 161
Work, 45, 50, 78, 107. *See also* Ca-
reer(s); Employer(s); Vocational ed-
ucation
Wyatt, John, 126–127

Yale Plan, 28
Yale University, ix, x, 12, 22, 40, 41;
early state support of, 23; financial
aid at, 35; in-house investment management department of, 25; and
Overlap Group, 98; wealth of, 26
Yankelovich, Daniel, 50

Zahra, Tara, 127
Zimmerman, David, 73, 99